Photoshop Type Magic

Photoshop Type Magic

by David Lai and Greg Simsic

Photoshop Type Magic

Library of Congress Catalog Number: 95-77739
ISBN: 1-56830-220-7

97 96 95 4 3 2 1

Interpretation of the printing code: the rightmost double-digit number is the year of the book's printing; the rightmost single-digit number is the number of the book's printing. For example, a printing code of 95-1 shows that the first printing of the book occurred in 1995.

This book was produced digitally by Macmillan Computer Publishing and manufactured using 100% computer-to-plate technology (filmless process), by Shepard Poorman Communications Corporation, Indianapolis, Indiana.

Trademark Acknowledgments

All products mentioned in this book are either trademarks of the companies referenced in this book, registered trademarks of the companies referenced in this book, or neither. We strongly advise that you investigate a particular product's name thoroughly before you use the name as your own.

Apple, Mac, and Macintosh are registered trademarks of Apple Computer, Inc.

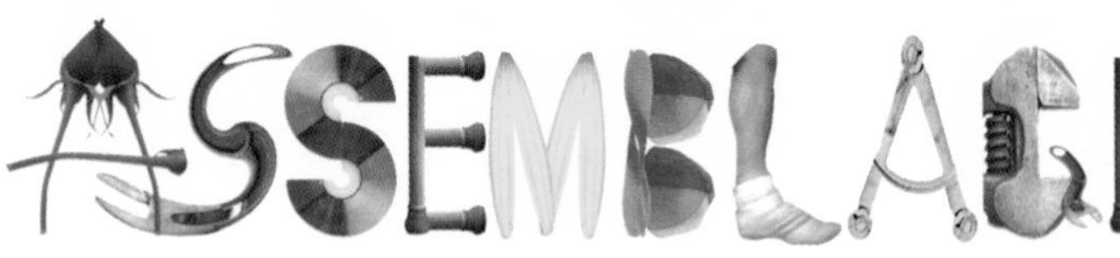

Page 18

Background

Page 24

Beveled

Page 28

Bitmap

Page 34

The Photoshop Type Magic Team

Publisher
David Rogelberg

Product Development Manager
Patrick Gibbons

Editor-In-Chief
Michael Nolan

Development Editor
Rebecca Tapley

Technical Editor
Dan Ryder

Editorial Contributor
Rich Evers

Publishing Coordinator
Rosemary Lewis

Blurred

Page 36

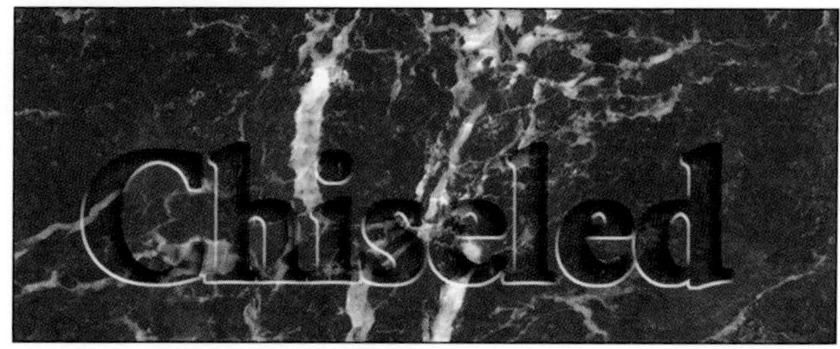

Page 40

CHROME

Page 44

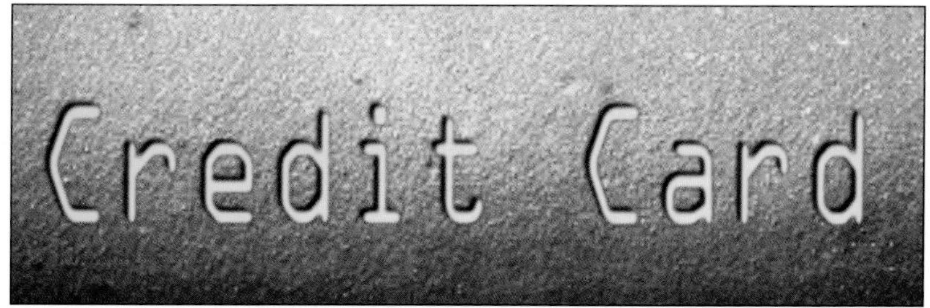

Page 48

Interior Design and Layout
Gary Adair

Cover Designer
Jason Grisham

Proofreaders
Beth Rago
Erich J. Richter
Christine Tyner

Composed in AGaramond and Gill Sans

Some thumbtab imagery provided by CMCD, Digital Stock, D'Pix, FotoSets, Image Club Graphics, and PhotoDisc, 1995.

Page 52

Earthquake

Page 54

Page 56

To Our Readers

Dear Friend,

Thank you on behalf of everyone at Hayden Books for choosing *Photoshop Type Magic* to help you to explore Photoshop type effects on the Macintosh. For many reasons, the Mac is the platform of choice for designers of every stripe, and the demand for quality type design on the Mac will continue to grow along with rising interest in multimedia, Web publishing, and 3D animation. This book will help you make your own contribution to these popular areas of design.

What you think of this book is important to our ability to better serve you in the future. If you have any comments, no matter how great or small, we'd appreciate you taking the time to contact us. And, as always, we'd love to hear your book ideas, too.

Sincerely yours,

David Rogelberg
Publisher, Hayden Books and Adobe Press

Page 60

Page 64

Page 68

Page 72

You can reach Hayden Books at the following:

Hayden Books
201 West 103rd Street
Indianapolis, IN 46290
(800) 428-5331 voice
(800) 448-3804 fax

Email addresses:

America Online: Hayden Bks
AppleLink: hayden.books
CompuServe: 76350,3014
Internet: hayden@hayden.com

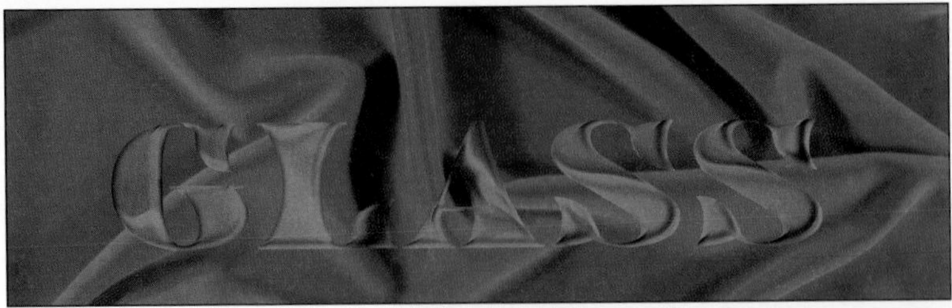

Page 76

Page 80

Gradient

Page 86

Page 90

About the Authors

David Lai is the author of *Icons for the Masses* published by Peachpit Press and the owner of Lai Design.

Greg Simsic uses Photoshop to do freelance work for the likes of BradyGAMES, though he prefers to spend his time lying in grassy fields and watching big, puffy clouds float by.

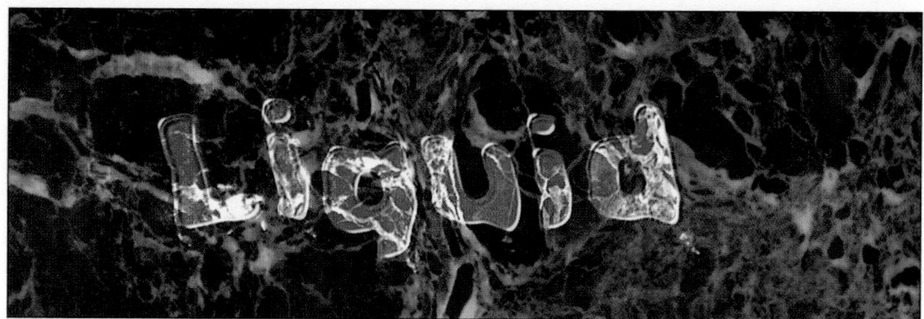

Page 96

MARQUEE

Page 102

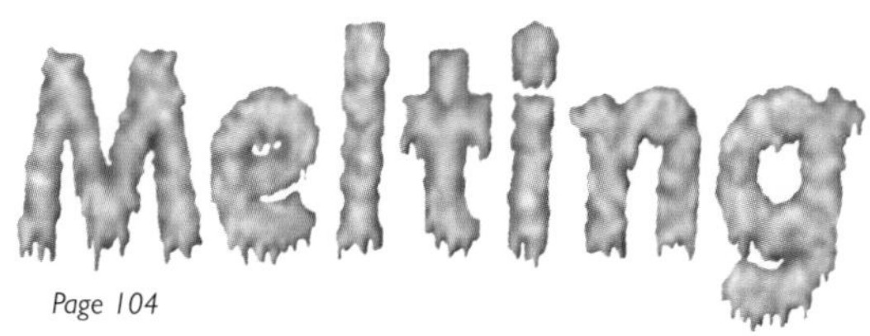

Page 104

Page 108

Acknowledgements

Special Thanks to:

Paul Celestin
Rich Evers
Robin Brandenberg Graham
The Macmillan Design team

Thanks for contributions from:

Tim Amrhein
Naoto Arakawa
Chris Cox
Ethan Dunham/Fonthead
Sal Giliberto
David Henderleiter/OPULUX
Geoff Heinricks/Chevalier Gris Digital Foundry
David Hull
Roger Morgan
Dave Nalle/Ragnarok
Eric Oehler/Kiwi Media
Patrick Quinn/pjq Design
Tim Rolands/Stylus Digital Typography
Neil Schulman
Raymond Snyder/Pat Snyder's Fonts
Don Synstelian/SynFonts
Susan Townsend/Hot Metal Type
Roger VanHorn
Adam Wunn/WUNNWAY fonts

Page 112

OVERGROWN

Page 118

Page 122

Dedications

This book is dedicated to my friends. - David

This book is dedicated to the Bunn Automatic. - Greg

Page 128

Peel-Away

Page 134

Perspective

Page 140

Page 144

Contents

Plastic

Page 148

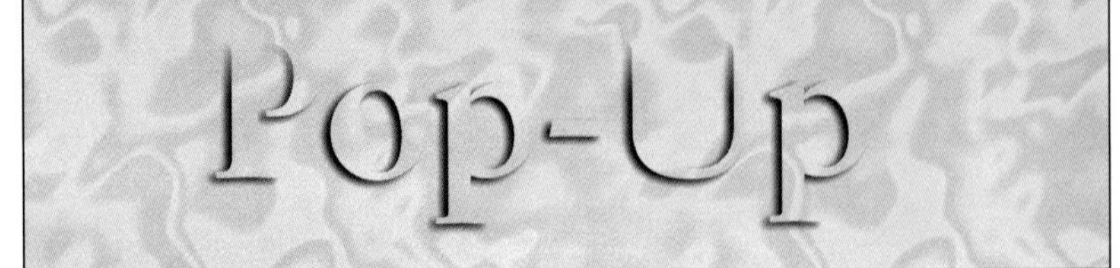

Page 152

Page 154

Rough Edges

Page 158

Page 164

Shadows

Page 168

Page 174

Page 176

Page 180

Page 184

Page 186

Page 192

Introduction

For a long time, artists have called for more recipe books on how to create type effects in Photoshop. This book is one of the first.

Photoshop Type Magic is the perfect guide for graphic designers, 3D animators, multimedia developers, and Web page designers of every proficiency level who've fallen in love with spectacular type effects and want to use Photoshop to make them.

This book is also very easy to use. Simply browse through the colorful thumbtabs to find the type effect you want to create and follow the step-by-step instructions. There aren't any big leaps between steps or assumptions about your knowledge of Photoshop—just simple, comprehensible guidelines so even the beginner can get working right away. Professional artists with lots of Photoshop experience can also use this book to help them create sophisticated type effects without feeling hampered by too many instructions. There's something here for everyone.

UNDERWATER

Page 194

Page 198

Page 202

We hope that *Photoshop Type Magic* will become a useful reference for your design work. Good luck with your designs, and may this book help turn your type into magic!

David Lai

Greg Simsic

About This Book

Welcome

This book is not intended to be a beginner's guide to Photoshop, but that doesn't mean beginners can't use this book. If you already have a working knowledge of Photoshop and you know how to operate a Macintosh or a PC, this book will help you create amazing type effects with ease. If you possess a general understanding of Photoshop but may need the occasional reminder, Part 2, *Photoshop Basics,* will help refresh your memory on fundamental tasks without slowing you down.

Recommended Setup

If you're a Macintosh user, we recommend exploring these type effects on a Mac with at least 16MB of RAM and plenty of room on the hard drive. It's also very important to have a CD-ROM drive so you can use the CD-ROM included in the back of the book. Some of these type effects require additional software and third-party filters, along with preset files we've created specifically to help you save time.

It is *not* necessary to run out and buy yourself a Power Mac, though generally speaking we understand the temptation—we created these chapters using a number of different Mac models, including a Centris. Keep in mind, though, that the less RAM your machine has, the longer it will take Photoshop to process the individual steps in these chapters. So if you can't afford extra memory, be prepared to exercise lots of patience.

We also recommend using Photoshop version 3.0 or later, since this is the software version we used to write this book. If you're working with version 2.5, you should still be able to create most of these effects without having to upgrade. Remember, though, that if you're attempting to duplicate our efforts using an earlier version of Photoshop, then your results will differ slightly or significantly compared to ours.

The Tools and Toolbox

If you're not familiar with Photoshop's Tool palette, there's no reason to panic. With a bit of experimentation, it doesn't take long to learn each tool's individual functions. To help the beginning Photoshop user along the way, here is a representation of Photoshop 3.0's toolbar with the common names of each tool.

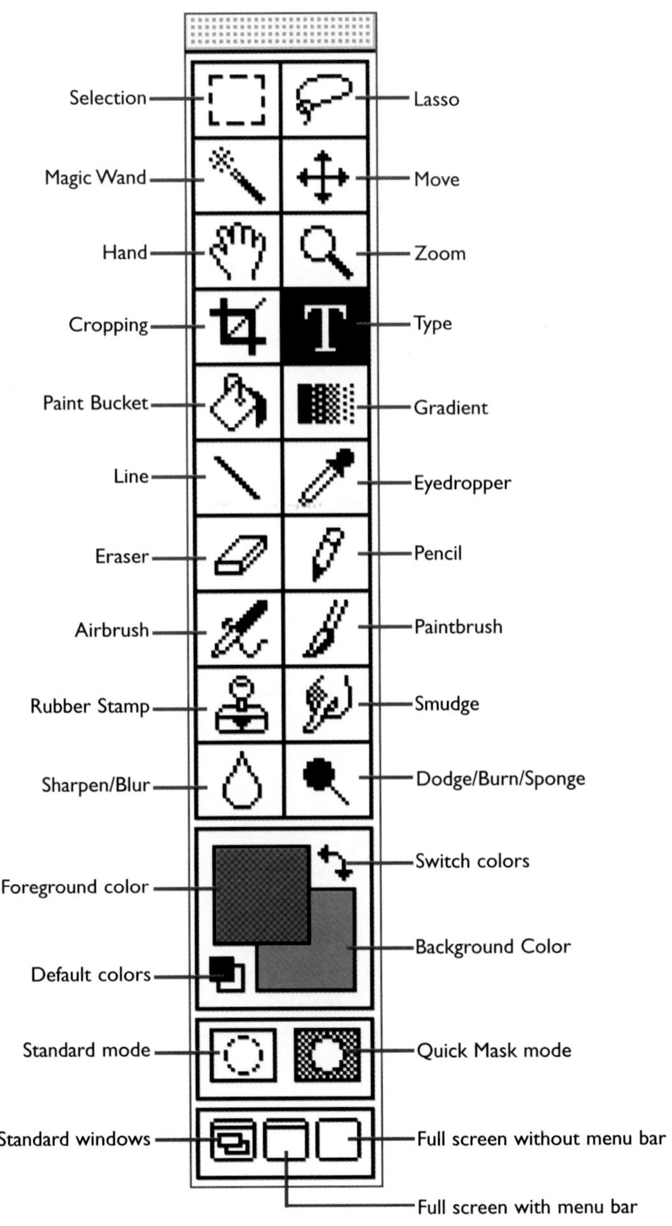

Also, to the side of the thumbtab on the first page of each chapter, you'll find a list of all the software, filters, and other stuff you'll need within a box called... the Toolbox. This contains everything you'll need to create each type effect and any of its variations other than what already comes included with Photoshop 3.0.

Resolution and Color

Up until the recent past, it could be safely assumed that any work done in Photoshop would eventually end up on paper. With the explosion of Web publishing, multimedia, 3D animation, and other onscreen design venues, the "paper assumption" no longer holds water.

In this book, we've created the majority of these type effects in RGB mode and we'll assume you'll do the same unless we give you a specific reason why CMYK might work better. The simplest rule of thumb for deciding which kind of file to open at the beginning of each chapter is this: use CMYK files for print and RGB files for the screen. (See page 8 in Part 2, *Photoshop Basics*, for how to switch modes. But be careful—some colors that look great in RGB mode may look like mud in CMYK.)

If you'd like more detailed information about the different color modes, refer to a good general Photoshop book like *Adobe Photoshop Classroom in a Book*, or to your Photoshop user manuals.

Channels and Layers

To the cheers of many, Adobe has introduced layers into Photoshop 3.0. Layers allow you to hold each piece of an image separately so you can make changes to it without affecting the rest of the image. It's like being able to stack several Photoshop files into one file. Then when you are satisfied with all the elements you can merge all the layers into one final image.

Channels, on the other hand, are essentially the same as they were in Photoshop 2.5—they are a holding place for selections that you want to keep for later use. If your initiation as a Photoshop user came with version 3.0, then you may get confused trying to figure out which one you should use in which cases. The first rule is: if it works, it works. Although there may be an easier route, at least you've got what you wanted.

The second rule is: you can't use a channel as a layer. A channel is merely a grayscale visual representation of a selection. White areas are included in the selection and black areas are not. Anything in between (i.e., grays) represent partially selected areas. The confusing part comes because often you can use a layer for the same use that you used to use a channel for—that is, to hold a selection.

Our general rule when creating these techniques was: if it's only going to be used as a selection, then we used a channel. Otherwise, when a channel wouldn't do the trick, we used a layer.

Filters

With a sweep of a filter, you can magically change plain type into gold or wood or just about anything else you can imagine. Although filters are really just programs that perform complex mathematical calculations, they can help you achieve some spectacular effects without having to do a lot of work.

This book uses filters that already come with Photoshop such as Blur and Emboss, but it also shows what many third-party filters can do. The CD-ROM that comes enclosed with this book contains many of these great filters—like a fully-functional version of Xaos Tools' Paint Alchemy 1.0—along with fonts, stock photos, and software demos from the likes of Specular International, Alien Skin, and Image Club Graphics.

Other Conventions and Instructions

All the type images created within the step-by-step examples in this book were 150 dpi, 5 by 2-inch files (with a few noted exceptions). Some of the variations and thumbtab images were created in 300 dpi files. If you are going to work in a resolution other than 150 dpi, remember that some of the filters and commands will require different settings than we used. Since there are fewer pixels in a 72 dpi image, a Gaussian Blur radius of 5 pixels will blur the image more than if it were a 150 dpi image. Just keep an eye on the figures next to the steps and match the outcome as close as you can.

Also, as you work through the Basics and type effect chapters you'll see instructions worded like this:

Filter ➥ Blur ➥ Gaussian Blur (2 pixels)

This is just an easy way to walk you through the right order of pull-down menus along the top of your screen. We've also included the settings we used to help you duplicate each effect. So when you actually execute the command we've typed out above, for example, it will look like this on the screen:

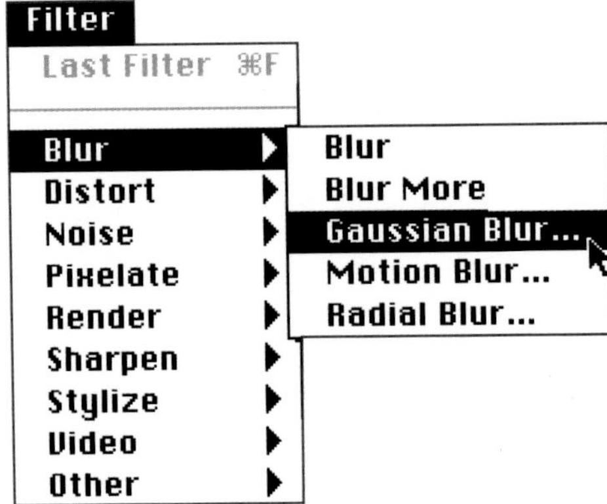

And, this is the dialog box that will appear, where you enter in the setting we provided in parentheses—2 pixels:

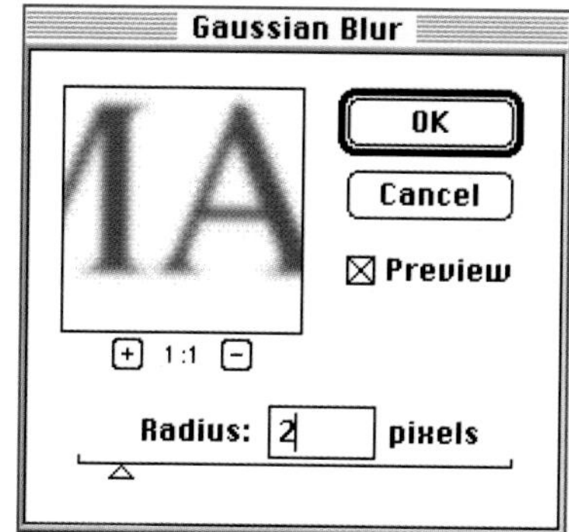

Occasionally in this book you'll also see some paragraphs of text that have been separated out to create Tips. Tips are additional bits of information that can help you render a better type effect by providing more information beyond the basic steps of each lesson.

Now, let's make some magic! ■

Photoshop Basics

How to use this section

This part of the book is intended to help new and novice users of Photoshop with the simple, basic tasks required to do the type effects we have created. Each of these tasks corresponds to the text highlighted in blue, so users can easily find the instructions they need in this chapter.

This chapter proceeds on two assumptions: that you're creating our type effects in Photoshop 3.0, and that you're keeping the Tool and Layer/Channel/Mask palettes open. If you're using Photoshop 2.5 and need help with channels and foreground and background default colors, it would be best for you to refer to your user manuals—also keep in mind that Photoshop 2.5 does not offer the ability to work in layers. And, if one or both of the Tool and Layer/Channel/Mask palettes are closed when you refer to this chapter, you can reopen them by name by using the Window menu at the top of the screen.

Basic Photoshop tasks

Apply a Photoshop filter

To apply one of the filters that comes with Photoshop, open the Filter menu along the top of the screen and choose the name of the filter you want to use. For example, if you wanted to apply Lighting Effects, you would choose **Filter ➥ Render ➥ Lighting Effects**.

Choose a foreground or background color

Shortcuts: Press D to change colors to default (black for the foreground, white for the background).

To change the foreground or background color from its default settings click on the Foreground or Background icon.

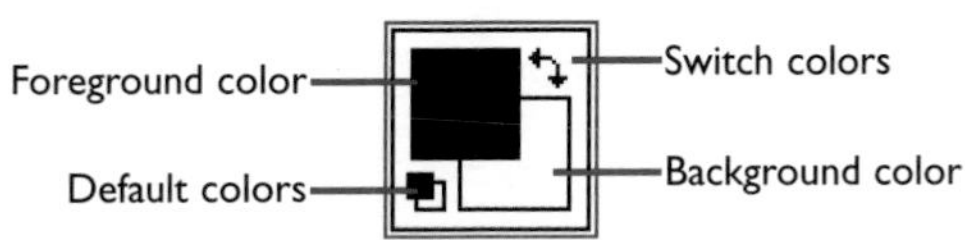

The Color Picker dialog box will appear, allowing you to choose a new foreground or background color by moving and clicking the cursor (now a circle) along the spectrum box, or by changing specific RGB, CMYK, or other percentage values. Note that the Foreground and Background icons on the Tool palette now reflect your color choices.

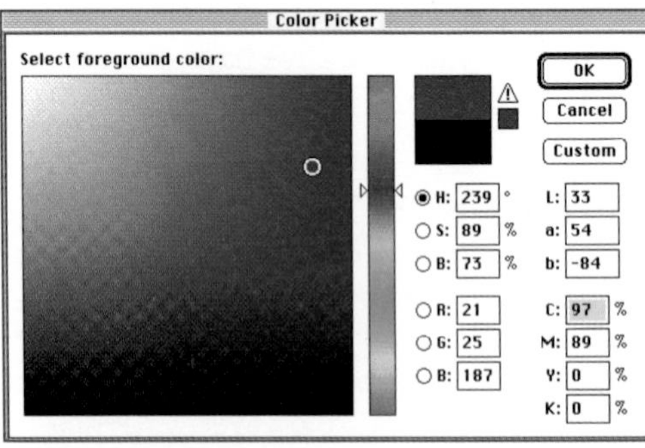

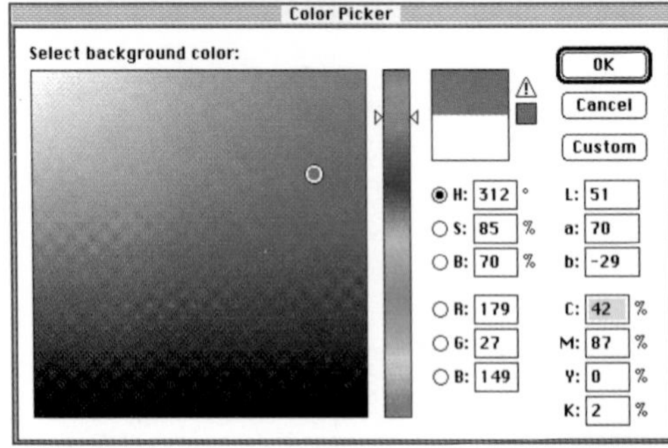

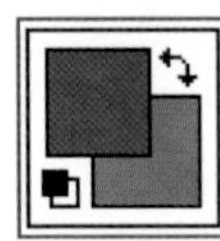

Convert to a new mode

To convert *from* one color mode *to* another color mode, click on the Mode menu at the top of the screen and scroll down to select your mode of preference. For example, if you wanted to switch from CMYK mode to Multichannel mode, you would choose **Mode ➡ Multichannel.** The check mark to the left of CMYK will move down to Multichannel, indicating you are now in Multichannel mode.

TIP

Remember, no matter what color mode the file is in on screen, your printer (if it prints in color) is going to print your work in CMYK. Since the color ranges for RGB and CMYK are different, you should convert your RGB image to CMYK before printing. Otherside, you may be in for a big surprise when your bright green prints out as a dull tan.

Create a layer mask

To create a layer mask, choose **Add Layer Mask** from the Layers palette pop-up menu. You can use a layer mask to mask out, or hide, specified parts of a layer.

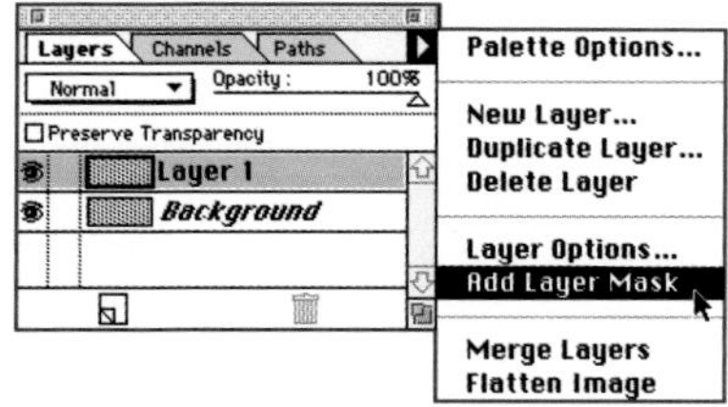

Create a new channel

Shortcuts: Hold down the Option key and click on the new channel icon on the Channels palette.

To create a new channel, choose **New Channel** from the Channels palette pop-up menu.

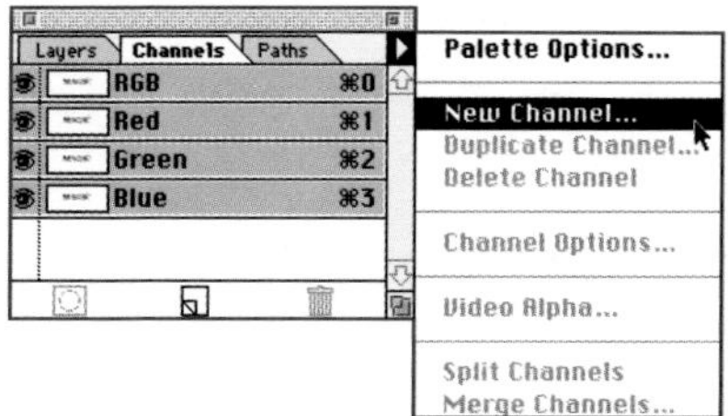

Use the Channel Options dialog box to establish your settings. Unless we note otherwise, we have always used Photoshop's defaults when creating a new channel. This figure shows Photoshop's default settings.

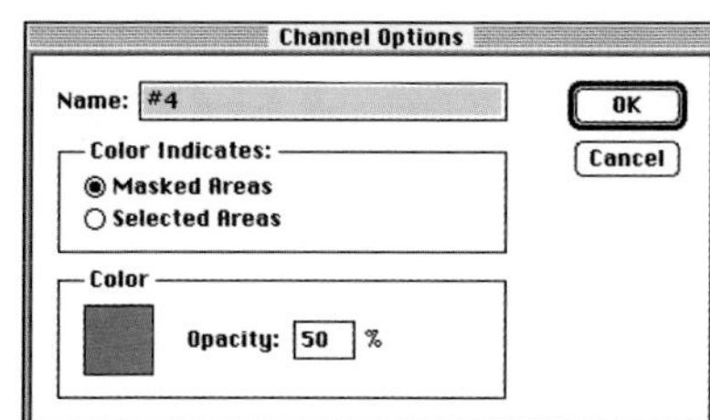

Create a new file

Shortcuts: Press Command-N.

To create a new file, choose **File ➥ New**. The New dialog box will appear, where you can name your new file and establish other settings. See Part I, *About this Book*, for information on the conventions we used when creating the type effect examples in this book.

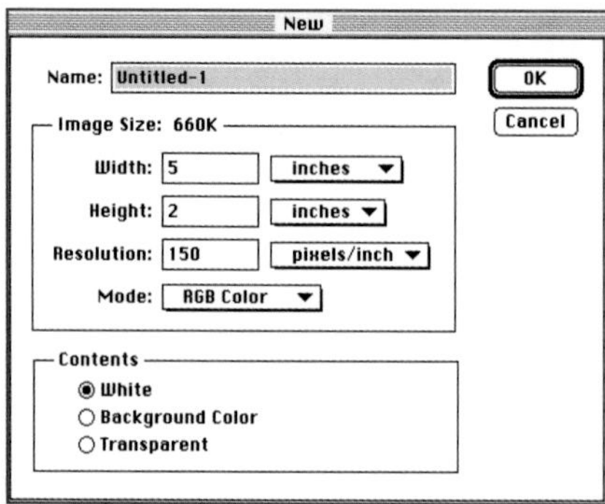

Create a new layer

To create a new layer, choose **New Layer** from the Layer palette pop-up menu.

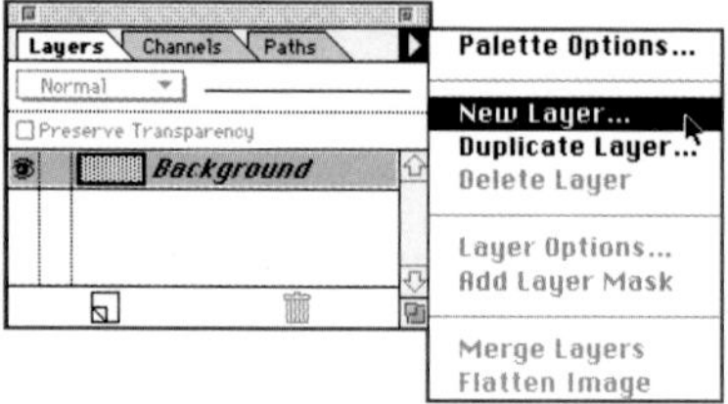

This brings up the New Layer dialog box, which enables you to name the channel and establish other settings.

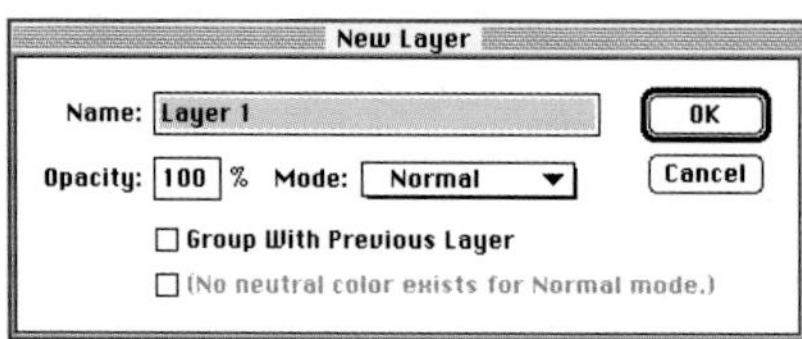

Delete a channel

To delete a channel, go to the Channel palette, select the channel you want to delete, and drag it to the Trash icon at the lower right hand corner—just like you would get rid of a document on the desktop by dragging it to the trash.

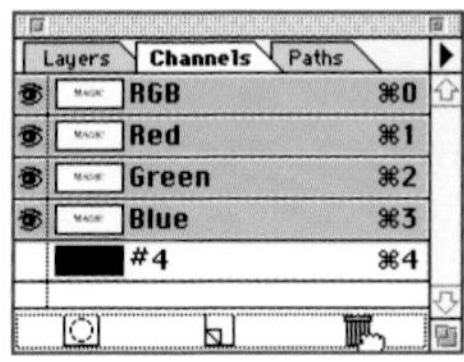

Deselect a selection

Shortcut: Press Command-D.

To deselect a selection, choose **Select ➥ None** or click anywhere outside of the marquee. The marquee will disappear.

Duplicate a channel

Shortcut: Hold down the Option key, click on the channel you want to duplicate, and drag it on top of the new channel icon.

To create a duplicate of a channel, select **Duplicate Channel** from the Channels palette pop-up menu.

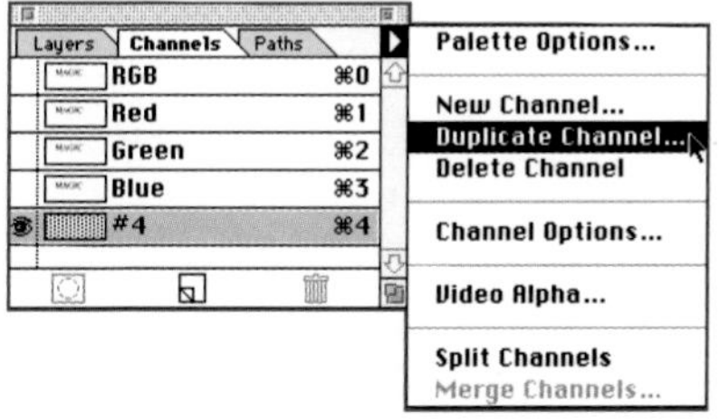

This automatically creates a new copy of the channel you selected for duplication, and causes the Duplicate Channel dialog box to appear.

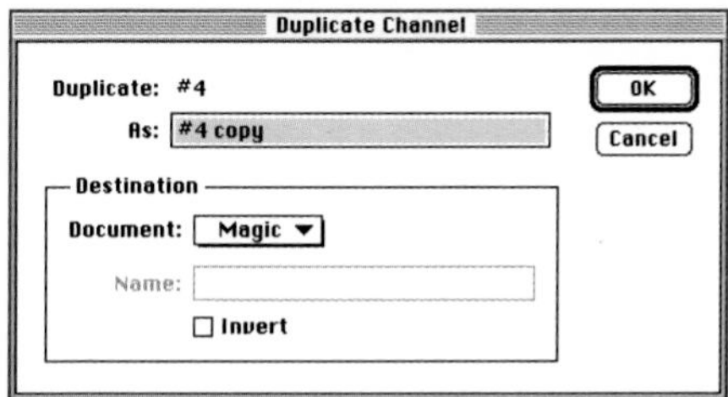

Enter/exit Quick Mask

Shortcuts: Press Q to enter and exit Quick Mask mode.

Click on the Quick Mask icon to switch to Quick Mask mode, and the Standard Mode icon to return to Standard Mode.

Essentially a Quick Mask is a temporary channel. When you're in Quick Mask mode you can use any of Photoshop's tools and functions to change the boundaries of the selection without changing the image. Then when you switch back to Standard Mode you'll have a new selection.

Enter the text

Before entering the text, make sure the foreground color is set to the color you want the text to be. Often, the instructions in this book ask you to enter text into a channel. Unless we note otherwise, we are assuming that you are entering white text onto the black background of the channel.

To enter the text, click on the Type tool to select it, and then click anywhere in the image to open the Type Tool dialog box. Type the text in the large box at the bottom of the dialog box, and make your attribute choices from the options above. Unless you're making Bitmapped type (page 34), always make sure you have the Anti-Aliased box checked.

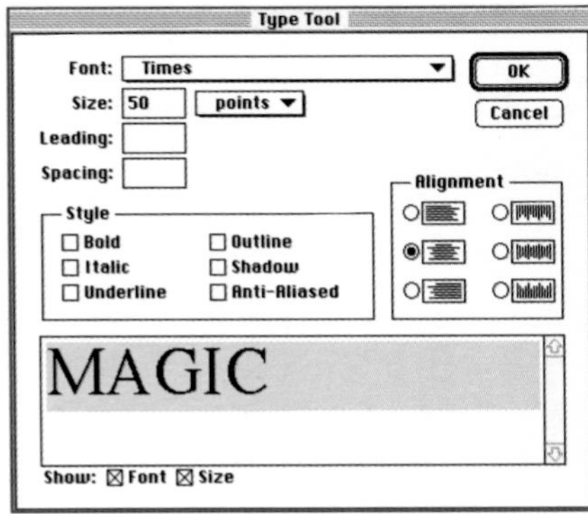

Fill a selection with foreground or background color

First, select the foreground or background color you wish to use (see page 7 in this section for instructions on how to do this). Keep the selection active and press Option-Delete to fill the selection with the foreground color. Press Delete if you want to fill in the selection with the background color. You can also fill in your selections by choosing **Edit ➥ Fill**.

This causes the Fill dialog box to appear, allowing you to establish which color you wish to use, and Opacity and Mode for blending.

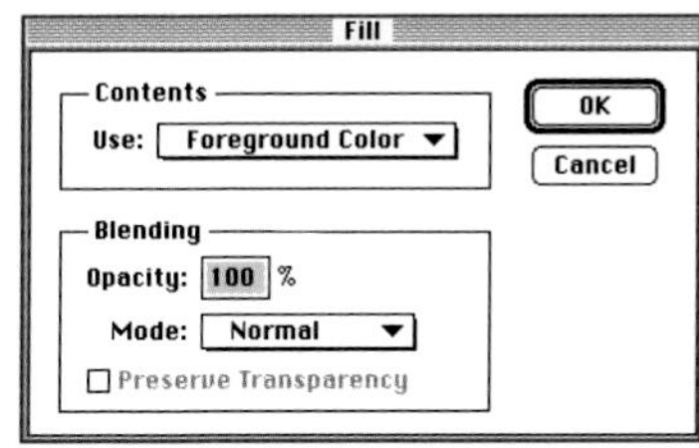

TIP

Be careful when using the Option-Delete combination—this only works if the selection is not floating. If it is a floating selection, then pressing Delete will delete the selection.

Flatten an image

To flatten an image (merge all the layers into a single layer), choose **Flatten Image** from the Layers palette pop-up menu.

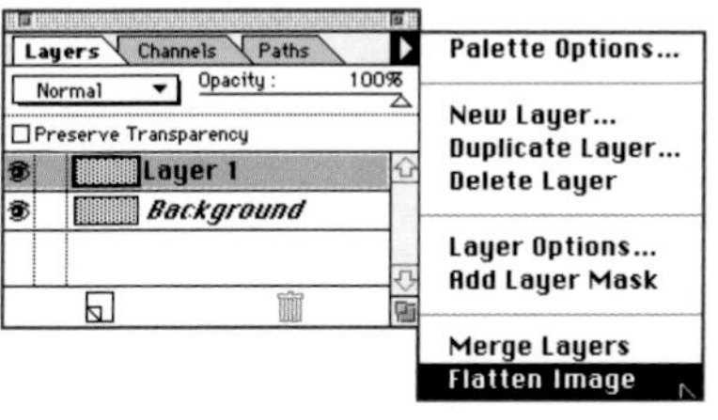

Load a selection/Load a channel selection/Load a channel

Shortcut: Hold down the Option key and click in the channel (on the Channels palette) containing the selection you want to load.

To load a selection, choose **Selection ➥ Load Selection**. This brings up the Load Selection dialog box, where you can establish document, channel, and operation variables.

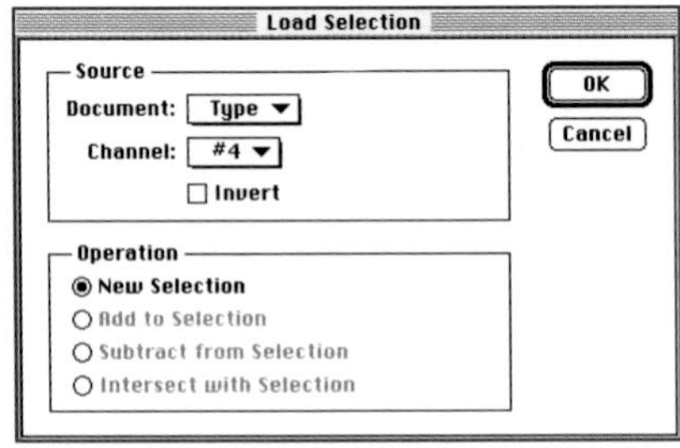

Make a channel active

To make a channel active for editing or modification, click on its thumbnail or title in the Channels palette.

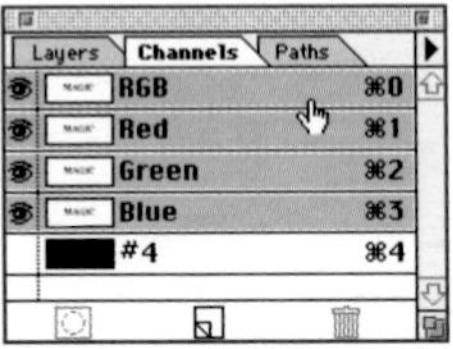

You can tell the channel is active if it's shaded gray.

Make a layer active

To make a layer active, click on its thumbnail or title in the Layers palette.

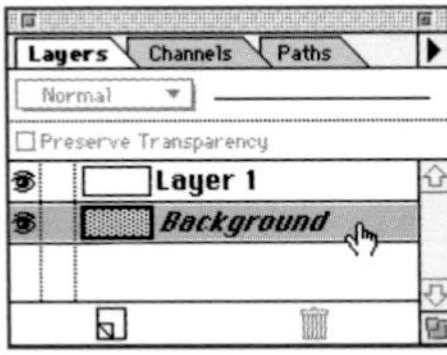

You can tell the layer is active if it's shaded gray.

Make a layer visible

To make a Layer visible, click in the leftmost column in the Layers palette. If an eye appears, then the layer is visible. If the column is empty, then that layer is hidden.

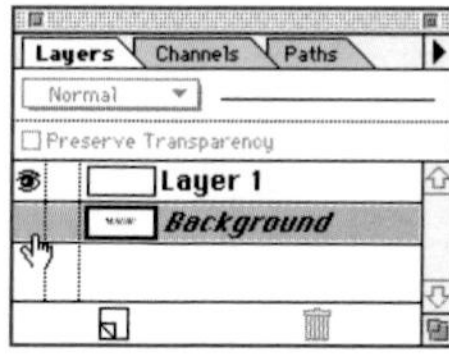

Move a layer

To move a Layer, click on the layer you want to move in the Layers palette and drag it up or down along the list of layers to the place you want to move it. As you drag the layer, the lines between the layers will darken indicating where the layer will fall if you let go.

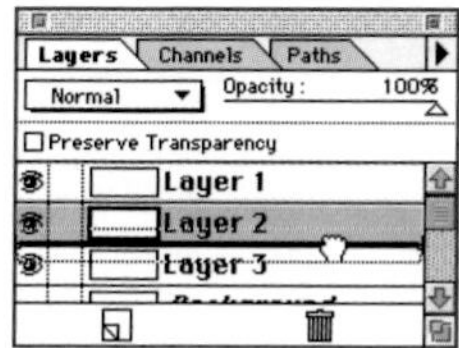

The layer you have moved will appear between layers, numerically "out of order."

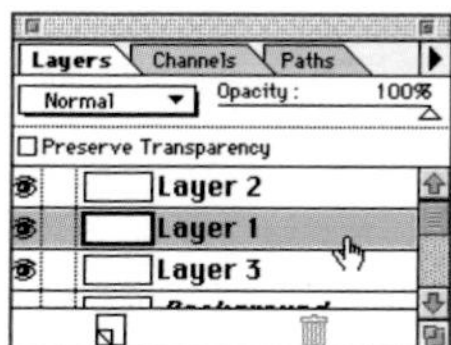

Return to the composite channel

Shortcut: Press Command-0 (this is a zero, not the letter O).

If you want to return to the composite channel, click on its thumbnail or title.

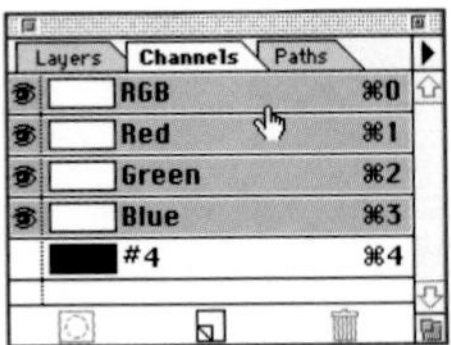

Channels 0 through 3 should now be active, since each of the R, G, and B channels are individual parts of the RGB channel.

Save a File

To save a file, choose **File ➡ Save As**. This will bring up the Save As dialog box, where you should name your new file and choose a format in which to save it.

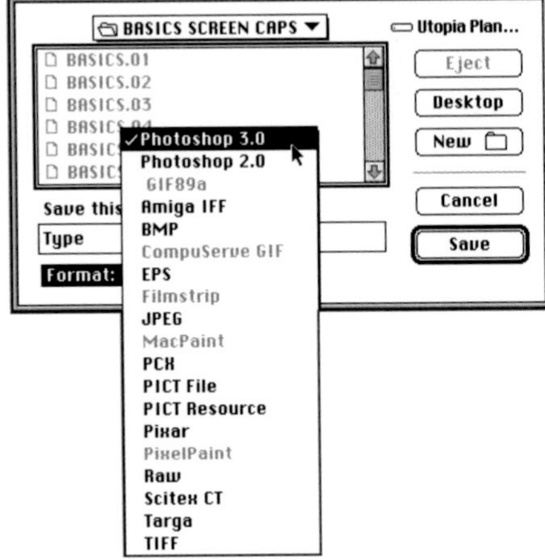

File format selection is going to depend on what you have in your file, what you want to keep when you save it, and what you're going to do with it afterward. Consult a detailed Photoshop book, such as *Adobe Photoshop Classroom in a Book*, for more guidance on which file format is best for your needs.

Save a Selection

Shortcut: Click on the save selection icon on the Channels palette.

To save a selection, choose **Select ➡ Save Selection** or press Command-S.

Switch Foreground/Background Colors

Shortcut: Press X to switch the foreground and background colors.

To switch the foreground and background colors, click on the Switch Colors icon. This flips the two colors shown in this icon only, and does not affect the rest of the image.

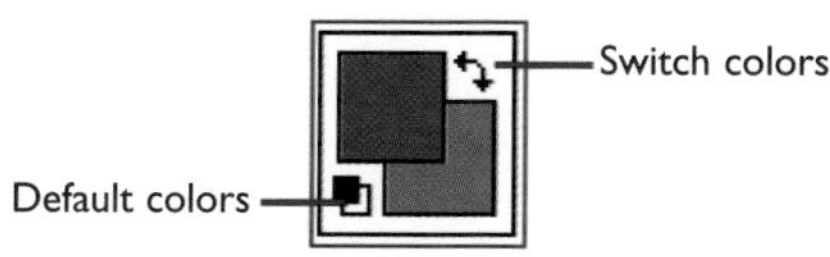

Switch to Default Colors

Shortcut: Press D to switch to default foreground and background colors.

To switch the foreground and background colors to black and white respectively, click on the Default Colors icon. ■

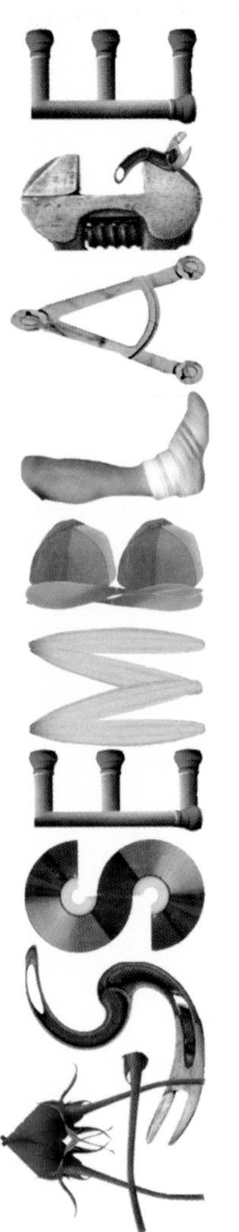

These steps provide some tips and tricks on how to work through the assembly process. Remember, though, that every assemblage project is going to present its own problems that require unique solutions.

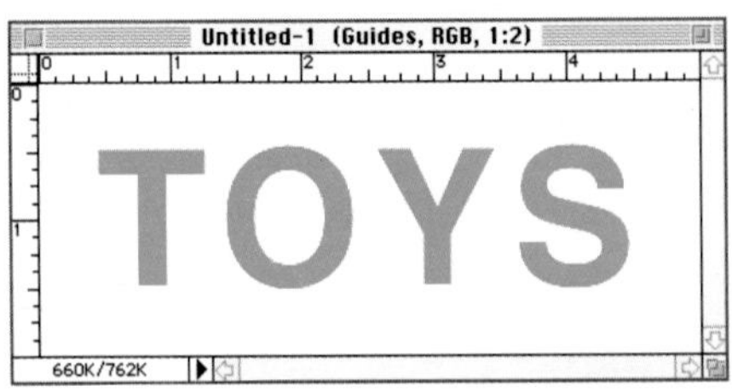

(1) Create a new file. Create a new layer and name it **Guides**. Use the Type tool to enter the text that will serve as a guide for the assembled type. We used a simple sans serif font—Helvetica, at 100 points. Now, deselect the text (Command-D).

©CMCD 1995

(2) Next, open the file containing the art you will use to assemble the type. We opened a stock photo from CMCD. Use Selection tools to select the item you want to use for assembling the type. Linear shapes will obviously be the easiest to work with when creating type. (We drew a path around the thumb, then turned the path into a selection.) After selecting the item, copy it to the clipboard.

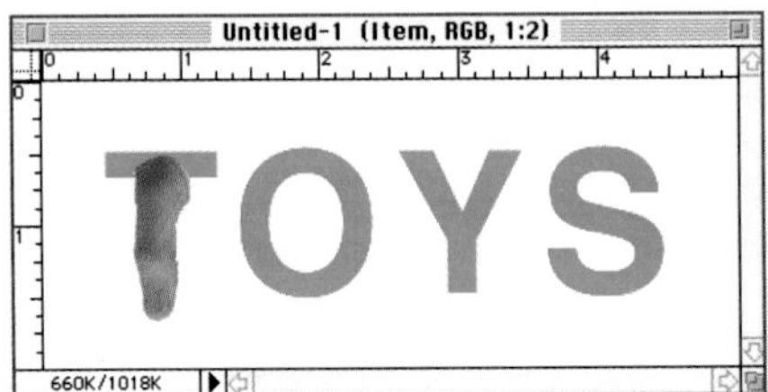

(3) Return to your text file, create a new layer named Item, and paste it in the clipboard (Command-V). We moved and rotated the thumb (Image ➥ Rotate ➥ Free) into position as the vertical member of the "T." This thumb will serve as the basic unit of our type's construction. If you need to scale your item to a good working size, choose Image ➥ Effects ➥ Scale. Deselect the item (Command-D).

④ Now make another new layer and name it **Type**. Our first thumb is already in place, but it's in the wrong layer, so make the Item layer active. Then press Command-Option-T to select the item, and copy it (Command-C). Then go back to the Type layer (the selection will remain active) and paste in the thumb (Command-V). Now you have the first line. Deselect the thumb.

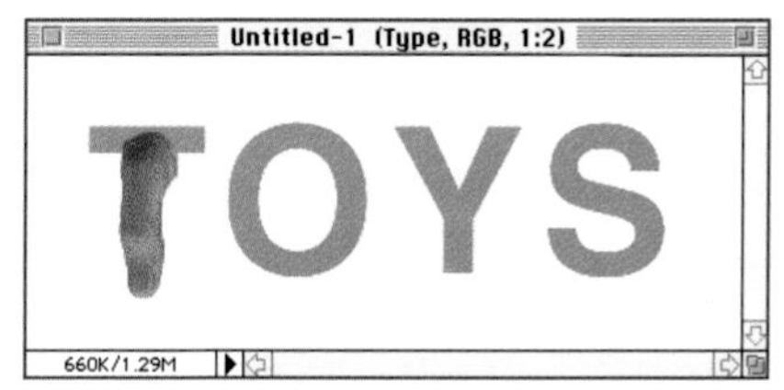

⑤ Press Command-V again to paste in another thumb. Then choose Image ➡ Rotate ➡ Free, and use the corner tabs to rotate the thumb into a horizontal position. Drag it into place and deselect it to finish the "T."

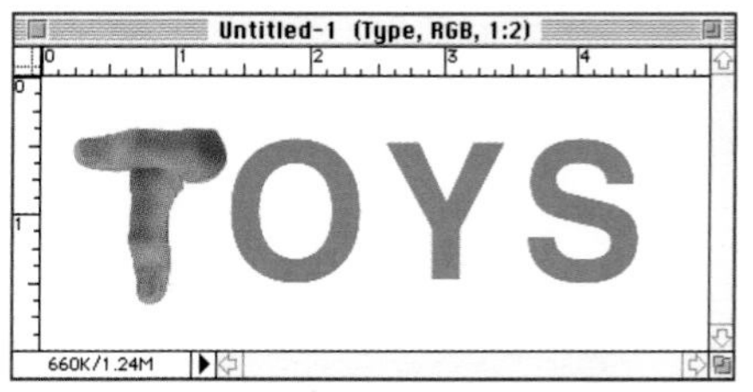

⑥ Make another new layer named Working, and paste in another thumb. Then deselect it. Photoshop has many distortion tools you can use for reshaping, including: Distort, Pinch, Polar Coordinates, Rotate, Shear, Skew, and Scale. Choose Filter ➡ Distort ➡ Shear and drag the points in the dialog box like this.

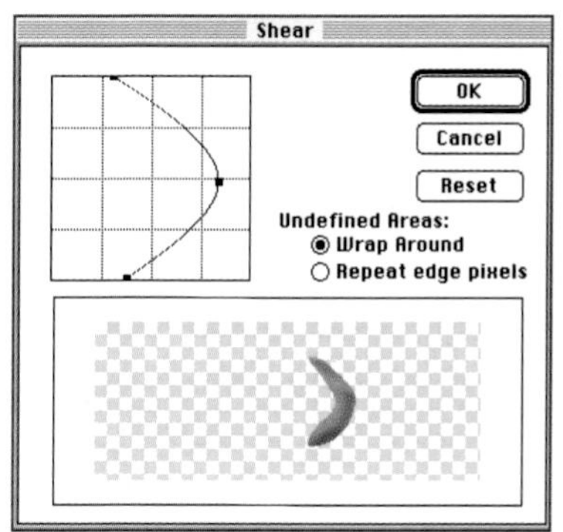

⑦ Then use the Move tool to move the thumb into place over the guides.

(8) Press Command-Option-T to select the thumb, then press Command-J to "float" a copy of the thumb. Choose Image ➡ Flip ➡ Horizontal, then drag the flipped thumb into place. Deselect the thumb.

(9) Select all (Command-A) and cut (Command-X) the contents of the Working layer. Make the Type layer active, paste in the "O" thumb, and move it back into position. Deselect it.

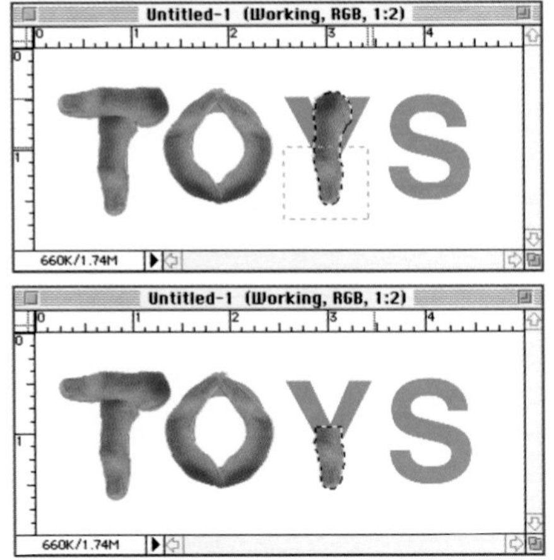

(10) Go back to the Item layer, press Command-Option-T, and copy the thumb. Then go to the Working layer and paste it in. Move the thumb over the "Y." Select the Marquee tool. While the selection is active, hold down the Command and Shift keys and draw a rectangle around only the part of the thumb you want to keep for the legs of the "Y."

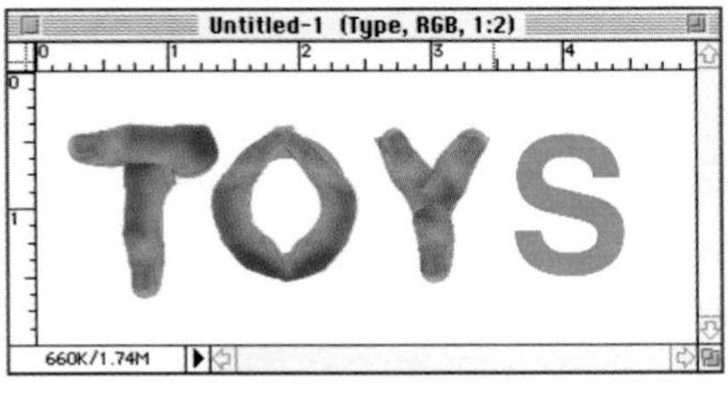

(11) Copy the partial thumb. Deselect the active thumb (Command-D) and paste in another. Rotate it (Image ➡ Rotate ➡ Free) and move it into place. Repeat this step for the third last arm of the "Y." As in Step 9, cut the contents of the working layer and paste them into the Type layer.

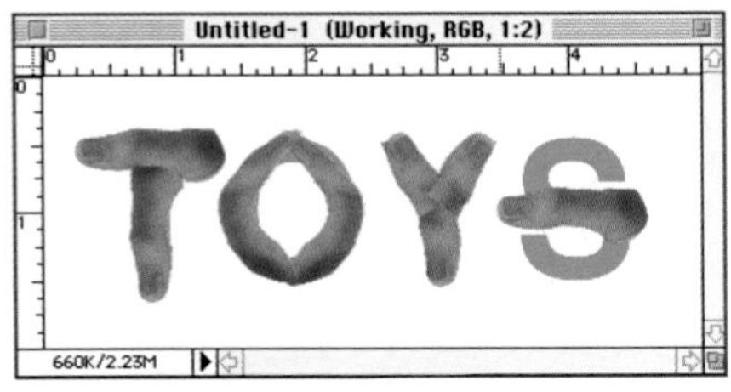

(12) Again, return to the Item layer, press Command-Option-T, and copy the thumb. Go to the Working layer, paste it in, and place it near the "S." Deselect it.

⑬ Use the Marquee tool to draw a selection like this.

Then apply Filter-Distort ➡ Polar Coordinates (Rectangular to Polar). If you didn't get what you see here, then undo (Command-Z) the filter, make a new selection, and try it again. Deselect the thumb.

⑭ Choose Image ➡ Effects ➡ Scale. Use the corner tabs to enlarge the thumb. (Hold the Shift key to keep it proportional.)

⑮ Use Image ➡ Rotate ➡ Free to rotate the thumb, and move it into place.

⑯ Moving and distorting selections often leaves traces of the selection behind. To get rid of them, choose Select ➡ Inverse, press delete, and choose Select ➡ Inverse again. Now, copy the thumb. Deselect it, then paste in the copy. Choose Image ➡ Rotate ➡ 180°, and move the thumb into place.

⑰ Save the selection to create Channel #4. Copy the thumb, delete it, then load the Channel #4 selection.

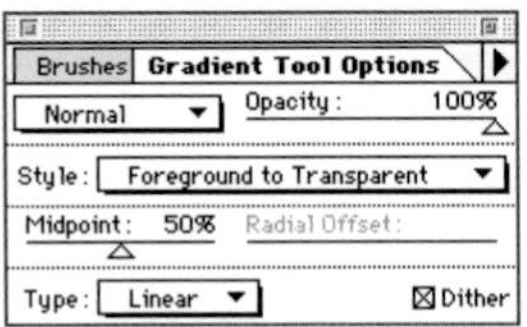

⑱ Press Q to enter Quick Mask mode. Change the foreground color to black. Double-click on the Gradient tool to select and open its floating palette. Match the settings to these.

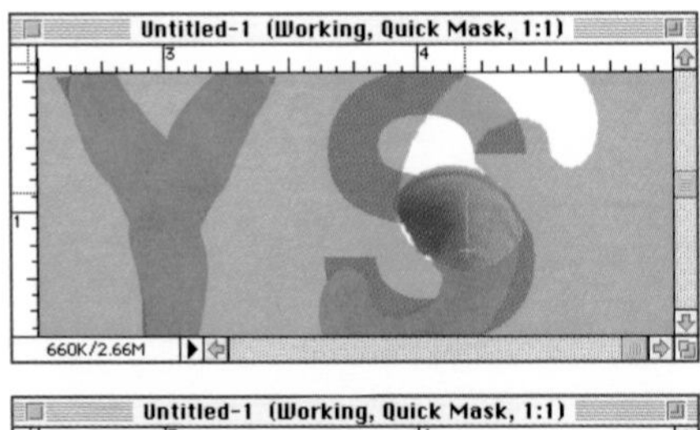

⑲ With the Gradient tool, click and drag from the bottom to the top as shown in the first figure to get what's in the second figure. Then press Q to exit Quick Mask mode.

⑳ Choose Edit ➥ Paste Into. The distorted thumb should paste right into the selection, and because of the gradient created in Step 19, it will blend smoothly into the bottom of the "S." If the two parts are not blended as you would like, then press delete, load the Channel #4 selection again, and go back to Step 18. Otherwise, deselect the thumb.

㉑ The "S" was crooked and too tall so we rotated it (Image ➥ Rotate-Free) and compressed it (Image ➥ Effects ➥ Scale). Then we repeated Step 9 to move the "S" to the Type layer.

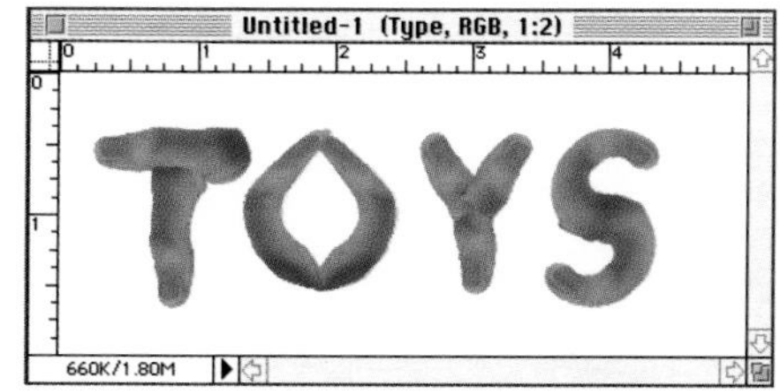

TIP **Use the Smudge tool for quick blending of parts like we did at the bottom of the two thumbs that make the "O."**

㉒ To finalize the image we deleted the other layers (Guides, Item, Working) and flattened the image. We also used the Smudge tool to smooth the transitions between the thumbs in the "Y," used Filter ➥ Distort ➥ Pinch to push down the tips of the "O," and then pasted a photograph inside the "O."

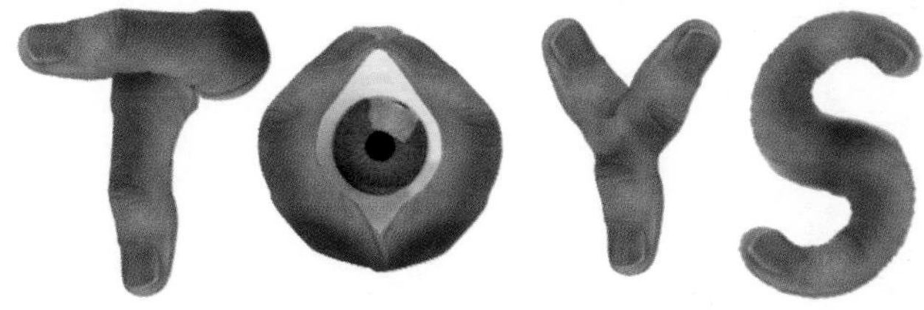

VARIATIONS

Of course, you can use more than one piece of art to assemble your type. Look at the "Assemblage" thumb tab on the opposite page. While working on this image we created several layers for the letters so we would have more room for working. This figure shows the naming convention we used to keep track of what letters were on what layers.

Layers | Channels | Paths
Normal | Opacity: 100%
Preserve Transparency
_______L
_______A
A__EM____GE
_SS____B
GUIDES
Background

Photo credits for this chapter: PhotoDisc, CMCD, D'Pix, Digital Stock, 1995. ■

Background

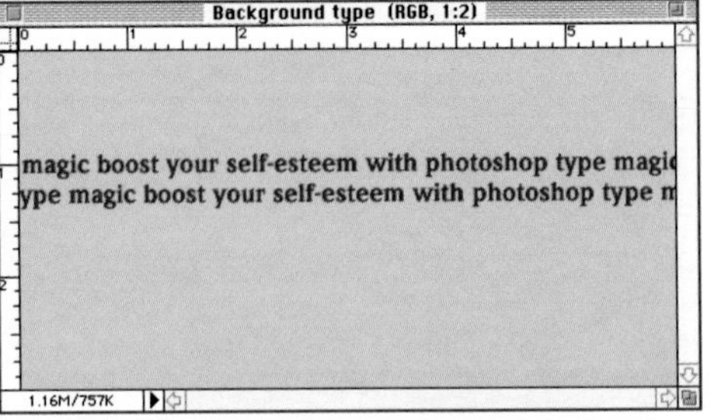

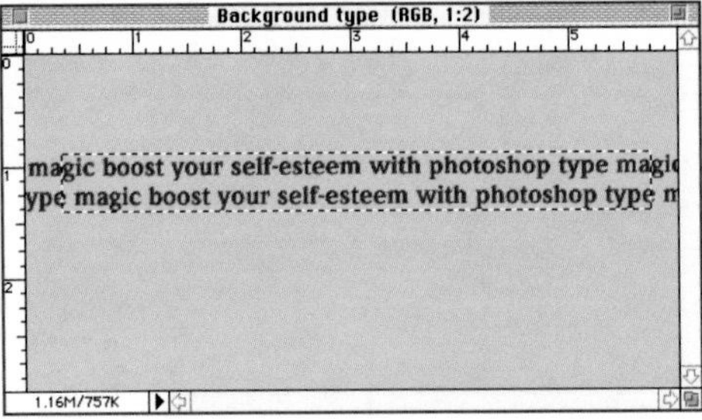

Need some cheap subliminal advertising? Here are two quick ways to create a background filled with text.

① Create a new file with the dimensions of the background you want to fill. Use the Type tool to enter the text you want repeated in the background. In the Type dialog box, type the text twice in the same row. We used Weideman Black at 17 points. After setting the type, we copied it, pasted it, and then offset the second copy.

② This is the most difficult step for this technique. You have to be careful what you select if you want to get the pattern to repeat correctly. Use the rectangular Selection tool to draw a box around the portion of the text that will be used as a pattern for the entire background. It's okay to cut the selection through the middle of a letter as long as the other end of the selection cuts through the same letter in the same place. You can control the spacing between lines in the final pattern by including more or less space in the selection rectangle above and/or below the text.

TIP

Make the area you wish to use for your pattern as large on the screen as you can. You can zoom in by holding down the Command key and Spacebar and clicking in the image. To zoom back out, click within the image while holding down the Option key and Spacebar.

③ Now choose Edit ➡ Define Pattern. Then Select ➡ All (Command-A) and choose Edit ➡ Fill (Pattern, Opacity: 100%, Normal).

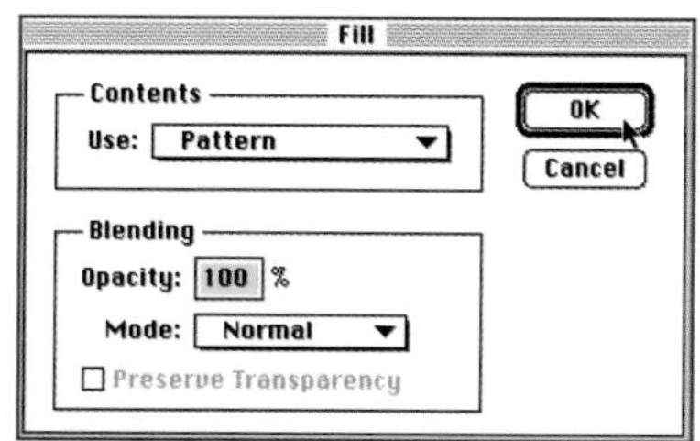

VARIATIONS

You now have a very simple background and can work on the rest of the image by creating new layers above it. Or you could…

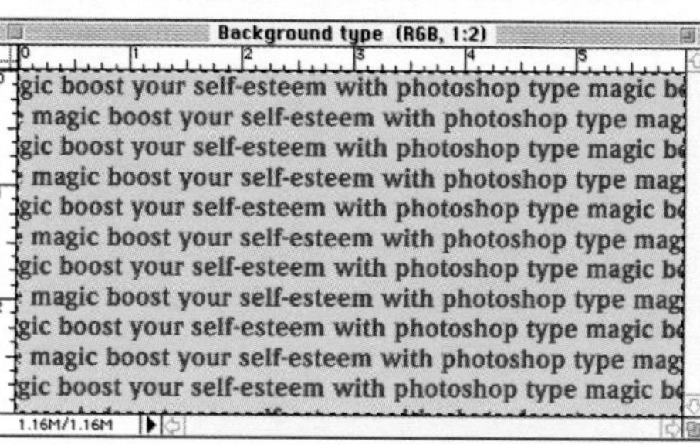

…blur the image and apply Photoshop's Emboss filter,

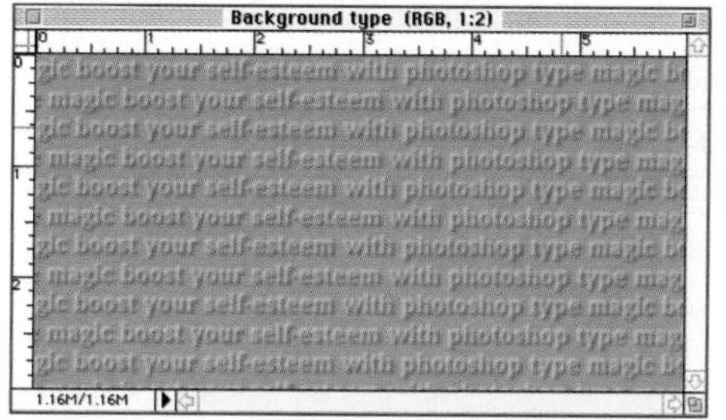

…or maybe combine it with a photograph, like this one from Digital Stock.

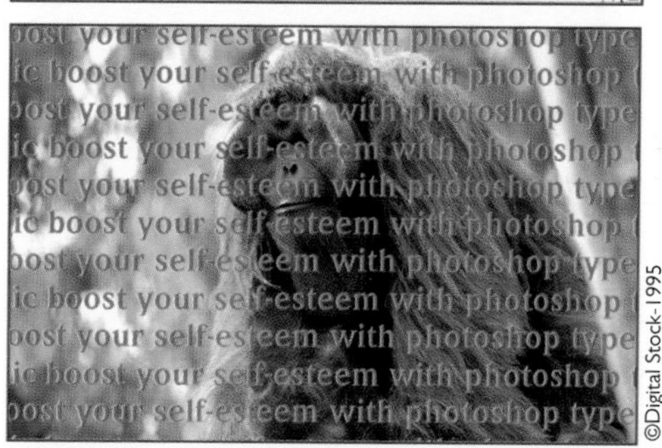

©Digital Stock-1995

…or maybe apply the Offset filter to only one channel,

...then add the Wave filter,

...then apply the Shear filter to only one channel,

...or maybe...

BACKGROUND 2

Another way to create a background filled with text is to use the Wave filter.

① In a separate file create the type you want to use for the background. For this example, we used the Plastic effect from page 148 to render this type. Copy the text (Command-C).

② Now, create a new file with the dimensions of the background you want to fill. Paste the text from first file into this background file (Command-V). Place the text in the middle of the background image, and deselect it (Command-D).

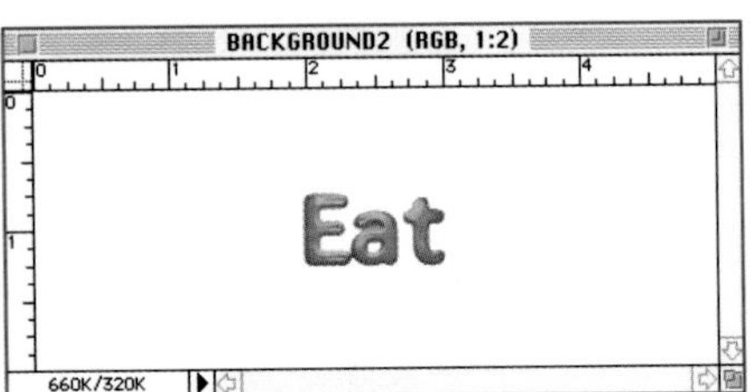

BACKGROUND 2

③ Choose Filter ➥ Distort ➥ Wave. Start with these values: Generators: 5; Wavelength: 500 & 660; Amplitude: 10 & 925; Horiz.: 100%; Vert.: 100%. Choose the Wrap Around option. Of course, this is only one of the countless possibilities for this filter. Use the Randomize button to see other options, or adjust the sliders until you see something you like. You could also apply the filter again for more variations. Simply choose Filter ➥ Last Filter (Command-F). Here are some of the variations we came up with. ■

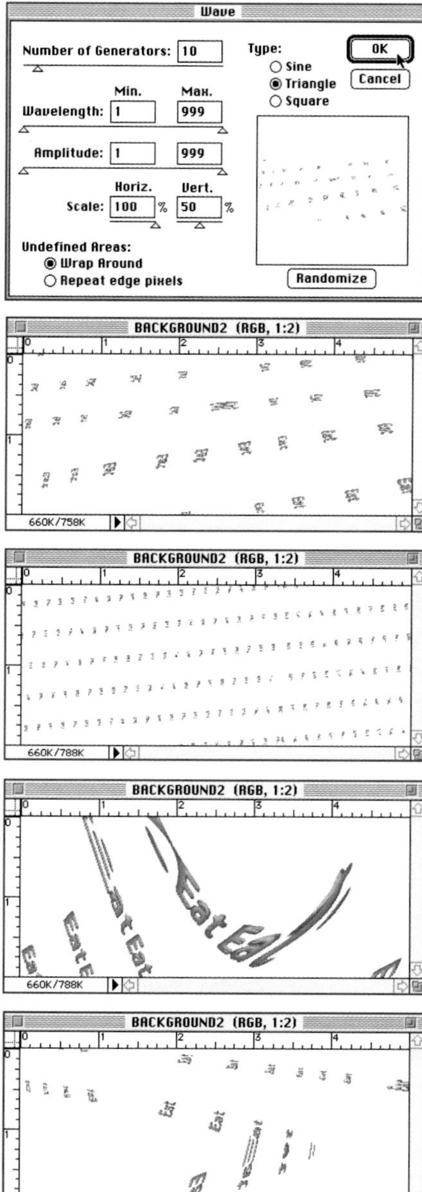

TOOLBOX

Adobe Dimensions 2.0
Alien Skin Inner Bevel 2.0
Alien Skin Outer Bevel 2.0
BevelLightStyles preset file
KPT Gradient Designer 2.1

Sometimes it's best to let Adobe's other software do some of the dirty work for you—and if it's beveled text you're looking for, then Adobe Dimensions gets the honor. A demo version of Dimensions 2.0 is included on the CD so you can try it for yourself. If you don't have Dimensions, skip to the Photoshop Bevel section, where you can learn how to create a bevel with Photoshop 3.0's new Lighting Effects filter.

Dimensions Bevel

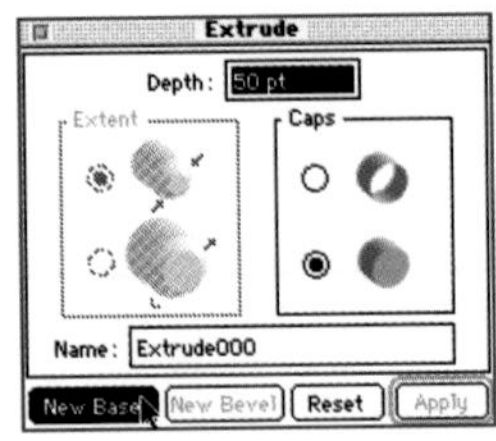

① Open Adobe Dimensions 2.0. A new document window will automatically open. Press Command-E to make sure that you are working in Edit Mode, where everything runs faster. Then choose Operations ➡ Extrude (Command-Shift-E). The Extrude floating palette will pop up on the screen. Click on the New Base button on the palette.

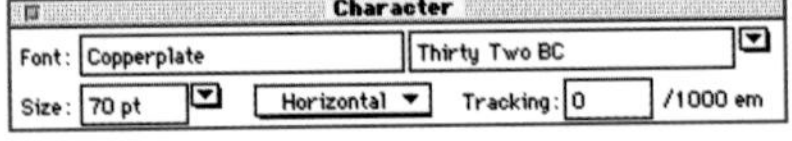

② A new untitled window will open, and the icons in the toolbar will change. Double-click on the Type tool to select it and open the Character floating palette. Make your selections in the Character palette. We use 70-point Copperplate 32BC.

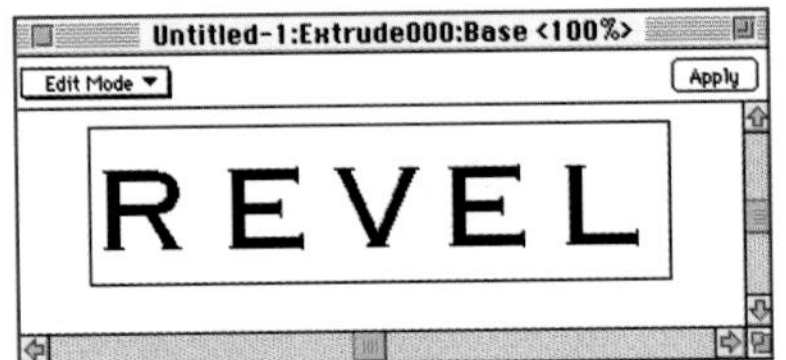

③ With the Type tool, click in the Extrude window that opened in Step 2. Type in the text. If you plan on having the bevels extend outward from the text, then make sure you increase the letter spacing by entering a positive value in the Tracking box. This gives them some room to spread. First, select the text by dragging the Type tool insertion bar over it. We set the tracking at 150.

TIP

If you don't like what you see, make changes to the text by selecting the text as described above, and making new selections in the Character palette. The text will change automatically.

④ Now click on the New Bevel button on the Extrude floating palette. Move through the directories to locate the Bevel Library within the Adobe Dimensions 2.0 folder on your hard drive. Adobe provides 22 preset bevels for you to use. We chose the Classic Normal bevel. Watch the preview window and click Import when you're done.

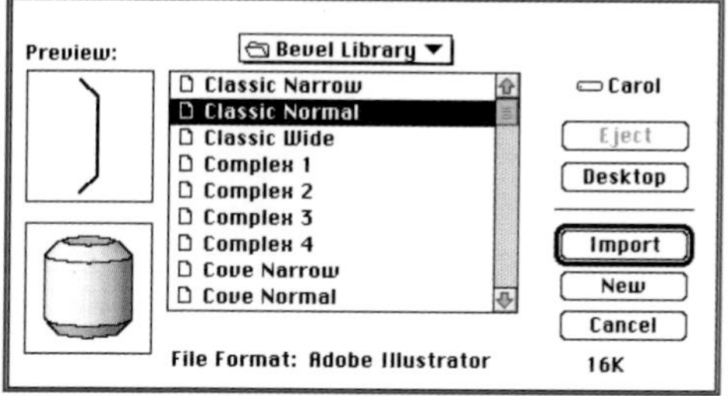

⑤ Another new window will open showing the contour of the bevel. Find the Extrude floating palette again. Enter, in points, the depth you want the text to extrude. Our text is going to be facing front so we entered an arbitrary medium depth of 20 points. We also choose an outer bevel and end caps.

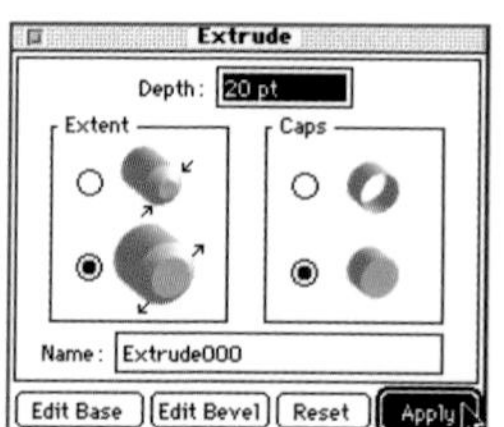

Click the Apply button on the Extrude floating palette.

⑥ If you can't see the original window that opened when you opened Dimensions, choose Window ➡ Untitled-1. Now you can see that the text has been extruded and beveled.

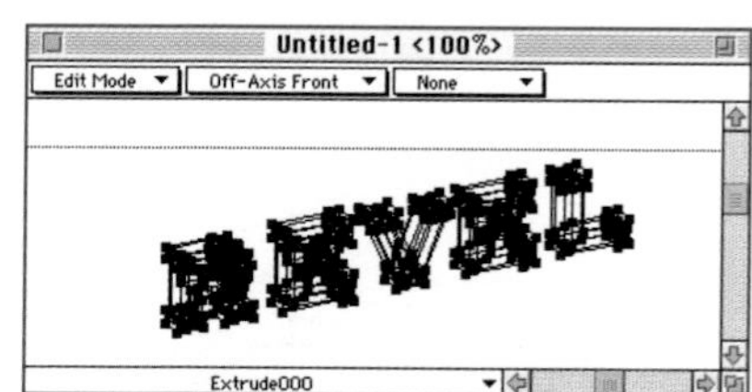

⑦ Choose View ➡ View Angles ➡ Front. Now, all you need to do is edit the surface properties of the text and render it.

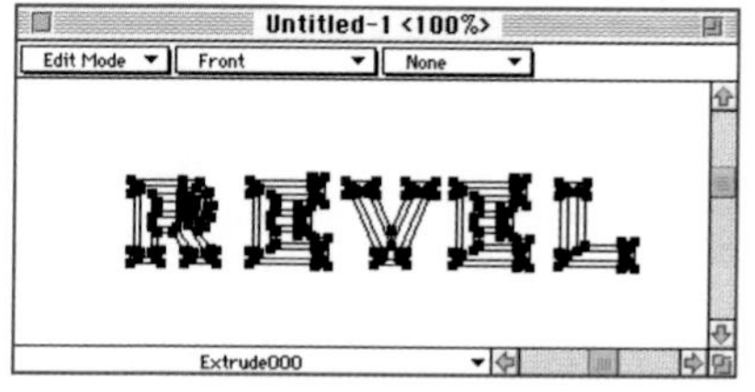

> **TIP** If you want to change the direction of the light source, choose Appearance ➥ Lighting, and make your selections in the Lighting floating palette.

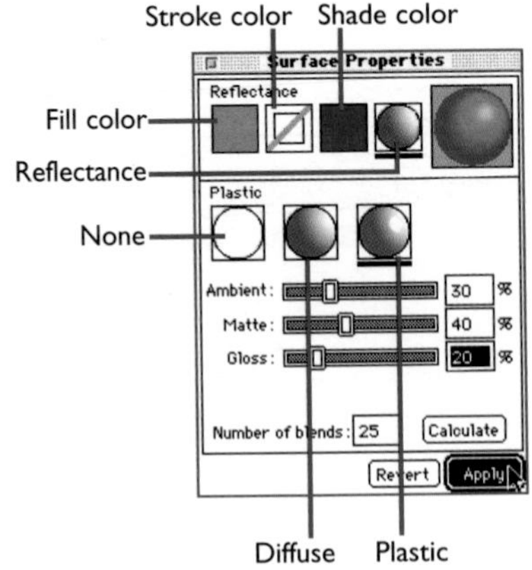

⑧ Choose Appearance ➥ Surface Properties. A floating palette will appear. The figure here explains its features. For the Fill (text) color, we used these CMYK values: 0/100/100/0. For the Shade (shadow) color, CMYK: 100/100/0/60. We left the Stroke (edge) color at none. Click on the Reflectance icon, then the Plastic icon, and use the values shown in the figure. Click the Apply button when you're finished.

> **TIP** Make sure that the Number of blends is at least 25 to avoid banding. If your text has a lot of curves you will probably want to increase it.

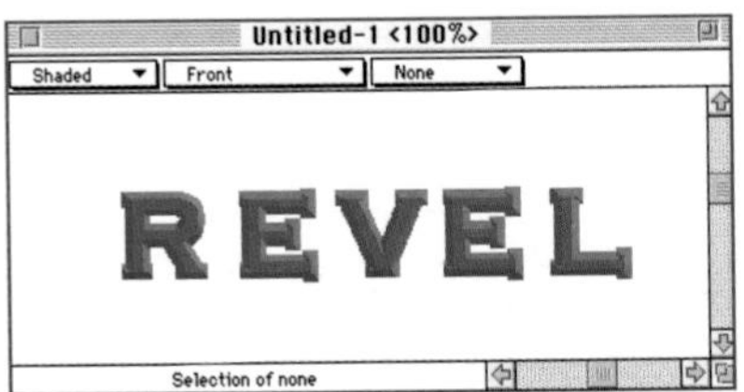

⑨ You won't see any changes in the text because you're not in a render mode yet. Choose View ➥ Shaded Render. (Complex text may take some time to render. Be patient.) If you don't like what you see, use the Surface Properties palette to make appearance changes or go back to the Extrude palette and use the Edit buttons to alter the text.

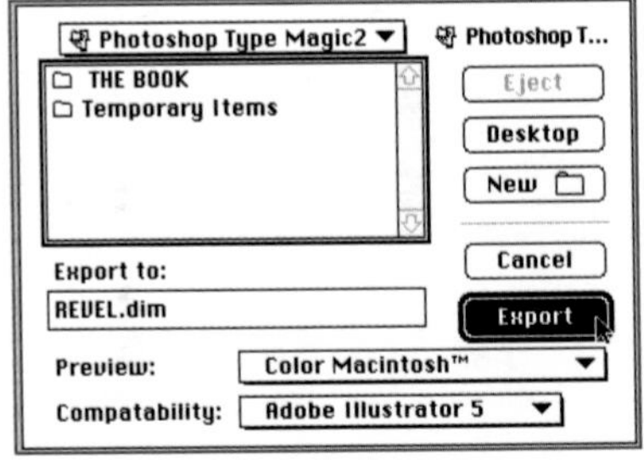

⑩ When you're satisfied, deselect the type (Command-Shift-A), and choose File ➥ Export. Choose Color Macintosh and Adobe Illustrator 5 and from the pop-up menus. Quit Dimensions (Command-Q). No need to save changes—we already exported what we wanted.

⑪ Open Photoshop, and open the file you just exported from Adobe Dimensions. Here are the settings we used in the Rasterize box:

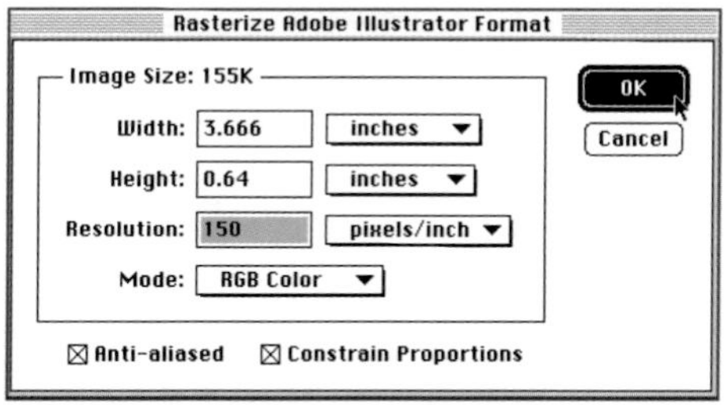

⑫ The text will open into Layer 1 and there will be no background layer.

⑬ If you simply want a white background, choose Flatten Image from the Layers palette pop-up menu. If not, take a look at the Variations.

VARIATIONS

If you want to make modifications to the text, don't flatten the image. Pressing Command-Option-T will select the text. Now you can use any of Photoshop's tools to alter the text.

To change the color of the text, choose Image ➡ Adjust ➡ Hue/Saturation, check the Colorize option and use the Hue slider to find or modify the color.

To add a background, create a new layer (Layer 2), and drag the layer in the Layers palette below Layer 1. The new layer will be the active one. Fill the background with a color or paste in an image.

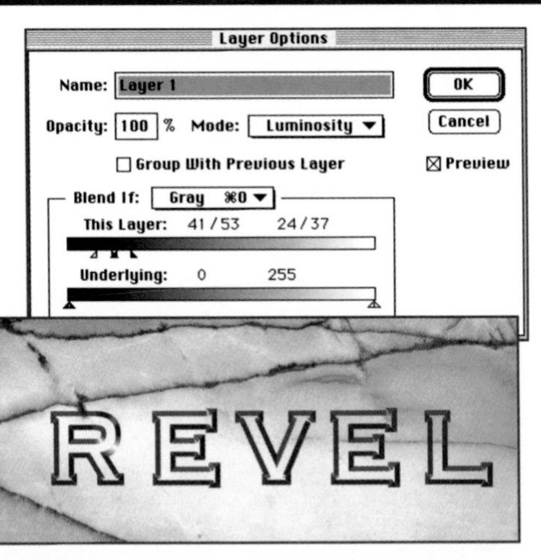

To get this transparent bevel, we put the same beveled text on a background, and double-clicked on Layer 1 (the beveled text layer) in the Layers palette to bring up the Layers Options dialog box. The settings we used are shown in this figure.

For this variation we used KPT Gradient Designer 2.1 to fill the selection with the Metal Sweep Cymbal II +a gradient. We chose Procedural Blend from the Options menu. After applying the blend, we raised the contrast using the Levels (Command-L) dialog box.

Photoshop Bevel

① Create a new file (it must be in RGB mode). Create a new channel (#4), and use the Type tool to enter the text. We used Frutiger Bold at 70 points.

② Duplicate the channel (#4) to create Channel #5. Deselect the text (Command-D). Choose Filter ➡ Blur ➡ Gaussian blur (5 pixels). The blurring creates the area for the bevel.

Untitled-1 (#5, 1:2) Devil 660K/381K

③ Load the original text channel selection (#4). Choose Select ➡ Modify ➡ Contract (3 pixels). Fill the selection with white so the bevel will have hard edges.

④ Return to the composite channel (Command-0). Load the channel #5 text selection. Fill the selection with a color for the type.

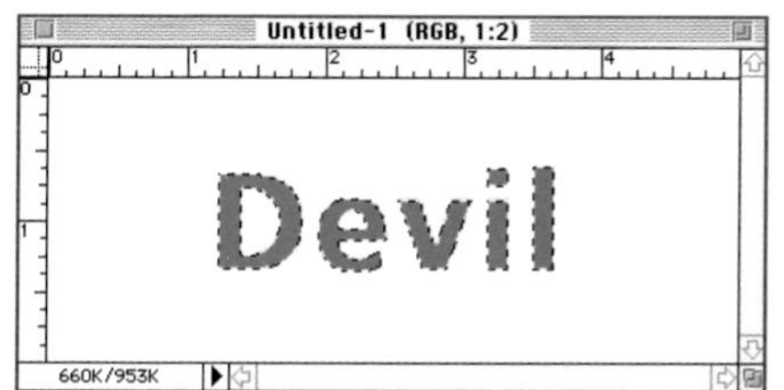

⑤ Choose Filter ➥ Render ➥ Lighting Effects. From the pop-up menu choose BevelLightStyles, or match the settings shown in this figure.

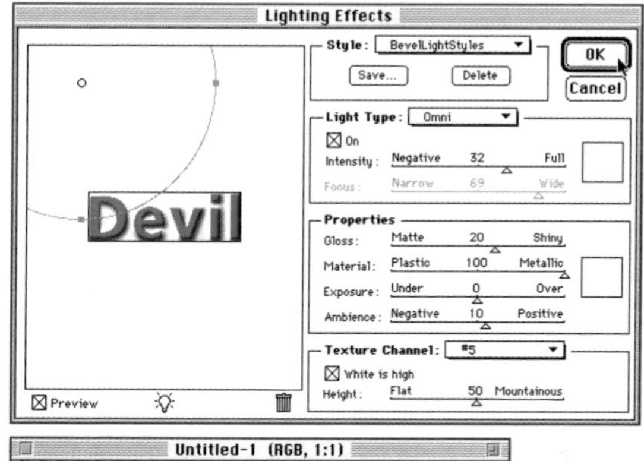

Click OK and you've got beveled text.

VARIATIONS

To bevel a surface, before Step 1 copy the surface into the clipboard. Then, in Step 4, instead of filling the text with a color, choose Edit ➥ Paste Into. Also, to automatically add a drop shadow we chose Select ➥ None at the end of Step 4.

©D'Pix 1995

Alien Skin's Outer Bevel 2.0 and Inner Bevel 2.0 filters make beveling a breeze. If you use the outer bevel, remember that the filter uses the color outside the text selection for the color of the beveled edges. If you want the bevels to be the same color as the text then the text should be placed on a background of the came color. For this variation, we placed white text on a stock photo from PhotoDisc. ■

©PhotoDisc 1995

Bitmap

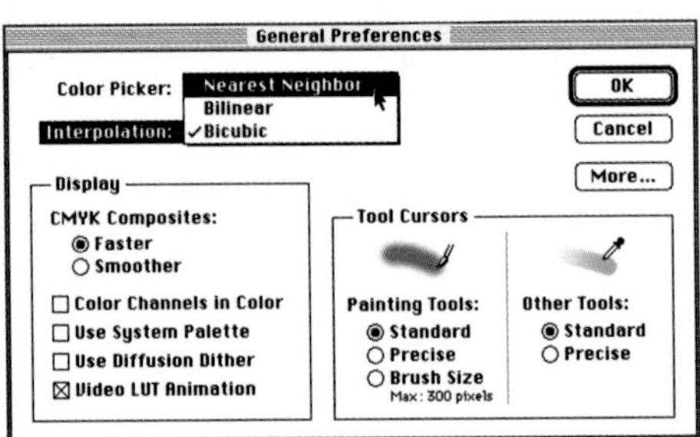

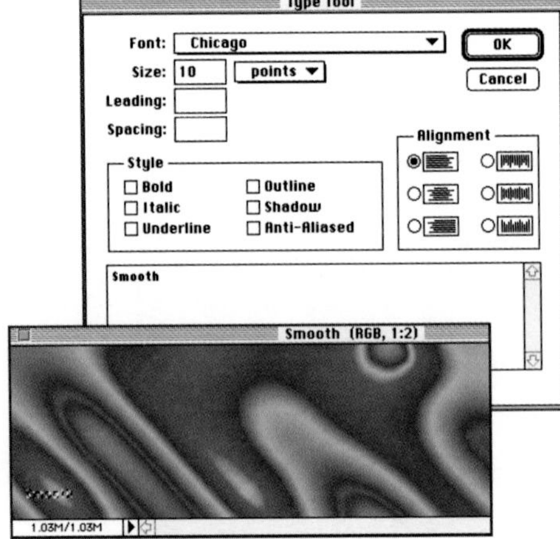

This technique is especially useful if you are trying to quickly get the bitmapped, computer look.

① In the File ➥ Preferences ➥ General (Command-K) menu, select "Nearest Neighbor" for the Interpolation Method. When this method is used, Photoshop simply duplicates the neighboring pixels when a selection is enlarged rather than averaging them.

② Enter the text. In the Type tool dialog box, select a small point size. We used Chicago at 10 points. This will allow your text to be very bitmapped when enlarged. Be sure that "Anti-Aliased" is not checked. Type your text and click OK.

③ With the type as the active selection, choose Image ➥ Effect ➥ Scale from the menu bar and enlarge the text. Holding down the Shift key keeps the selection in proportion.

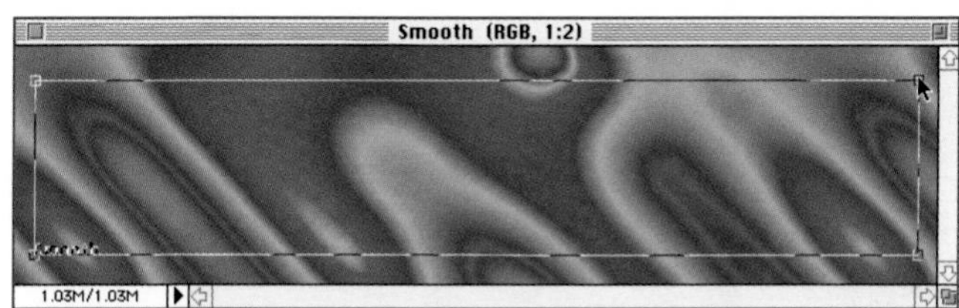

Because the "Nearest Neighbor" interpolation method was selected in Step 1, the enlarged selection gets blocky.

That's all there is to it!

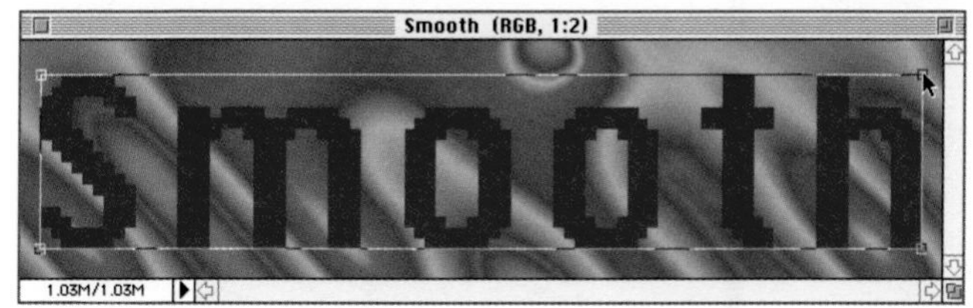

VARIATIONS

Add smooth text to contrast the "jaggies" for a nice effect.

Bit
Boyeez

You can get an outline around your text by using Edit ➥ Stroke. This command strokes the selection with the foreground color, so be sure it's not the same color as your text!

Mint
Chocolate
Chunk

After enlarging the text a little (about 25%), choose Filter ➥ Noise ➥ Add Noise. Then enlarge the text even more. The noisy pixels inside the text enlarge right along with the text, complementing the bitmappy look.

Blaring

Or, instead of using Filter ➥ Noise, try Filter ➥ Midnights TV (from the Sucking Fish Series of filters). ■

TTFN

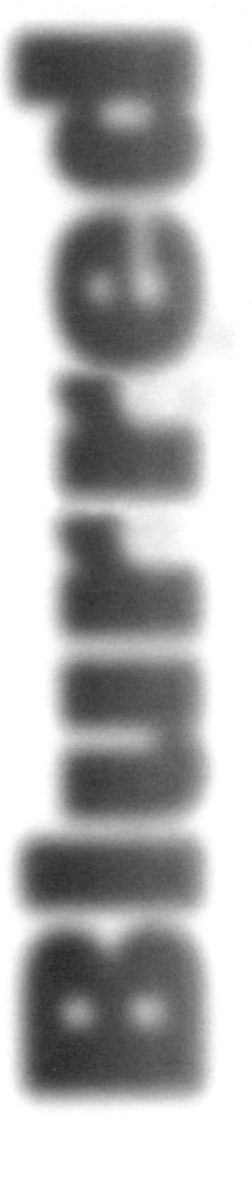

① Create a new file. Use the Type tool to enter the text you want to blur. We used Folio Bold Condensed at 100 points in this example.

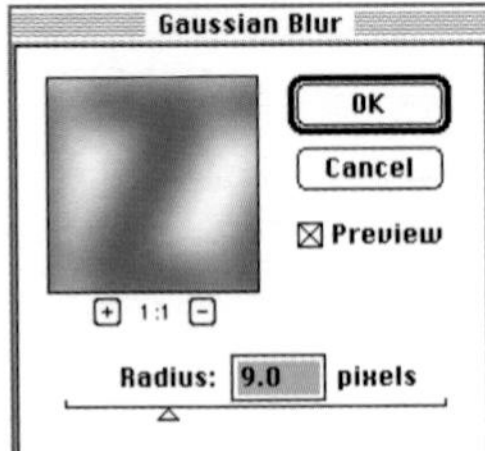

② Select ➥ None (Command-D). Then apply Filter ➥ Blur ➥ Gaussian Blur. We used a radius of 9 pixels.

You should get something like this.

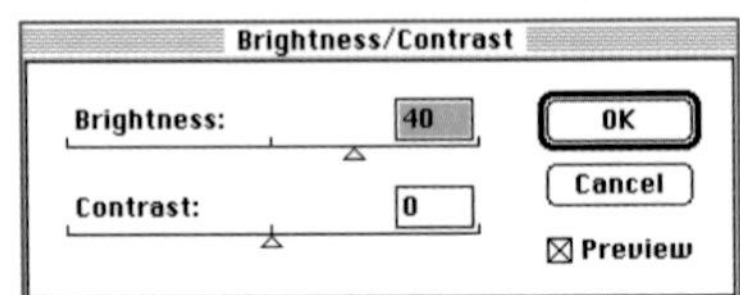

③ In order to lighten the type, choose Image ➥ Adjust ➥ Brightness/Contrast (Brightness: +40). This will add some haziness to the image.

Your type should now look something like this.

VARIATIONS

Blurred text looks particularly good when contrasted against unblurred text.

After applying Photoshop's Gaussian Blur filter, choose Filter ➥ Other ➥ Minimum to beef up the blur. The higher the setting, the wider the blur. A setting of 8 pixels was used here.

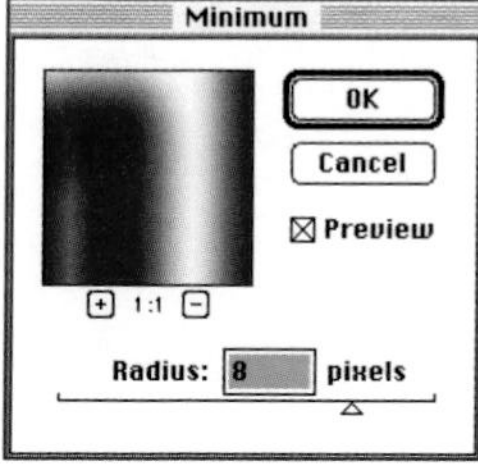

The result is a more robust blur.

You could also use Filter ➥ Other ➥ Maximum to thin down the type. A setting of 9 pixels was used here.

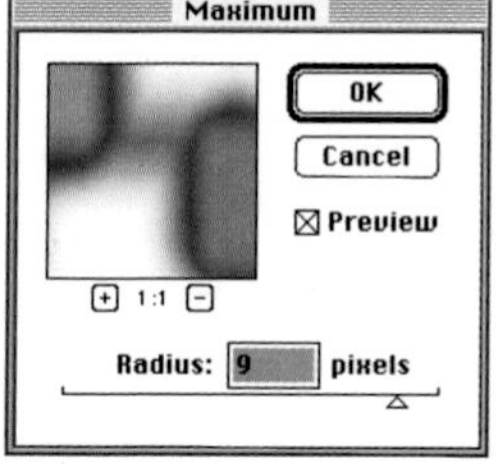

Some interesting residue is left between the letters.

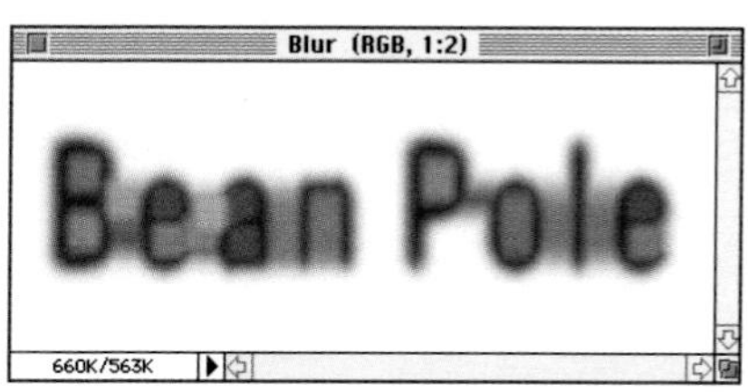

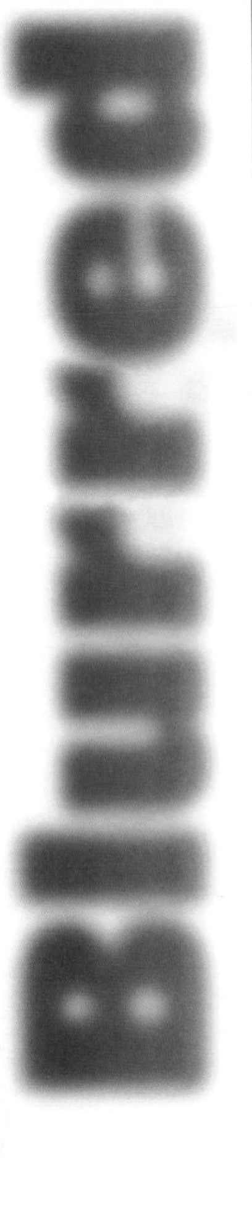

Clouds

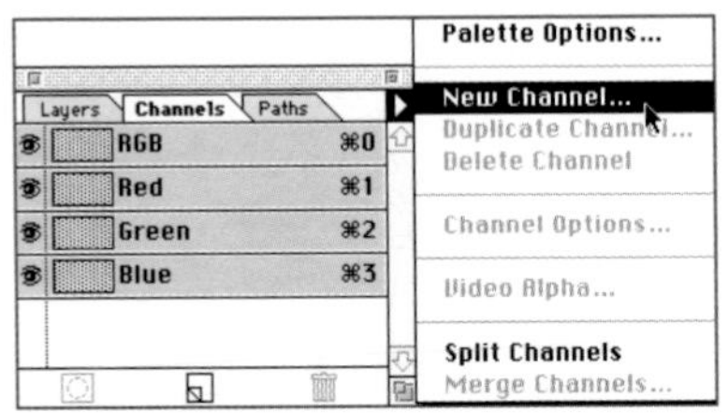

① Create a new file, and create a new channel, Channel #4.

② Set the foreground color to white. Enter your text into Channel #4. A round-edged font such as VAG Rounded, which we used here at 80 points, works best.

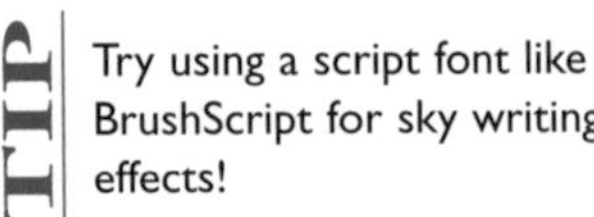

Try using a script font like BrushScript for sky writing effects!

③ Return to the composite channel and Select ➥ All. Change the background color to a sky blue and press Delete to fill the selection with the color. Apply Filter ➥ Render ➥ Clouds.

Load Selection

Source	
Document:	Clouds
Channel:	#4
☐ Invert	
Operation	
◉ New Selection	
○ Add to Selection	
○ Subtract from Selection	
○ Intersect with Selection	

OK / Cancel

④ Choose Select ➥ Load ➥ Selection, and load the Channel #4 selection.

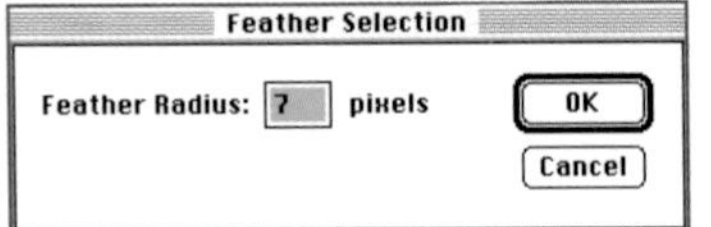

⑤ Now choose Select ➥ Feather and use a setting of 7 pixels.

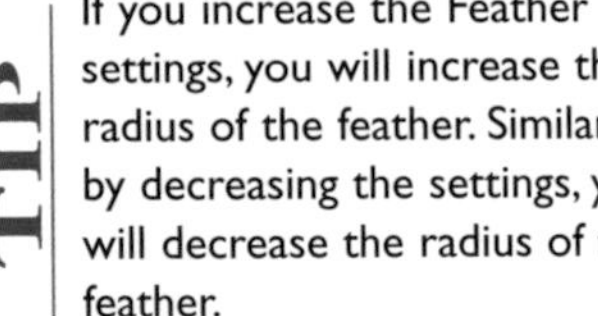

If you increase the Feather settings, you will increase the radius of the feather. Similarly, by decreasing the settings, you will decrease the radius of the feather.

⑥ Press Option-Delete to fill the selection with white. ■

created by Craig Swanson

©D'Pix 1995

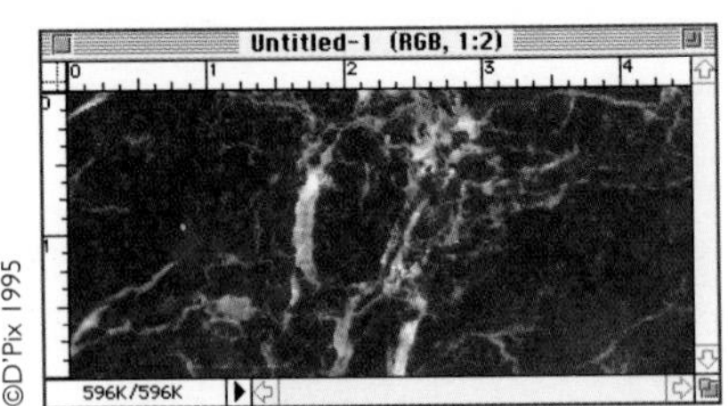

① Open a file containing the background you wish to chisel. Obviously, a marble or stone texture will work best for this effect. We used a stock photo of a piece of marble from D'Pix for this example.

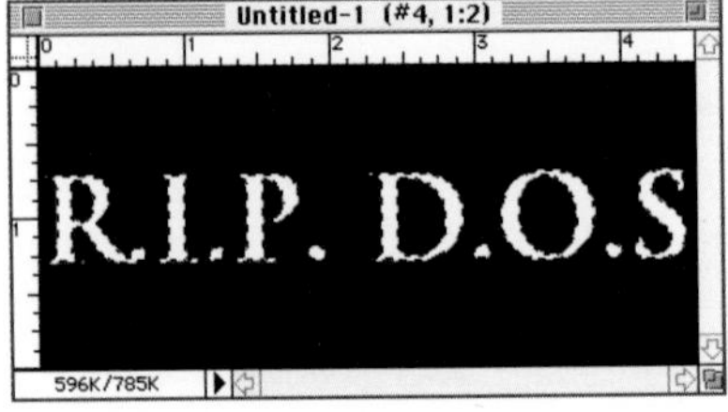

② Create a new channel (Channel #4), and change the foreground color to white. Use the Type tool to enter the text in the new channel. This epitaph appears in Trajan Bold at 55 points.

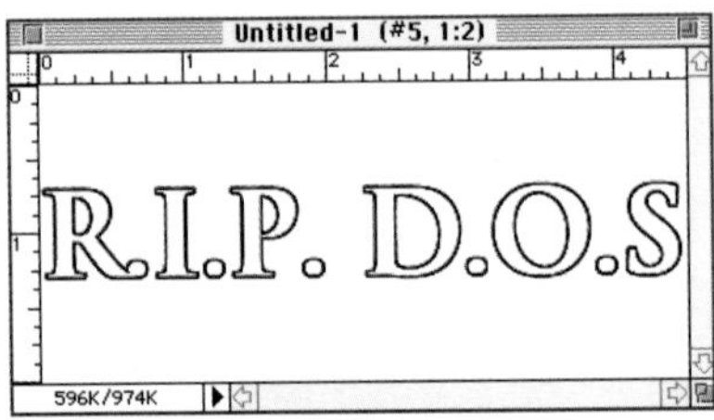

③ Create another new channel (Channel #5). Choose Edit ➡ Stroke (3 pixels, Outside, 100%, Normal). Choose Select ➡ None (Command-D) and Image ➡ Map ➡ Invert (Command-I).

④ Go back to Channel #4 and duplicate it to create Channel #4 copy. Choose Filter ➡ Blur ➡ Gaussian Blur (6 pixels). Choose Filter ➡ Stylize ➡ Emboss (240°, 3 pixels, 200%).

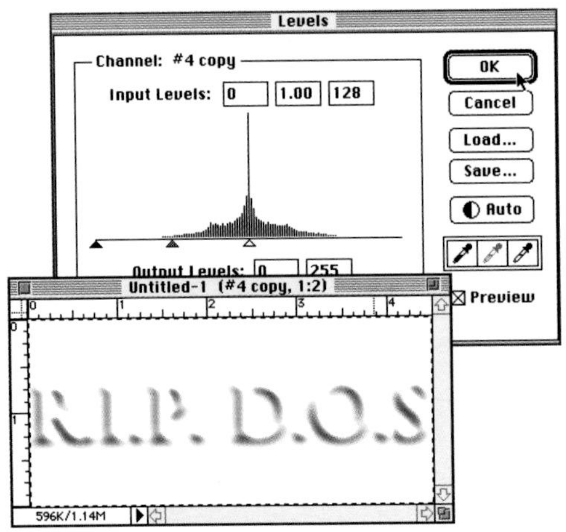

⑤ Select ➡ All (Command-A) and Copy (Command-C) the image to the clipboard. Choose Image ➡ Adjust ➡ Levels (Input Levels: 0, 1, 128).

⑥ Select ➥ Load Selection (Channel #5). Press Option-Delete to fill the background with white. Deselect the text. Choose Image ➥ Map ➥ Invert (Command-I).

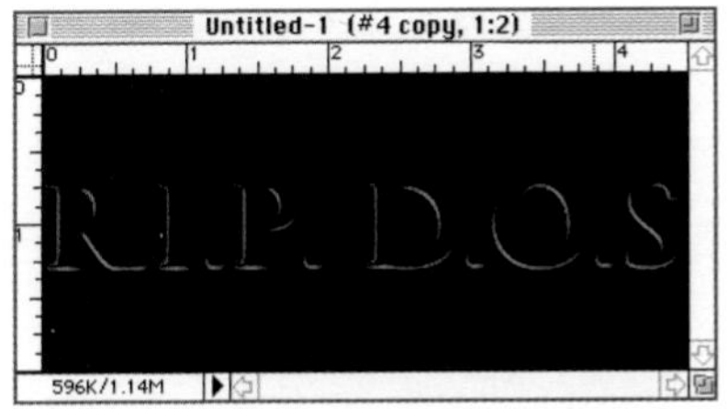

⑦ Create a new channel (#6) and paste (Command-V) in the clipboard. Choose Image ➥ Map ➥ Invert (Command-I), then Image ➥ Adjust ➥ Levels (Input Levels: 0, 1, 128).

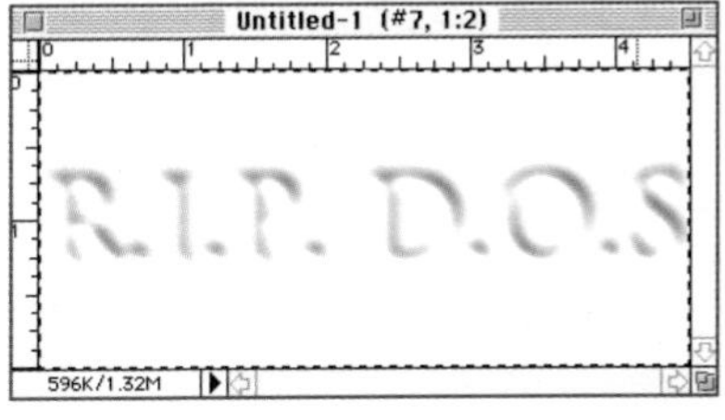

⑧ Select ➥ Load Selection (Channel #5). Press Option-Delete to fill the background with white. Deselect the text. Choose Image ➥ Map ➥ Invert (Command-I).

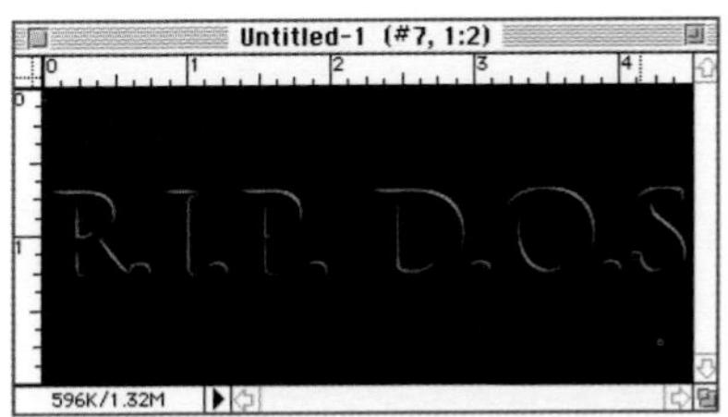

⑨ Go back to Channel #4 and duplicate it to create Channel #4 copy 2. Choose Image ➥ Adjust ➥ Invert (Command-I). Apply Filter ➥ Blur ➥ Gaussian Blur (3 pixels). Change the background color to white. Select ➥ All (Command-A) and press the left arrow key and down arrow key four times to offset the image.

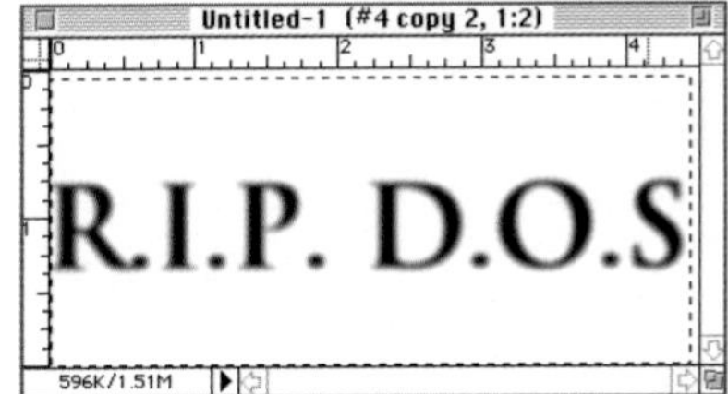

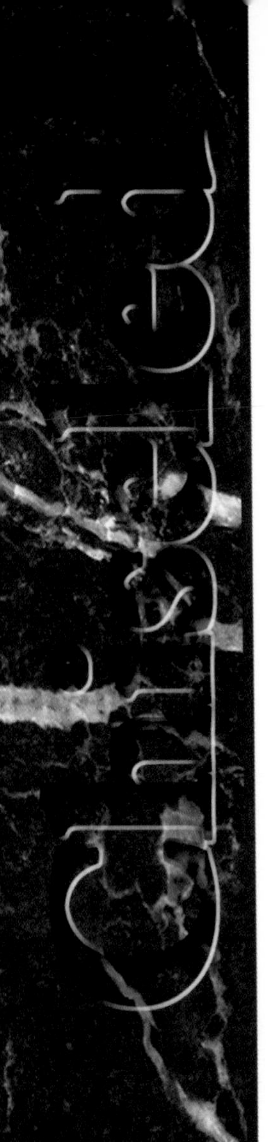

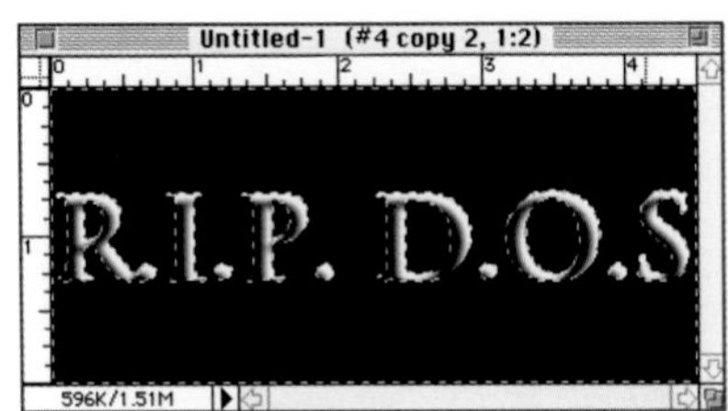

⑩ Select ➥ Load Selection (Channel #4). Choose Select ➥ Inverse. Change the foreground color to black and press Option-Delete to fill the selection.

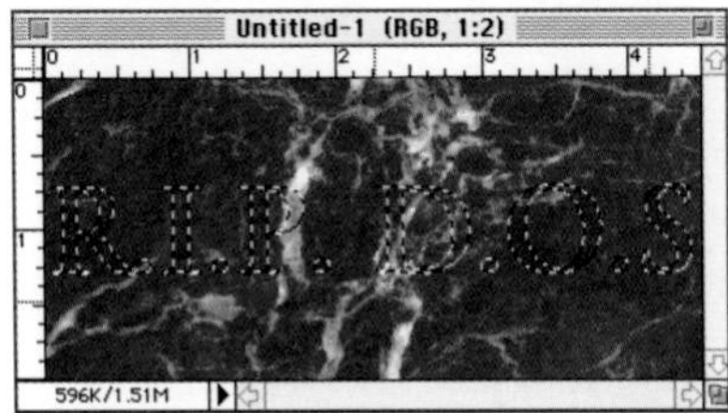

⑪ Return to the RGB window. Make sure the foreground color is black. Choose Select ➥ Load Selection (Channel #4) and Edit ➥ Fill (Foreground Color, 15%, Normal).

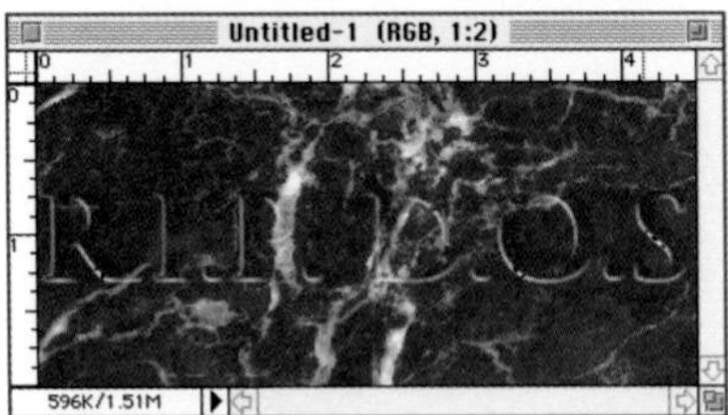

⑫ Select ➥ Load Selection (Channel #4 copy) and change the foreground color to white. Press Option-Delete twice to fill the selection twice.

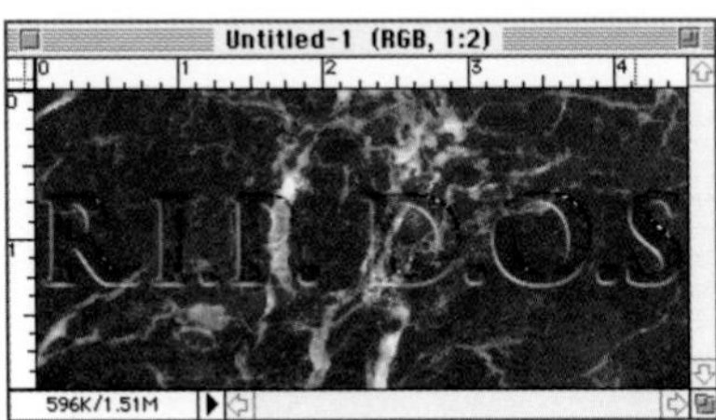

⑬ Select ➥ Load Selection (Channel #7) and change the foreground color to black. Press Option-Delete twice to fill the selection twice.

⑭ Choose Select ➥ Load Selection (Channel #4 copy 2) then Edit ➥ Fill (Foreground Color, 85%, Normal). ■

CHROME

created by Patrick Quinn, pjq Design

① Create a new file. Select Mode ➡ Grayscale, then select Mode ➡ Multichannel. Create a new channel (#2). You should now see a blank, black image area.

② Make sure that the foreground color is white (press D, then X). Click on the Type tool, choose the font you wish to use (In this example, we used Copperplate 33bc, 50 point), and enter the text you want to work with in the new channel.

③ Set the foreground color to black and the background color to white (Press D).

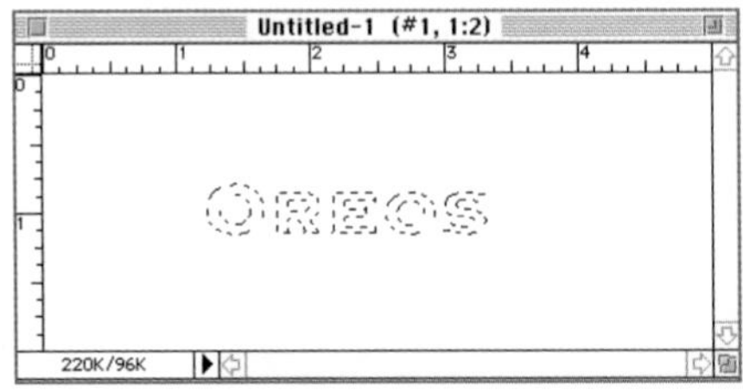

④ Return to the Channel #1 window (press Command-1). You should still be able to see the active selection. If you don't, then choose Select ➡ Load Selection (Channel #2) to make the area inside the type active.

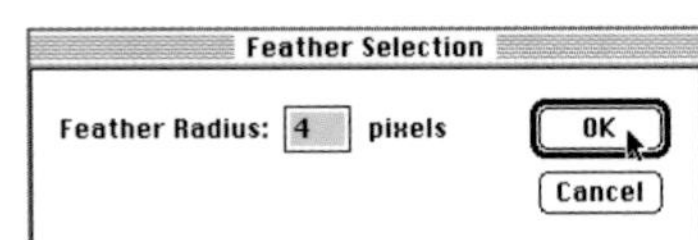

⑤ Now, choose Select ➡ Feather and set the amount to 4 pixels. You may find that varying this number will produce a better effect—it will depend on the typeface that you choose. Choose Edit ➡ Fill (Foreground Color, Opacity: 100%, Normal). Choose Select ➡ None (Command-D).

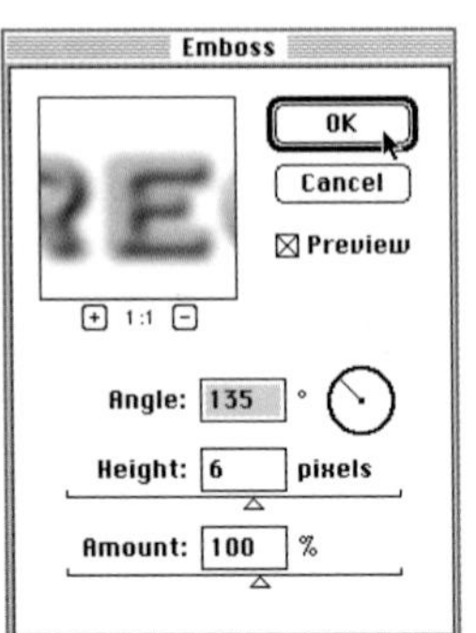

⑥ Apply Filter ➡ Stylize ➡ Emboss (Angle: 135°, Height: 6, Amount: 100%) to raise the text. The angle setting will determine the direction of the primary source of light.

MagicCurve file

⑦ Choose Select ➡ Load Selection (Channel #2, with the invert box checked). Click on the foreground color and change it to 50% gray by changing the "B" setting of the HSB to 50%.

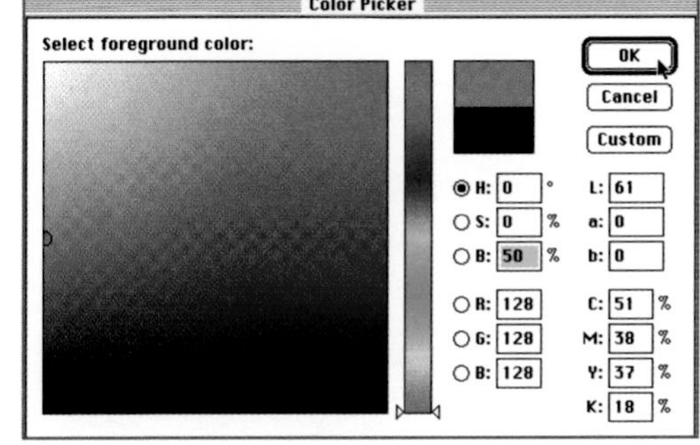

⑧ Choose Edit ➡ Fill (Foreground Color, Opacity: 100%, Normal). Choose Select ➡ None (or Command-D).

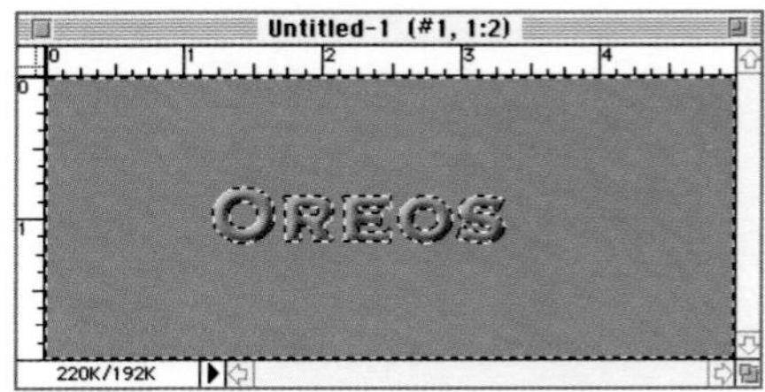

⑨ This is the magic step. Go to Image ➡ Adjust ➡ Curves (Command-M). Click on the Load button and find the MagicCurve file, or re-create the curve you see here. The more precise it is, the better it will work. Click OK.

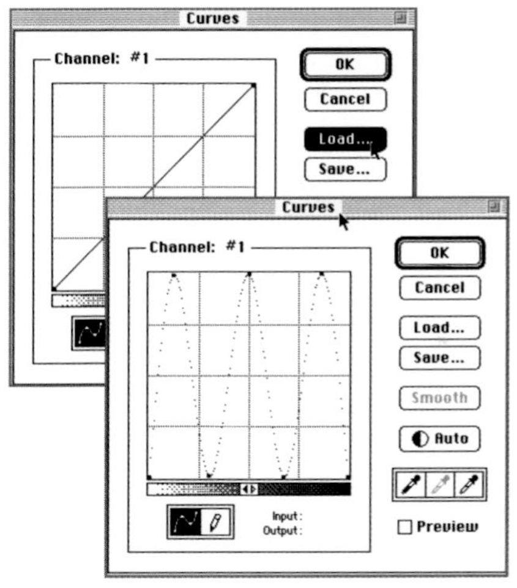

Do you see this?

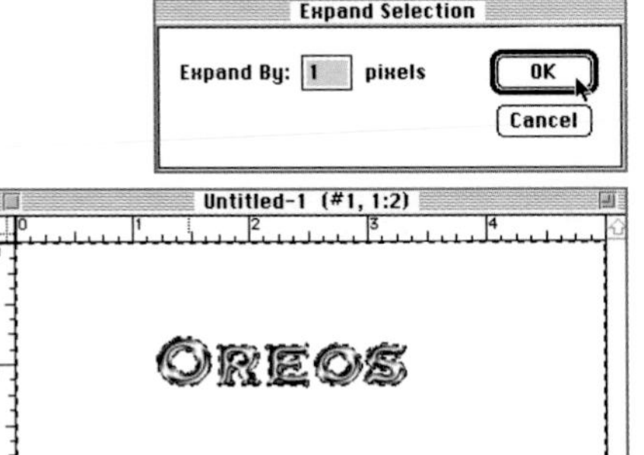

⑩ Choose Select ➥ Load Selection (Channel #2). Then choose Image ➥ Map ➥ Invert (Command-I).

⑪ Choose Select ➥ Modify ➥ Expand (1 pixel). Choose Select ➥ Inverse. Set the foreground color to white (press X) and press Option-Delete to make the background white.

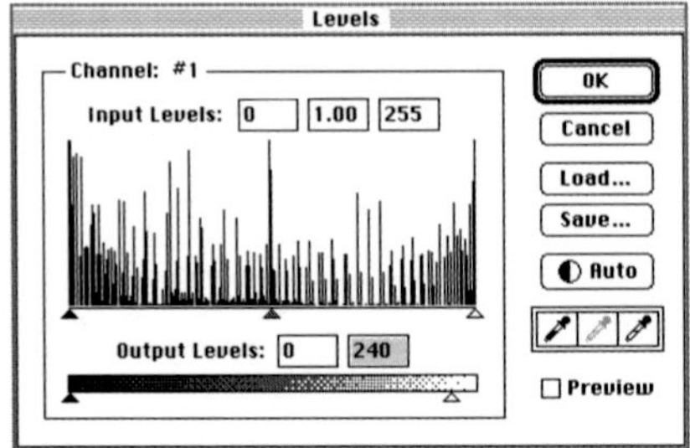

⑫ Go to Select ➥ Inverse, then Image ➥ Adjust ➥ Levels (Command-L). In this dialog, change the "Output Levels" white point (the lower right box) from 255 to 240 and click OK.

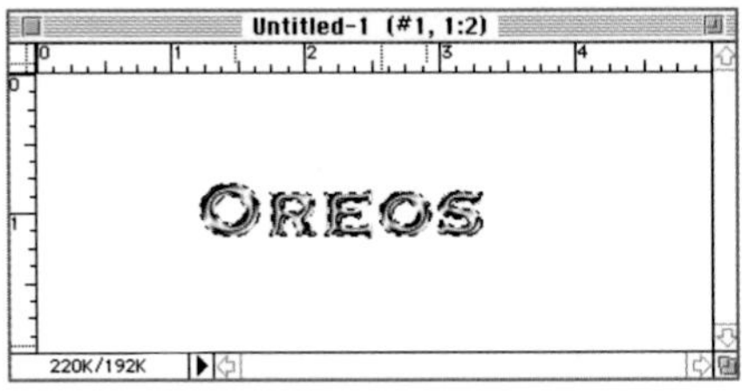

TIP

You can use the Input Levels in the Levels dialog box to fine tune the greys in the chrome. Moving the middle (gray) slider to the left will brighten things up.

CHROME 2

Follow the steps for creating Plastic type (page 148) with the following exceptions:

Step ④ : do not deselect the selection;

Step ⑤ : skip this step;

Step ⑥ : deselect the text (Command-D) after this step;

Step ⑦ : skip this step.

Now, choose Filter ➥ Stylize ➥ Find Edges. You may prefer using Find Edges & Invert. Choose Edit ➥ Select All, then copy (Command-C) the image. Go to the RGB channel (Command-0), and paste (Command-V) the text into this composite channel. That's it.

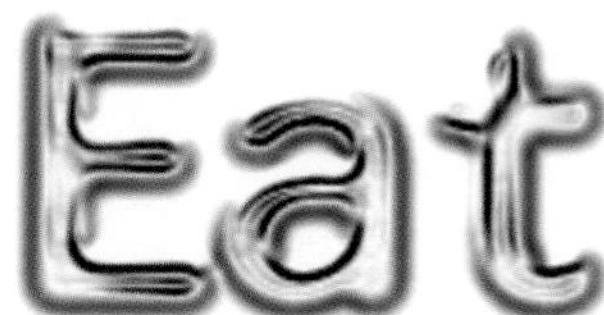

VARIATIONS

Adding a little color to the chrome might be the final touch it needs. Choose Image ➥ Adjust ➥ Curves (Command-M). Best results will come from working in the color channels one at a time. In these two variations, we bent the Cyan curve up a little, then down a little. You may find it easier to use the Hue/Saturation (Command-U) dialog box, in which you can slide the Hue slider to the left and right to produce subtle color changes.

Adding a lot of color can change your chrome to something that looks more like gold. You will need to convert the file to a color mode first. We chose CMYK (choose Mode ➥ CMYK). Choose Image ➥ Adjust ➥ Hue/Saturation (Command-U). Make sure the preview box is checked so you can see what you're doing. Click on the Colorize checkbox in the lower right, and try these values: Hue: 27, Saturation: 59, Lightness: 0. ■

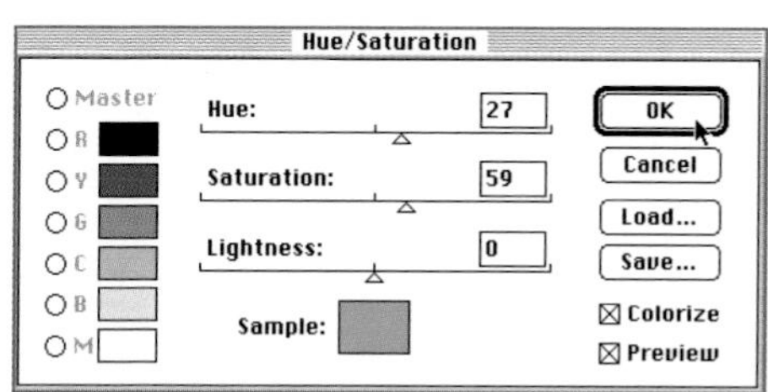

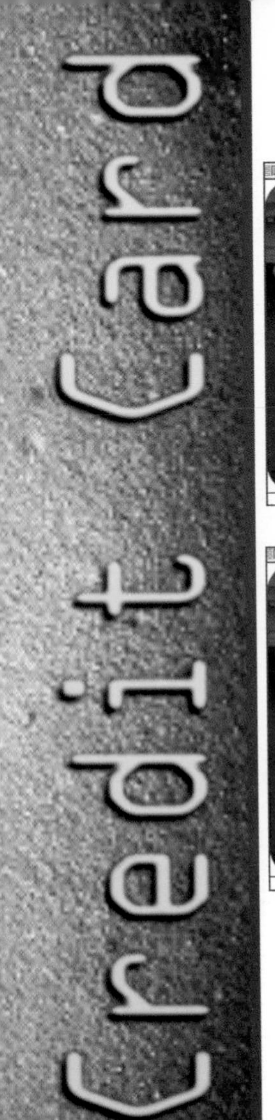

©Fotosets 1995

① Open the picture you'd like use as your credit card background or create a new file. This stock photo comes from Fotosets.

② Use the Type tool to enter the text and move it to where you'd like it to fall on the image. We used OCR-A font at 40 points to achieve a more realistic look.

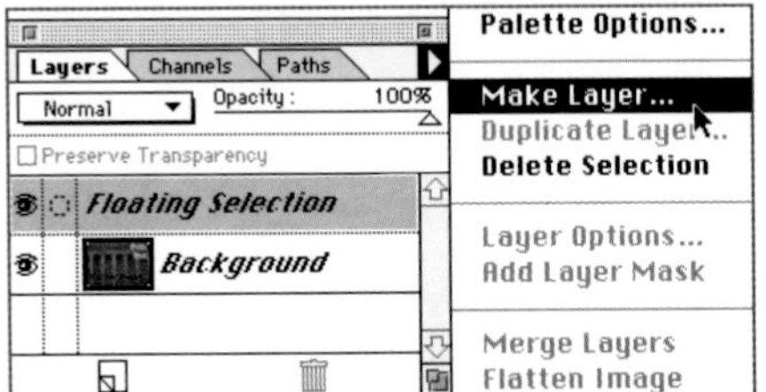

③ In the Layers palette, select **Make Layer** from the pullout menu. This will make the floating selection (your type) fall onto a layer of its own. Change the layer name to "Text" and leave all other settings at their default.

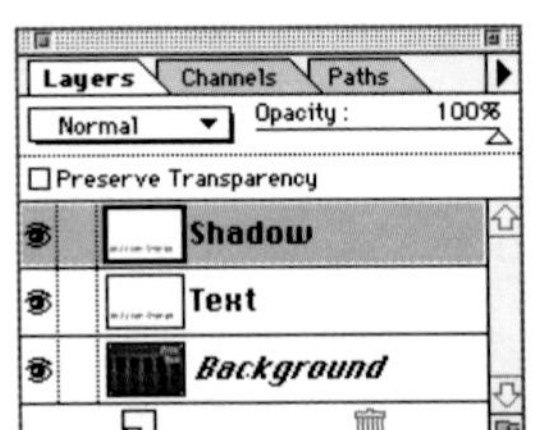

④ Select **Duplicate layer** from the pullout menu and name it "Shadow." You should now have a total of three layers in your file.

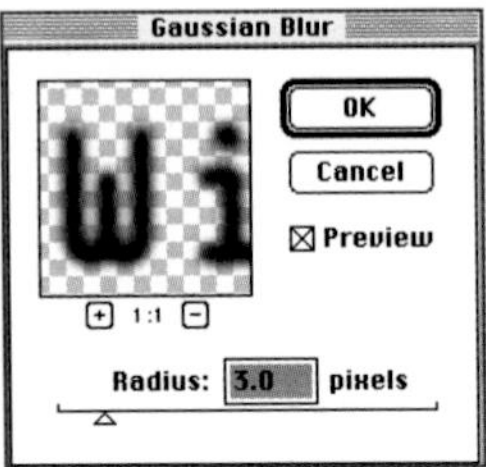

⑤ Make the Text layer the active layer. For ease, you might also want to make it the only visible layer, too. Apply Filter ➡ Blur ➡ Gaussian Blur. A setting of 3 pixels was used for this image. If your type is considerably larger, use a higher pixel setting.

⑥ Apply Filter ➥ Stylize ➥ Find Edges to the text layer. This is the beginning of the raised effect.

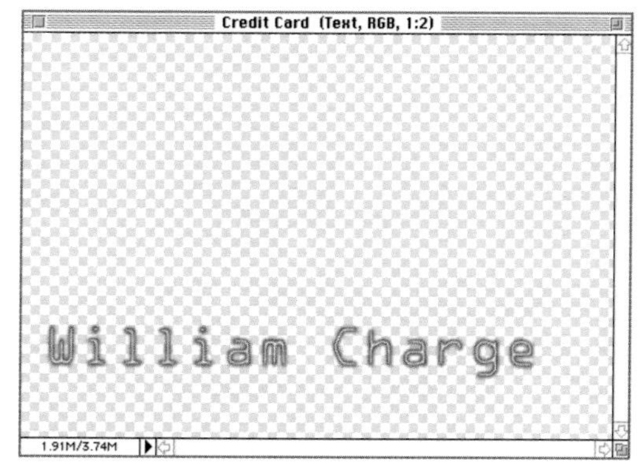

⑦ Next, apply Filter ➥ Other ➥ Offset to the text layer. For this example, we used settings of 3 pixels right and 2 pixels down. This filter moves the text slightly so that the Shadow layer will show on the top and left sides.

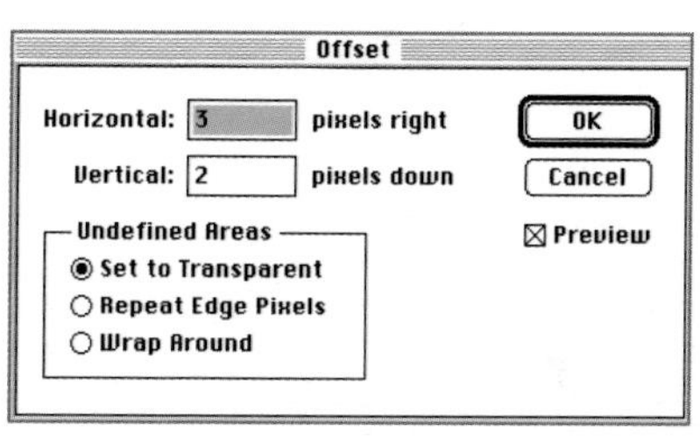

⑧ Make the Shadow layer the active layer. Apply Filter ➥ Blur ➥ Gaussian Blur. Use a setting of 3, like you did in Step 5.

⑨ Click the eye icon next to the Text layer so it's visible, but keep the Shadow layer the active one, so you can see what you're doing.

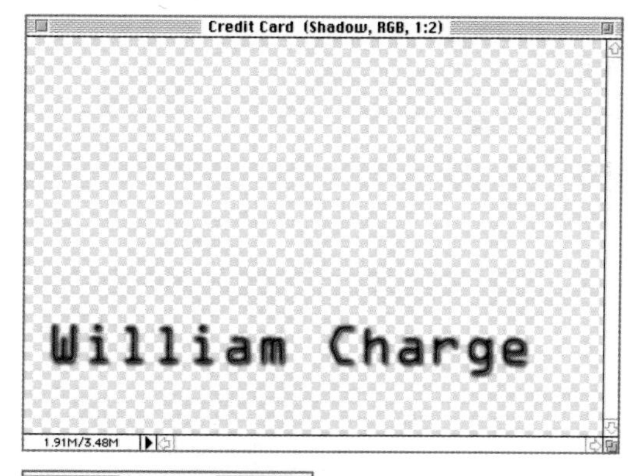

Use Filter ➥ Other ➥ Maximum to thin down the text on the Shadow layer. This text will be the shadow side of the letters (which is why we named it "Shadow"—convenient, eh?). A setting of 3 pixels was used here.

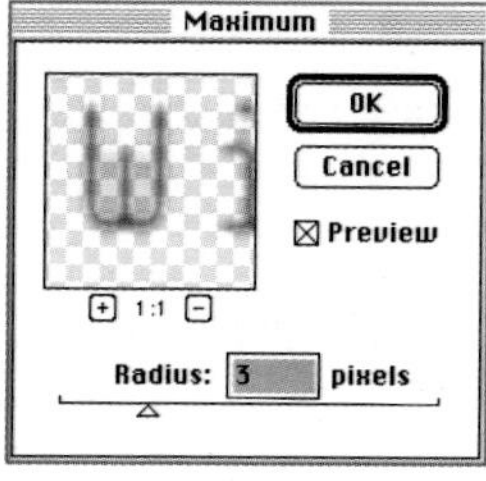

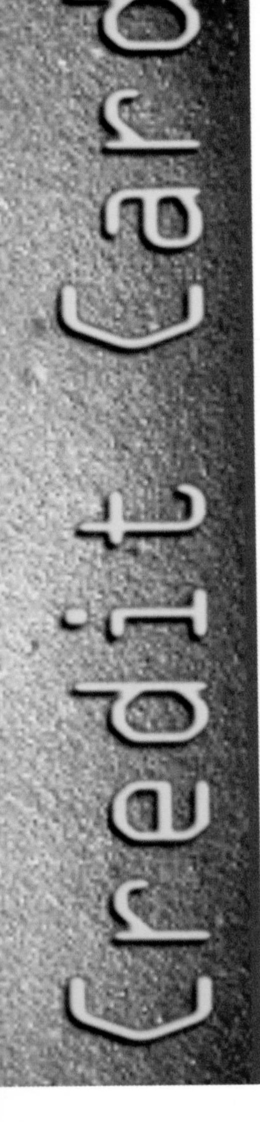

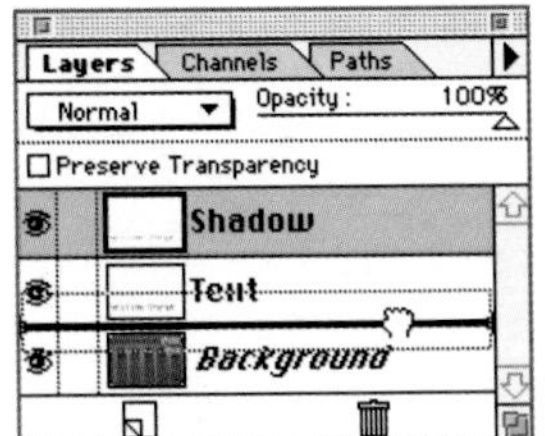

(10) Make all three layers visible. Move the Shadow layer to make it the layer directly below the Text layer. This puts the Shadow layer behind the Text layer so it doesn't obscure the words.

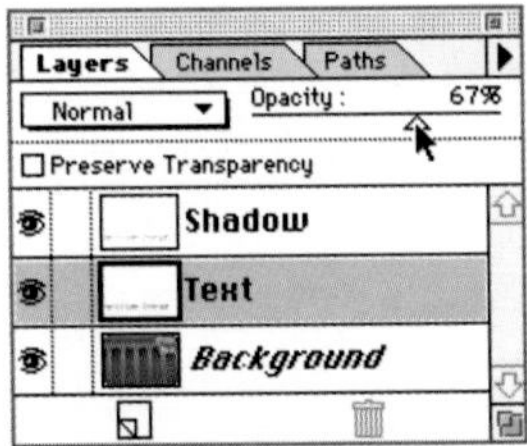

(11) Make the Text layer the active one. Adjust the Opacity level to 67%. This lets the background image show through and reduces the harshness of the shadows.

If you like the way the image shows through the text, you can flatten the image and stop now.

But, if you want the look of ink printed onto the "raised" letters keep going.

(12) To add the ink, make the shadow layer active and duplicate it by choosing Duplicate layer from the Layers pullout menu. Name the layer "Ink."

Use Filter ➡ Other ➡ Offset to move this layer the same amount that you moved the Text layer in Step 7. The Offset dialog box will have the same settings you used the last time the effect was applied, so all you need to do is click OK.

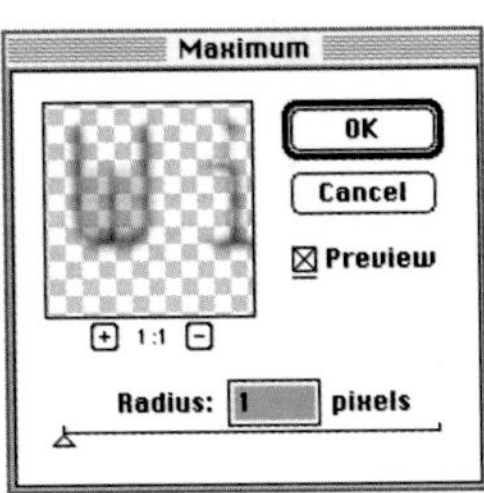

Use Filter ➡ Other ➡ Maximum with a setting of 1 pixel to thin the text even more. At higher settings, the letters may start to fill in, so do some experimenting first!

⑬ Select Image ➥ Map ➥ Invert (Command-I) to make the text white.

⑭ To colorize the type, choose Image ➥ Adjust ➥ Hue/Saturation. Be sure to click on the "Colorize" checkbox first to give you the appropriate sliders to work with. Adjust the sliders until you've achieved the color you want.

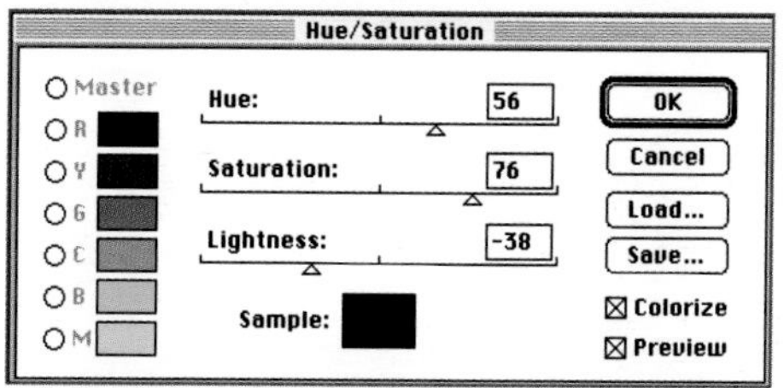

Flatten the image and charge it! ■

© PhotoDisc 1995

① Open a new file or a file with an image you want to cut the text from. This stock photo comes from PhotoDisc.

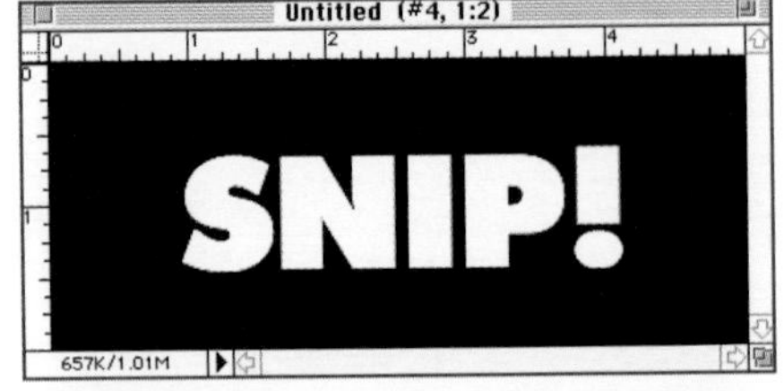

② Create a new channel (Channel #4). Use the Type tool to enter the text. While the text selection is still active, save the selection (to Channel #5).

Deselect the text (Command-D).

③ Now, apply Filter ➥ Blur ➥ Gaussian Blur (3.5 pixels). Then choose Filter ➥ Other ➥ Offset (10 pixels right, 10 pixels down, and make sure to select the **Repeat Edge Pixels** option). This channel is the shadow that will appear behind the text.

④ Return to the composite channel (Command-0), and create a new layer (Layer #1).

⑤ Load the selection you saved in Step 2 (Channel #5), and fill it with black, or any other color you want to use for the shadow.

⑥ Keep the selection active. Now, choose Select ➥ Load Selection, select the shadow channel (#4), and choose the Intersect with Selection option. The active selection should look like this.

⑦ Change the foreground color to the color you want to make the background. Press Option-Delete to fill selection, deselect it (Command-D) and you're done. No cuts, no bleeding, no errors.

TIP

If you want to fine tune the shadow (brighten, soften, change its color), then load Channel #5. Now choose Select ➥ Load Selection, choose the shadow channel (#4), and click on the **Subtract from Selection** option. The shadow is now selected.

VARIATIONS

If you want to cut through one image to see another underneath, before opening the file containing the foreground image in Step 1, open the file containing the background image. Copy the part of the image you want to use as the background. Complete all the steps above except Step 7. Instead choose Edit ➥ Paste Into. Presto! If you need to move the background image, drag it around using the Selection tool pointer—but only if you didn't deselect it first.

Both stock photos ©Image Club Graphics 1995

In Step 1 open a new file with a white image area and do the entire exercise. In step 7, choose white as the foreground color. The type needs a soft outline to separate the foreground from white background, so load the selection you saved in Step 2, and choose Edit ➥ Stroke (1 pixel, Center, 10% Opacity, Normal).

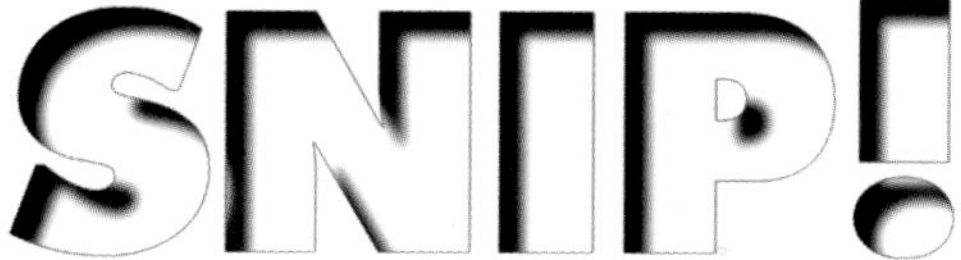

Anything you can put in a channel, can be cut out. Try using a hard-edge paintbrush and scrawling text into the channel. ■

©D'Pix 1995

Earthquake

TOOLBOX

QuakeStripes preset file

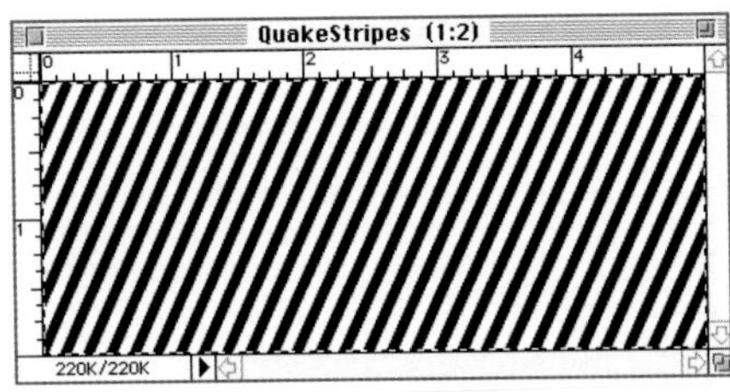

① Open the QuakeStripes preset file included on the CD, choose Select ➡ All and copy the image to the clipboard (Command-C). Close the file (Command-W).

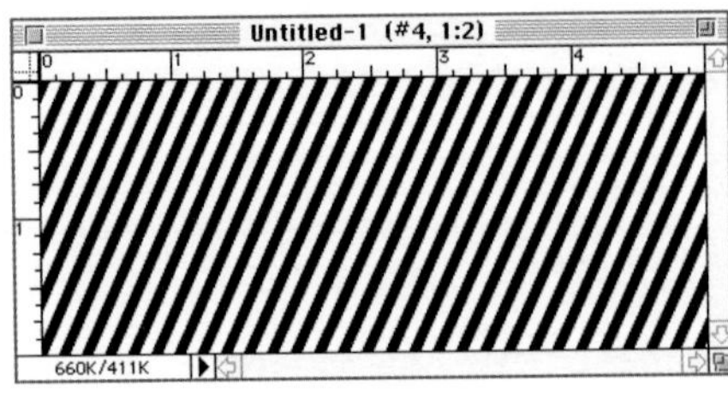

② Create a new file. Create a new channel. Paste the clipboard into this new channel (Command-V). Use the Scale tool to fill the channel with the stripes.

TIP

The width of the stripes in this file may not be a good width the for the size of text that you want to distort. If they are too small, then use the Scale tool to make them larger. If they are too big, then scale them down, copy them, paste the copy back in to the channel and move the copy so it continues the striped pattern. Repeat if necessary.

③ Return to the composite channel (Command-0). Change the foreground color to a color for the text. Use the Type tool to enter the text. We used Helvetica BoldOblique at 65 points for this example. If you do not choose an oblique font, then check the Italic style option. It is also important to give the letters some room to move. We increased the spacing to 10.

④ While the text is still the active selection, save the selection (to create Channel #5).

⑤ We're going to move the letters in pieces by using the two channels to select only certain parts of the letters. To select the first part, choose Select ➥ Load Selection, and choose Channel #4 with the Subtract from Selection option checked.

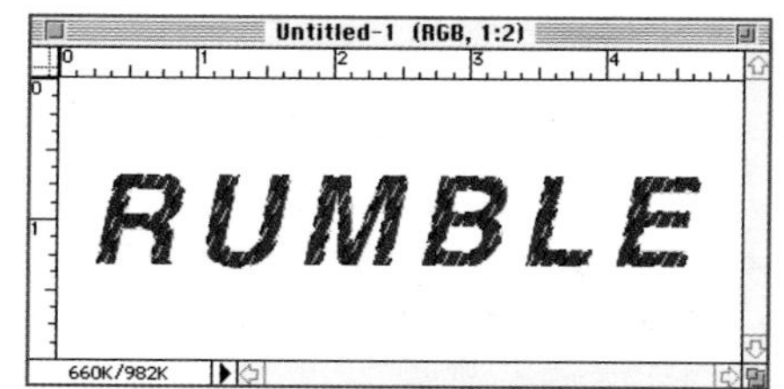

⑥ Press Command-J to float the selection. Now use the arrow keys to move the text to the left and upward. We pressed the up arrow key 2 times and the left arrow key 4 times. Deselect the text (Command-D).

⑦ Load the text selection (Channel #5), then load the stripes selection (Channel #4) with the **Intersect with Selection** option checked.

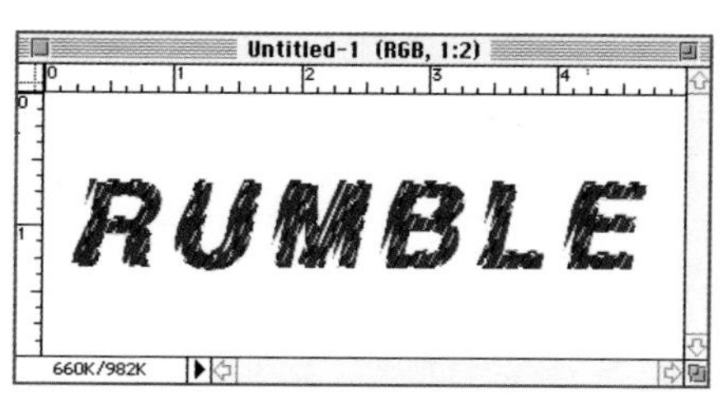

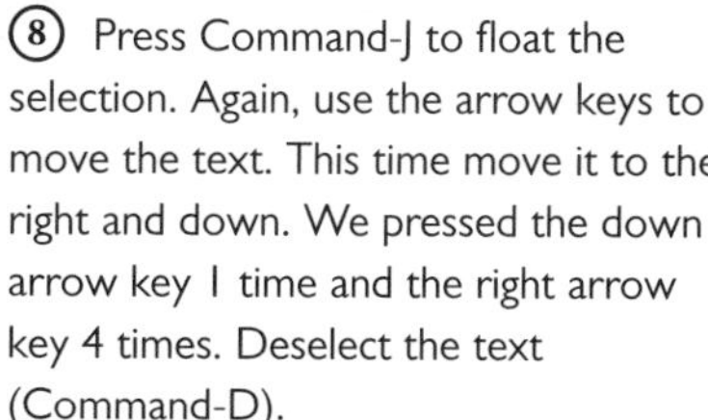

⑧ Press Command-J to float the selection. Again, use the arrow keys to move the text. This time move it to the right and down. We pressed the down arrow key 1 time and the right arrow key 4 times. Deselect the text (Command-D).

VARIATIONS

Two extra steps make this variation. Before Step 5, and after loading the text selection in Step 7, we chose Select ➥ Modify ➥ Border (7 pixels).

Add color. After floating the text selection in Steps 6 and 8, change the foreground color and press Option-Delete to fill the slices with the new color. ■

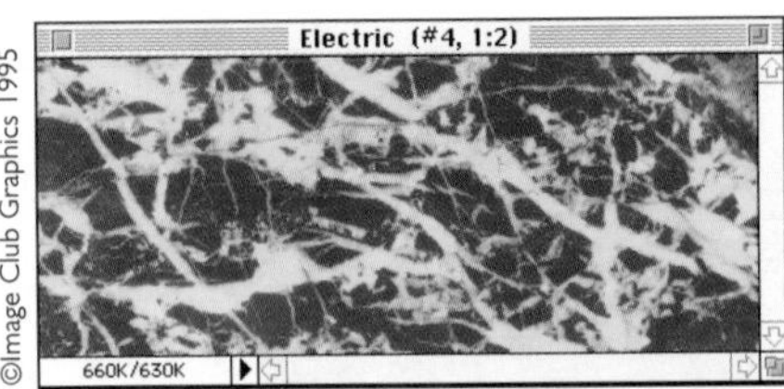

©Image Club Graphics 1995

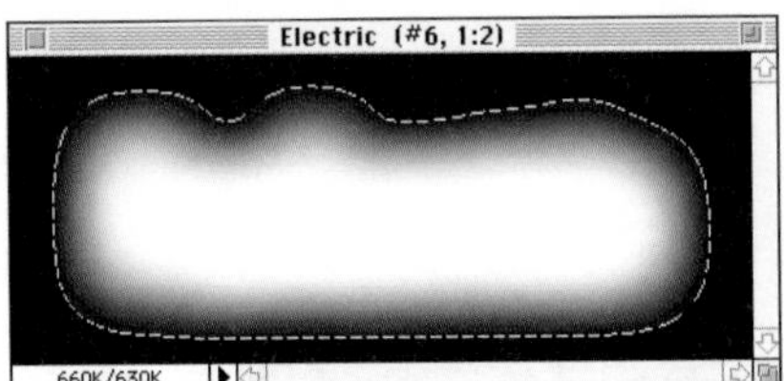

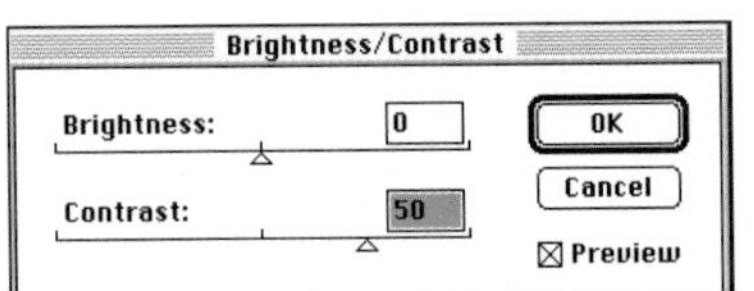

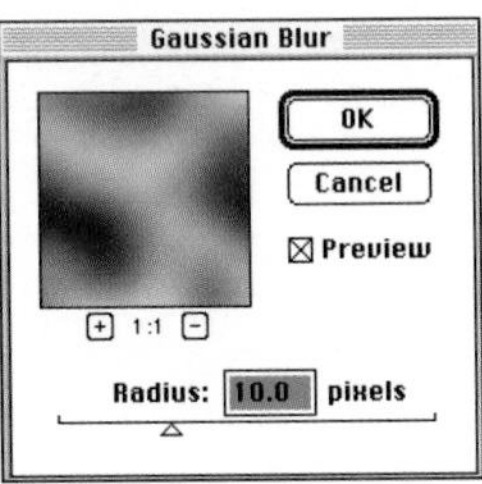

1. Open the MARBLE_04.TIF file from Image Club Graphics or another marble image. Choose Select ➥ All and Copy the image to the clipboard. Close the file.

2. Create a new file for your final image. Create a new channel (#4), and paste in the marble image from the clipboard. Move it around so a fair amount of white streaks are in view.

3. Create a new channel (#5). Use the Type tool to enter the text that will sit behind the electric sparks. We used Futura Condensed, Regular at 65 points.

4. Create another new channel (#6). Load Channel #5 (text channel) and choose Select ➥ Feather (30 pixels). Press Delete several times to generously fill the selection with white. We pressed the delete key 13 times for this example. Choose Select ➥ None. This channel, when used later, will keep the arcs visible only around the letters, rather than filling the entire image.

5. Return to Channel #4. Then Image ➥ Adjust ➥ Brightness/Contrast (Command-B) and kick the Contrast up to 50.

6. Apply Filter ➥ Blur ➥ Gaussian Blur (10 pixels).

⑦ Apply Filter ➡ Other ➡ Minimum (10 pixels). This step creates the bright bolts.

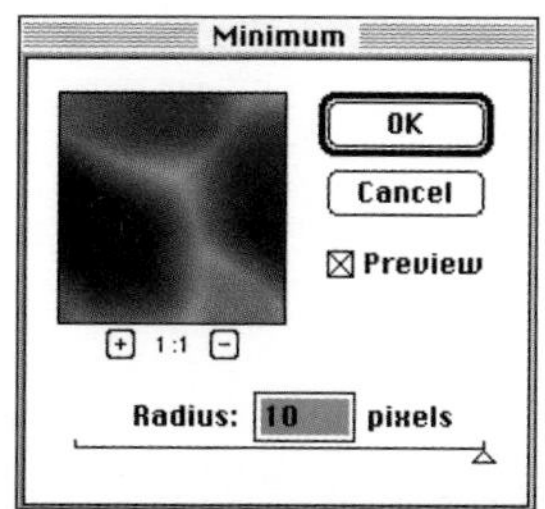

You should now have something like this.

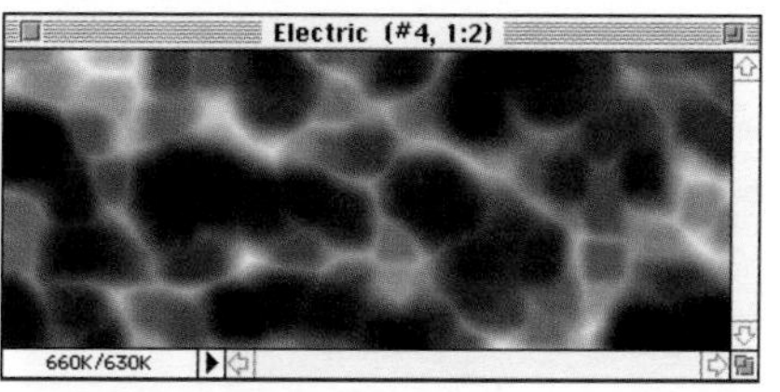

⑧ Apply Filter ➡ Sharpen ➡ Unsharp Mask (344%, 9.1 pixels, 9 levels).

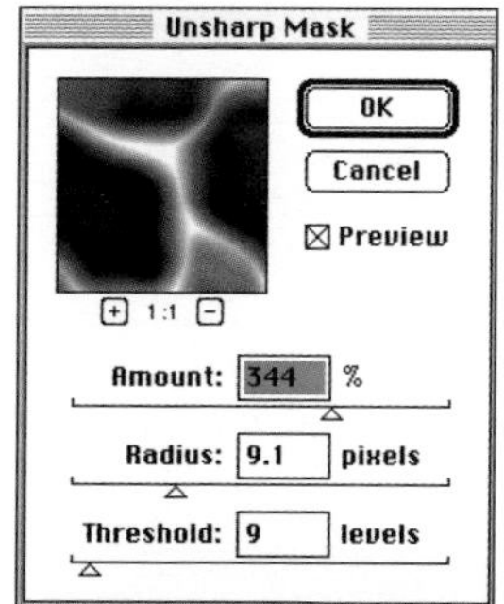

You should have something like this.

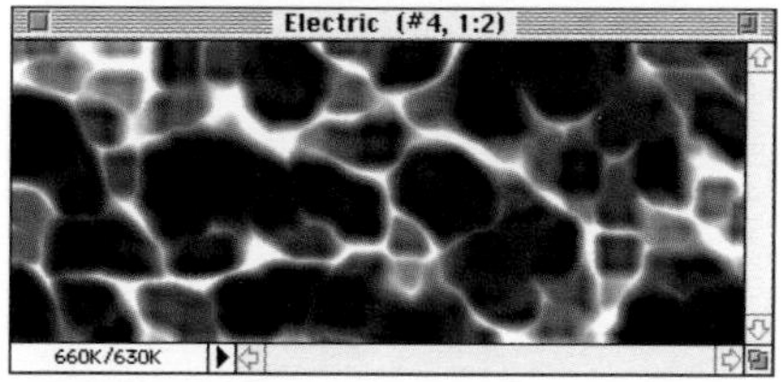

⑨ Return to the composite channel and fill the image with black. Load Channel #5 (the text channel.) Set the foreground color to the color you want the text to be. We chose a medium blue-green. Press Option-Delete to fill the selection.

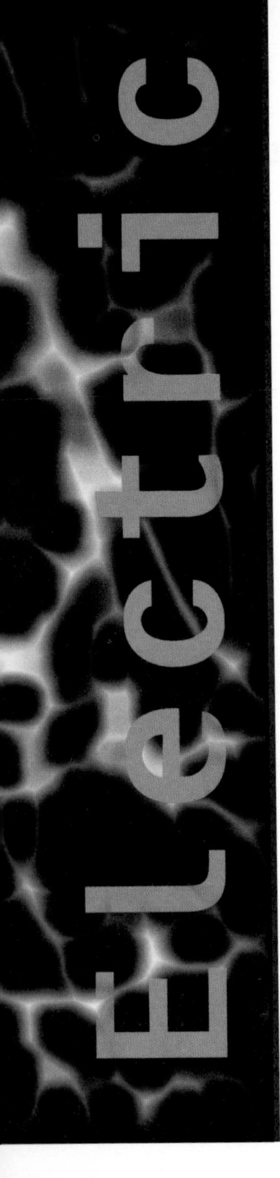

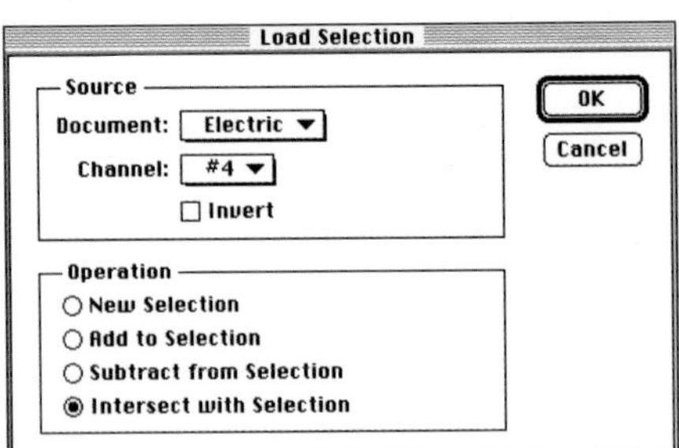

⑩ Load Channel #6 (the blurred text channel.) With that selection still active, Select ➡ Load Selection. Be sure the Intersect with Selection option is on and Load Channel #4 (the arc channel).

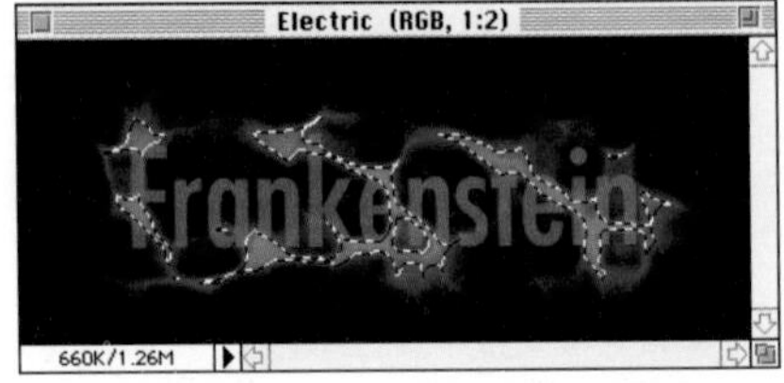

⑪ Set the foreground color to a medium purple, or whatever color you want, for the lighting. Press Option-Delete to fill the selection. You should get some arcs like this.

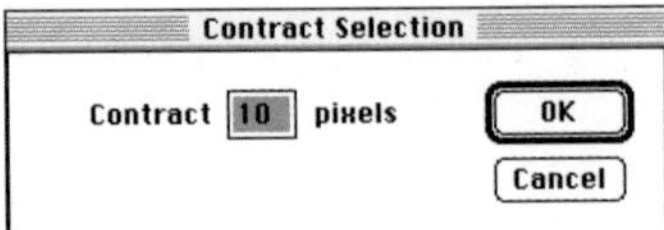

⑫ With the selection still active, choose Select ➡ Modify ➡ Contract. Use a setting of 10 pixels. This will shrink the selection.

⑬ Set the background color to white and press Delete to fill the contracted selection. This will add the white-hot highlights.

VARIATIONS

① To give the image some depth, reload the text channel (Channel #5). Then, while holding down the Command key and the Lasso tool, deselect the parts of the text that you want to leave behind the arcs. The parts that you want in front of the bolts should be left selected. For this example, we want the top of the *F*, the first *n*, the top of the *k*, the second *n*, the *t*, the *i* and the back half of the final *n* to be in front of the arcs.

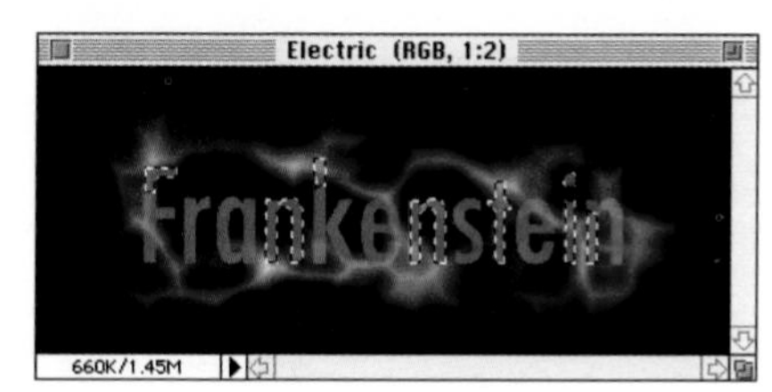

② Set the foreground color to the same color as your text and press Option-Delete to fill the selection.

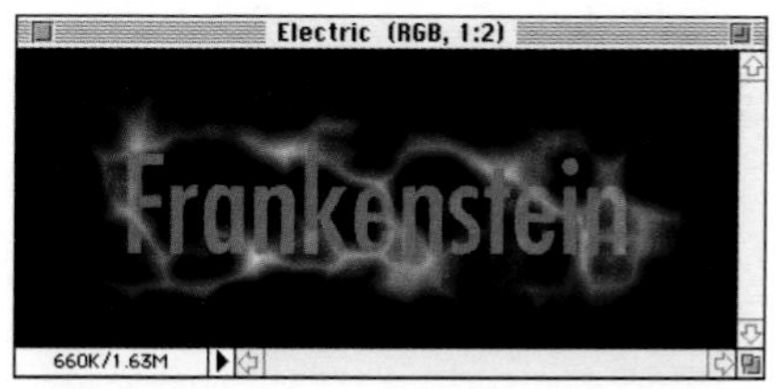

If you want all of the text in front of the arcs, do step 9 last.

This effect and any of its variations can also be done on a white background. ■

There are a number of ways to raise text in Photoshop. The first method shown here is a shortcut to embossing type. It uses Photoshop 3.0's new Lighting Effects filter, relieving you from having to find the highlights and shadows. The second method is the traditional (Can you use that word when you're talking about Photoshop?) method that uses separate channels for the highlights and shadows, allowing you to edit and re-edit those areas of the type.

Embossed 1

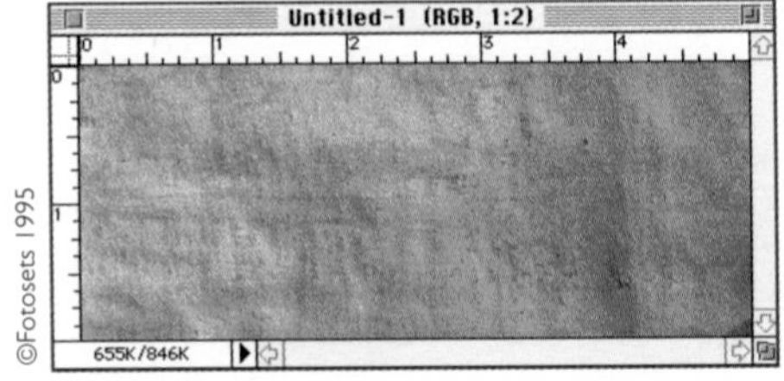

©Fotosets 1995

① Create a new RGB file, or open a file containing the surface you want to emboss. We used a clip from a stock photo from Fotosets. Whichever you choose, the file must be in RGB mode since the Lighting Effects filter only works in RGB mode.

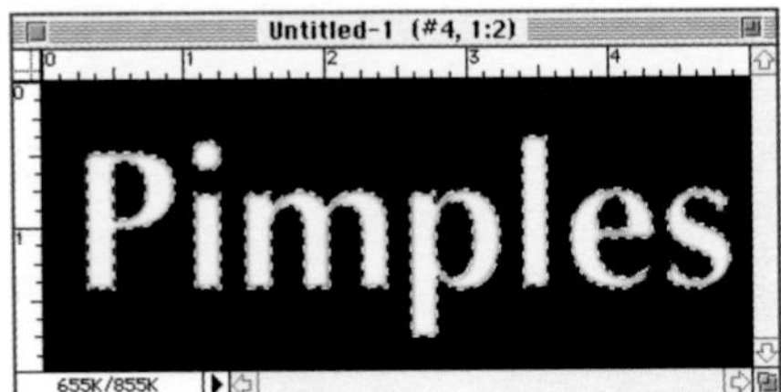

② Create a new channel, and use the Type tool to enter the text. We used B Optima Bold at 100 points. Press Command-J to defloat the text. Keep the selection active, and choose Filter ➥ Blur ➥ Gaussian Blur (4 pixels) to only blur the inside of the type. The lower the pixel radius you use when blurring, the softer and slighter the edges of the text will be. Deselect the text (Command-D).

③ Choose Filter ➥ Render ➥ Lighting Effects. Either choose the EmbossLightStyles preset from the pop-up menu or adjust the settings as you see them here. Make sure that you position the light far enough away from the text that the letters aren't completely washed out. The texture channel should be the type channel created in Step 2 (Channel #4). Click OK and you're done.

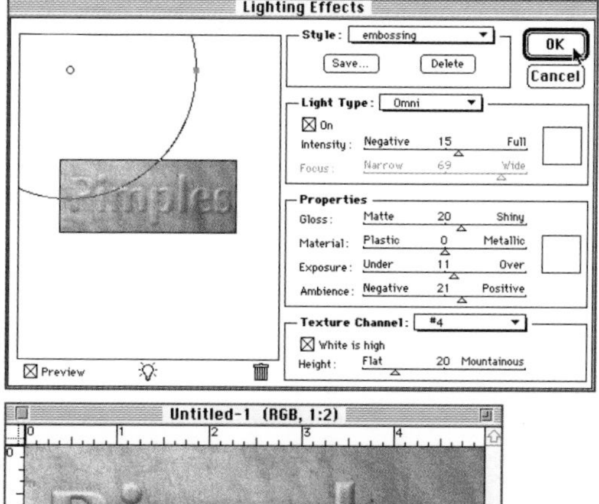

TIP If you want to leave the background flat and unaffected by the light, then don't deselect the text at the end of Step 2.

Embossed 2

created by Craig Swanson

① Create a new file, or open a file containing the surface you want to emboss.

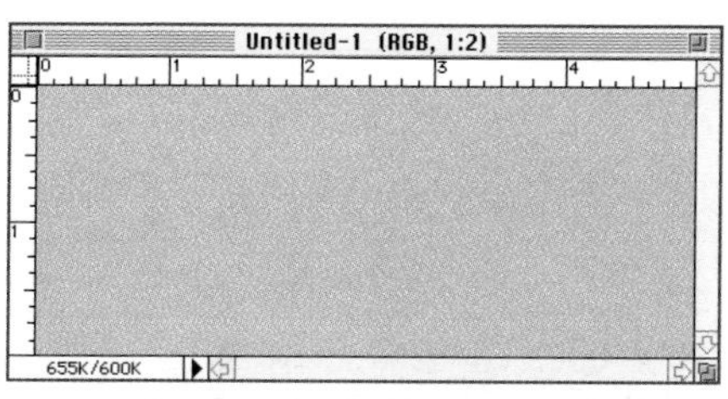

② Create a new channel (Channel #4). Use the Type tool to enter the text you want to apply the effect to in the new channel. Again, we used B Optima Bold at 100 points. Deselect the text (Command-D).

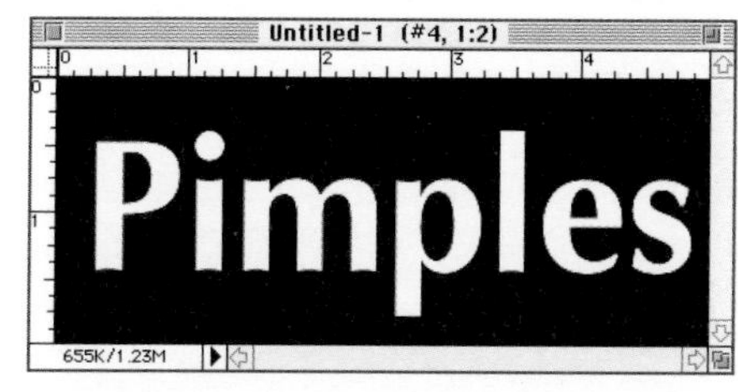

③ Duplicate Channel #4 to create Channel #5. To soften the edges, apply Filter ➥ Blur ➥ Gaussian Blur (8 pixels). Apply Filter ➥ Stylize ➥ Emboss (135°, 4 pixels, 200%). The type should now look like this.

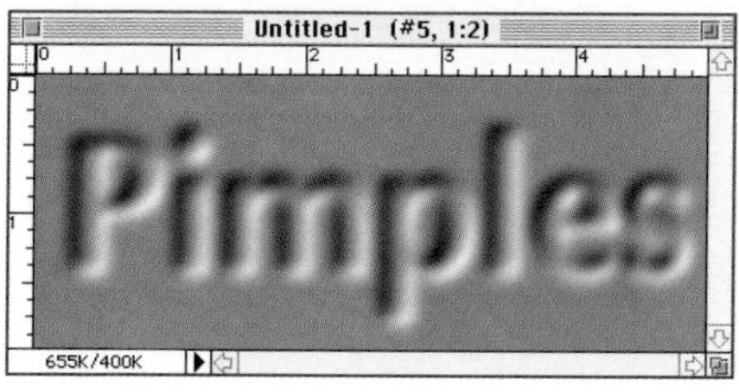

④ Duplicate Channel #5 and name it Channel #6. To isolate the shadow areas, choose Image ➡ Adjust ➡ Levels (Input Levels: 0, 1, 128).

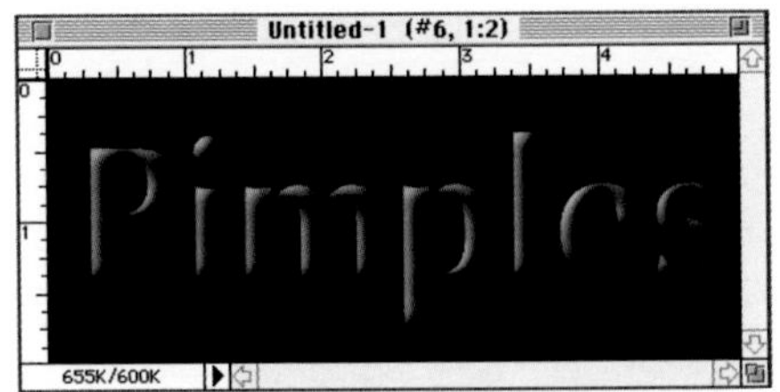

⑤ Select ➡ Load Selection (Channel #4). Check the Invert box. Change the background color to white and press the Delete key. Deselect the background (Command-D). Invert the image (Image ➡ Adjust ➡ Invert). This channel we will use as the selection for the highlights.

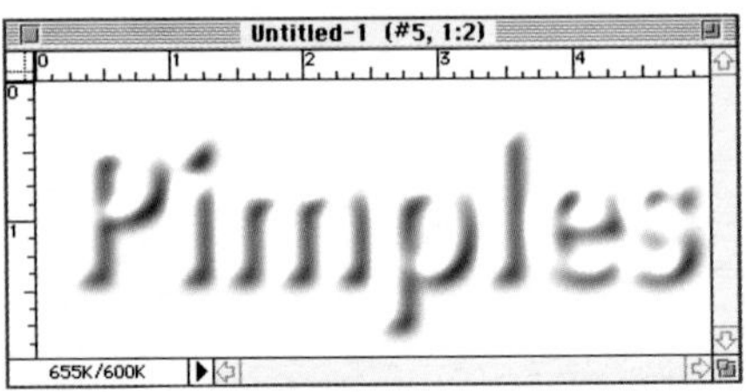

⑥ Now, to make the channel for the highlights, return to Channel #5. Choose Image ➡ Map ➡ Invert and then Image ➡ Adjust ➡ Levels (Input Levels: 0, 1, 128).

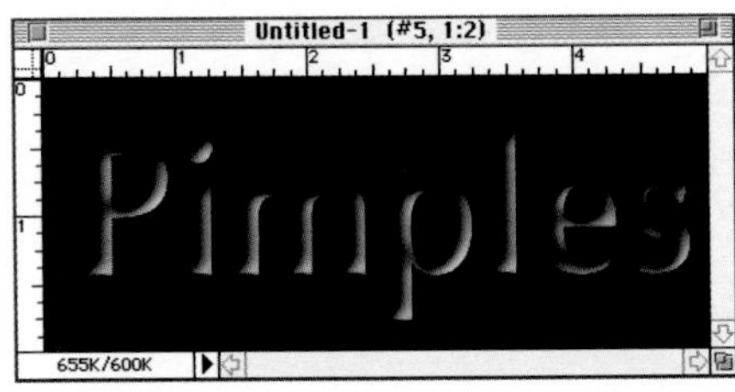

⑦ Select ➡ Load Selection (Channel #4). Check the Invert box. Change the background color to white and press the Delete key. Deselect the background (Command-D). Choose Image ➡ Map ➡ Invert. Now you've got a selection channel for the highlights.

⑧ Return to the composite channel (Command-0), and choose Select ➡ Load Selection (Channel #6). Change the foreground color to black. Now press Option-Delete to fill in the shadows.

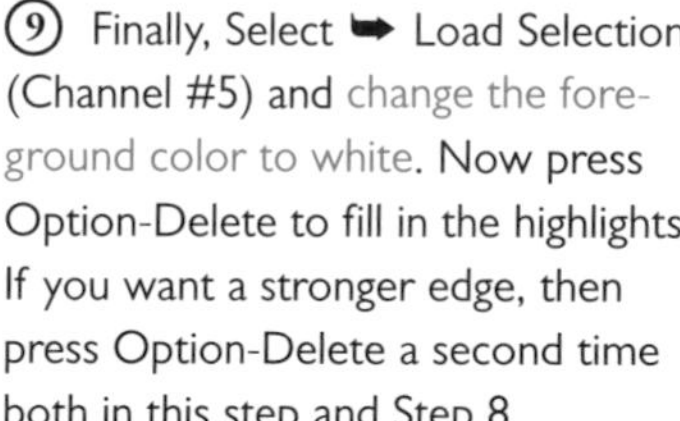

⑨ Finally, Select ➡ Load Selection (Channel #5) and change the foreground color to white. Now press Option-Delete to fill in the highlights. If you want a stronger edge, then press Option-Delete a second time both in this step and Step 8.

TIP The advantage to this technique is that you can load the highlight and shadow selections again if you want to make alterations.

VARIATIONS

Another quick way to create embossed type is with The Boss filter—part of Alien Skin's Black Box collection of filters.

Create a new file. Use the Type tool to enter the text you want to apply the effect to in the new channel. Keep the selection active as you return to the composite channel (Command-0). Choose Select ➡ Inverse and apply Filter ➡ Alien Skin ➡ The Boss. Experiment with settings. Here's what we came up with after loading the selection again and raising the contrast inside the text. ■

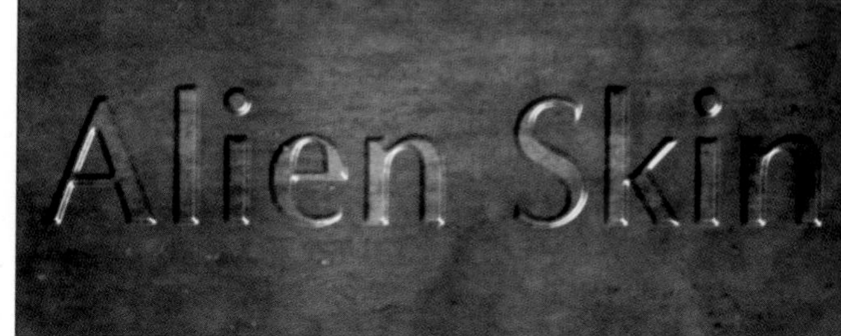

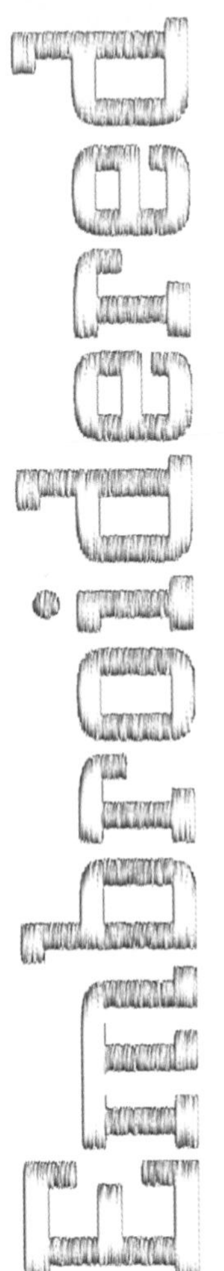

① Create a new file. Set the foreground color to black (press D). Use the Type tool to enter the text. We used City Medium at 70 points for this example. Deselect the text (Command-D).

TIP The point size and thickness of the font are important in this technique, because the Wind filter can really blow smaller and thinner type away. If you want smaller type, we still suggest you use 70 points and choose Image ➥ Effects ➥ Scale to reduce the type when you're finished.

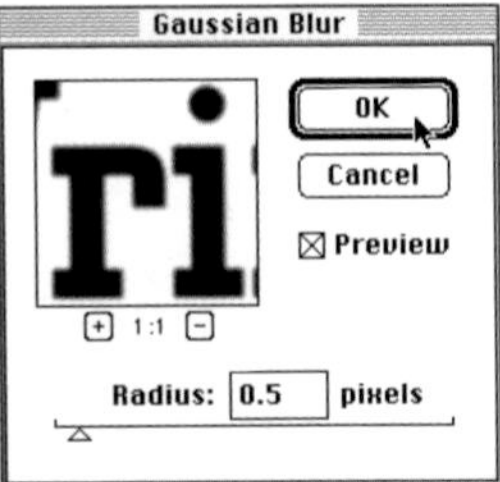

② Choose Filter ➥ Blur ➥ Gaussian Blur (.5 pixels). The thicker the font, the higher the pixel radius should be.

③ Choose Filter ➥ Stylize ➥ Wind (Wind, Left). Press Command-Option-F to bring back the last filter dialog box, and switch the Wind direction to Right.

④ Choose Image ➥ Map ➥ Invert (Command-I).

⑤ Duplicate the background layer to create the Background copy layer.

⑥ Double-click on the Magic Wand tool. Find the Magic Wand floating palette (it's hiding somewhere on your screen) and change the Tolerance setting to 25. With the Magic Wand, click in the black area of the image. You will also need to select the enclosed areas within letters like *e* and *o*, by holding the Shift key and clicking within these areas. Press Delete.

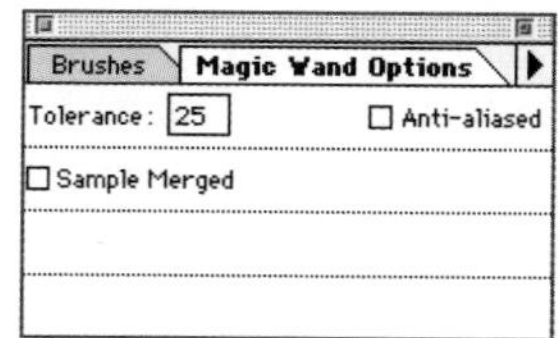

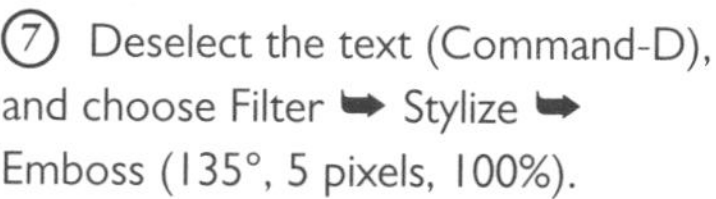

⑦ Deselect the text (Command-D), and choose Filter ➡ Stylize ➡ Emboss (135°, 5 pixels, 100%).

⑧ In the Layers palette click on the pop-up composite control menu and choose Lighten. Leave the opacity at 100%.

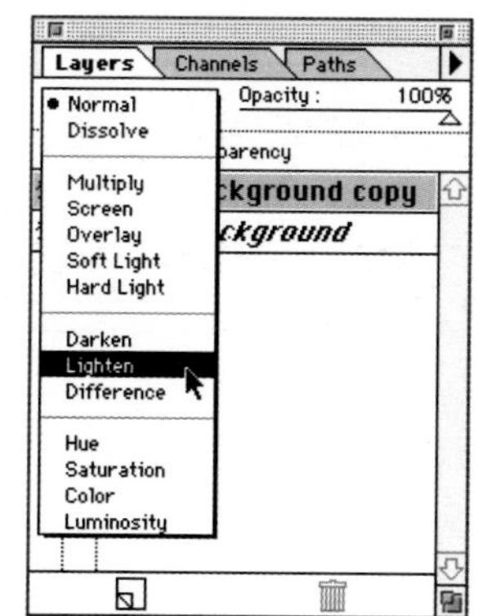

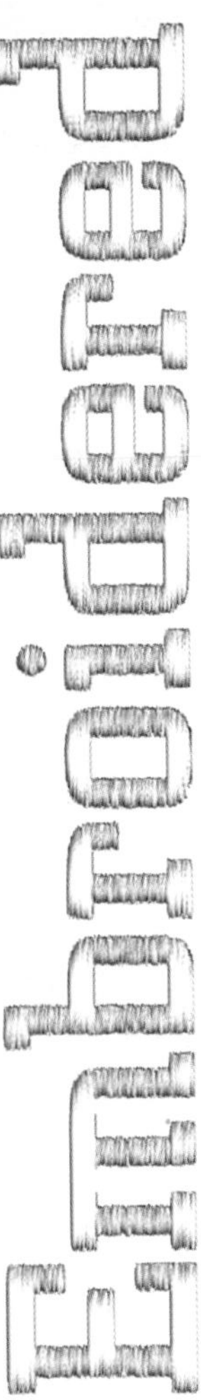

⑨ Flatten the image.

TIP

To copy the type onto another background, use the Magic Wand tool again to select the black area around the type (as in Step 6). Choose Select ➥ Inverse, then Copy the type (Command-C). Go to the file you want to paste the text into, and, well, paste it in (Command-V).

VARIATIONS

Add subtle color to the thread Use the Magic Wand tool to select the area around the type (as in Step 6). Choose Select ➡ Inverse. Then choose Hue/Saturation, and click on the Colorize checkbox. Use the Hue slider to find the color you're looking for, and drop the Saturation slider to control the brightness of the color. For this variation we set the Saturation at 20.

Change the color of the thread Before entering the text in Step 1, fill the background with a dark version of a color near the complement of the thread color you want to use (for example, a dark blue if you are using orange thread). Don't use black for the foreground color. Instead, change the foreground color to a light version of the color of thread you want. Complete the rest of the steps and you're done. ■

Flaming

created by Sal Giliberto

① Create a new file. Select Mode ➥ Grayscale and press D to set the foreground color to black. Press Option-Delete to fill the image with black.

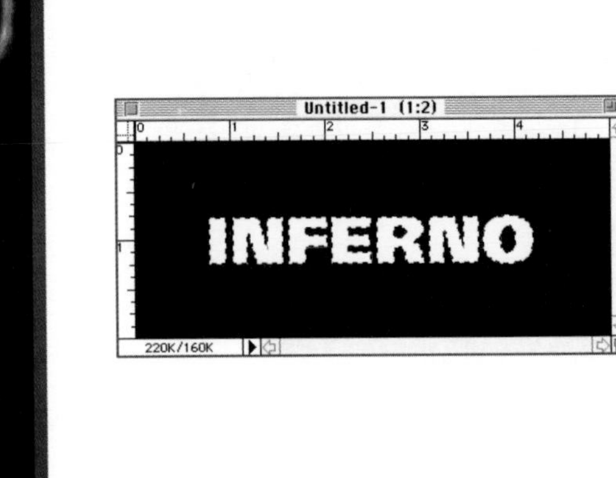

② Switch the foreground color to white (press X) and use the Type tool to enter the text. For best results, use a large Sans Serif Font (in this example, we used Frutiger UltraBlack at 50 points). Set the text towards the bottom of the picture frame so there will be enough room for the flames.

③ With the text selection still active, save the current selection.

④ Deselect the text (Command-D), and rotate the image 90 degrees counterclockwise (Image ➥ Rotate ➥ 90° CCW).

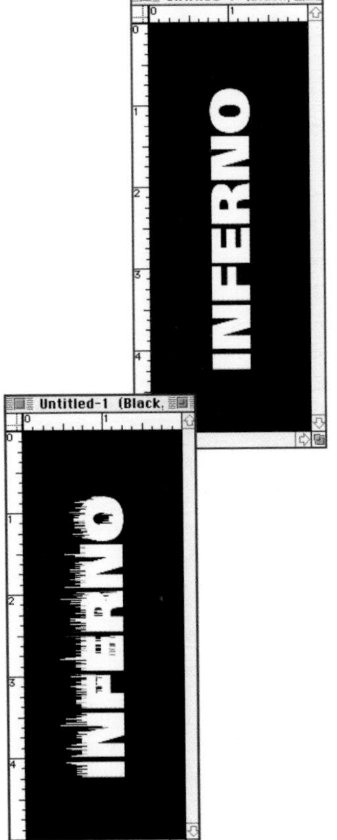

⑤ Apply Filter ➥ Stylize ➥ Wind (Blast, Left). The larger your text the more wind it needs. If you are using a smaller point size then Wind might do the job. Larger text might need the Blast applied twice. You should see something like this.

TOOLBOX

Natural Gas palette

⑥ Return the image to its original orientation by rotating it 90 degrees clockwise (Image ➡ Rotate ➡ 90° CW).

⑦ Apply Filter ➡ Stylize ➡ Diffuse (Normal).

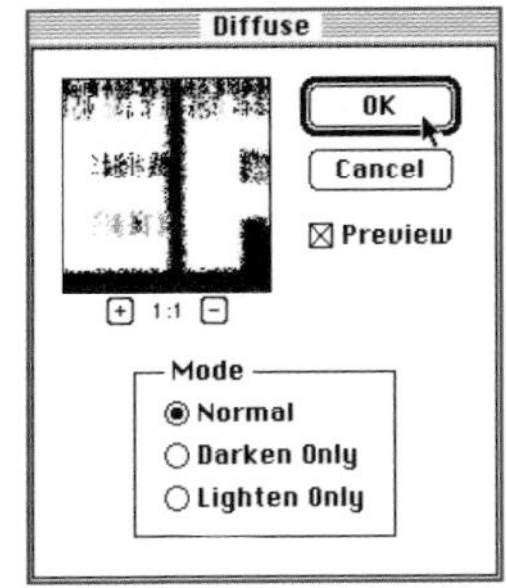

⑧ Apply Filter ➡ Blur ➡ Gaussian Blur (Radius: 2.5).

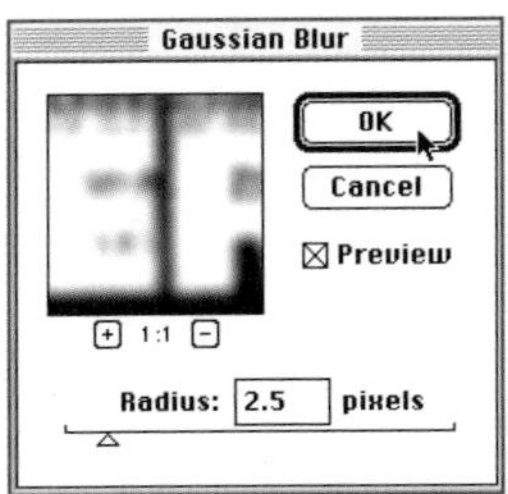

The image should now look like this.

⑨ Apply Filter ➡ Distort ➡ Ripple. Use the default settings (100, Medium).

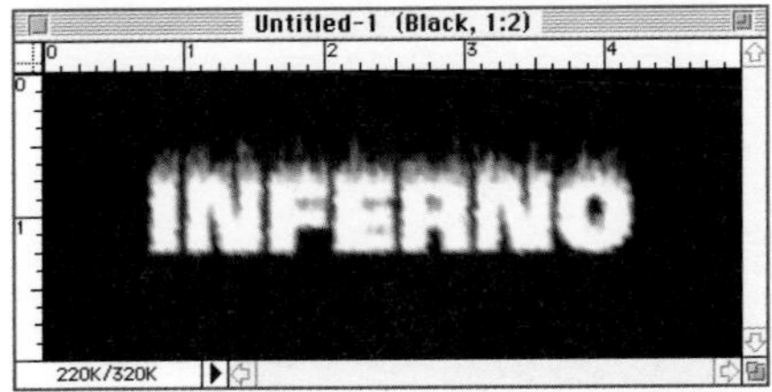

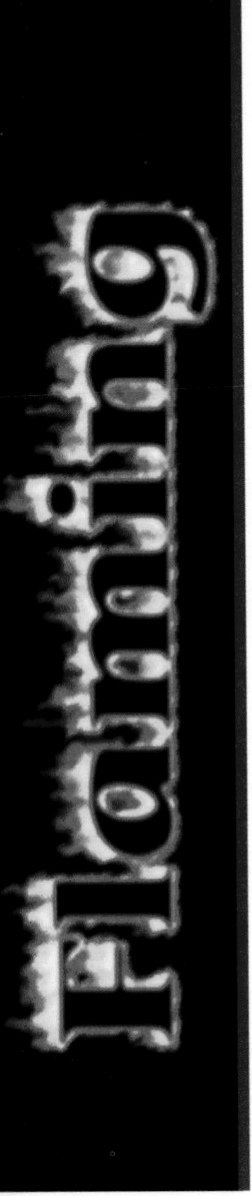

(10) Load the selection you saved in Step 3. Choose Select ➥ Modify ➥ Contract (2 pixels). Choose Select ➥ Feather (1 pixel). Change the foreground color to black (press D) and press Option-Delete to fill the selection. Choose Select ➥ None (Command-D).

TIP If you want a lighter, more realistic-looking flame, adjust the gray values before converting the image to color. Choose ➥ Image ➥ Adjust ➥ Levels (Command-L). Try these settings for the Input Levels values: 0, 3.46, 190.

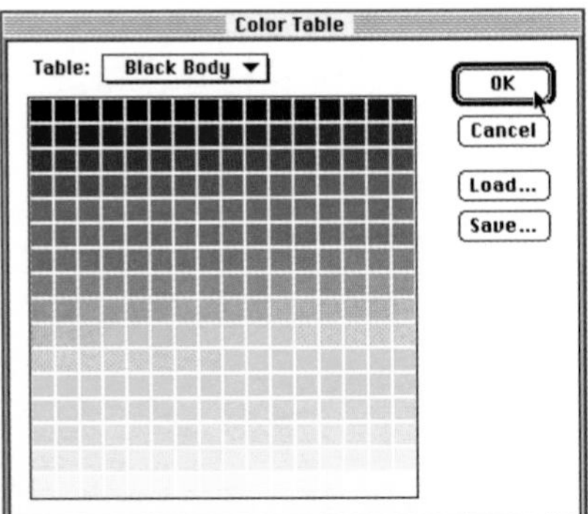

(11) Convert the image to Indexed color mode (Mode ➥ Indexed Color). Select Mode ➥ Color Table and choose Black Body from the pop-up menu.

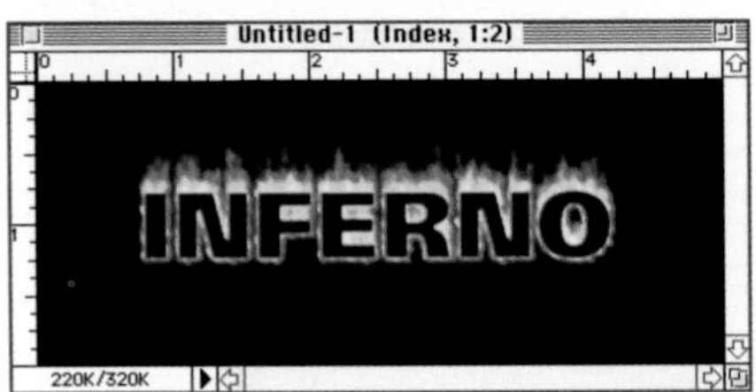

After changing color tables, your type should look like it's on fire.

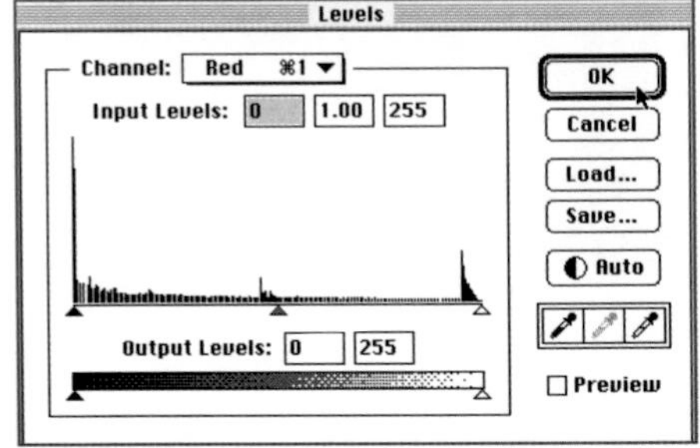

TIP You can use the Levels dialog box to adjust the color and height of the flames. Choose Image ➥ Adjust ➥ Levels (Command-L). It helps to work in the Red and Green channels separately.

VARIATIONS

For this variation, we used black text on a white background. Use all the same steps except skip Step 10.

After Step 10, adjust the Output Levels (Command-L) white point to 240. In Step 11, use the Natural Gas palette (included on the CD) instead of the Black Body palette, then convert the image to RGB and apply Filter ➡ Blur ➡ Blur.

Now don't light any matches.

Create a flaming shadow by choosing Image ➡ Map ➡ Invert (Command-I) right before doing Step 11.

In a grayscale file, enter the text into a new channel. Return to the Black channel. Load the selection. Fill it with black. Deselect the text. Apply Gaussian Blur (5 pixels). Load the selection. Fill it with black. Choose Filter ➡ Render ➡ Difference Clouds. Deslect the text. Choose Filter ➡ Render ➡ Difference Clouds. Do Step 11. ■

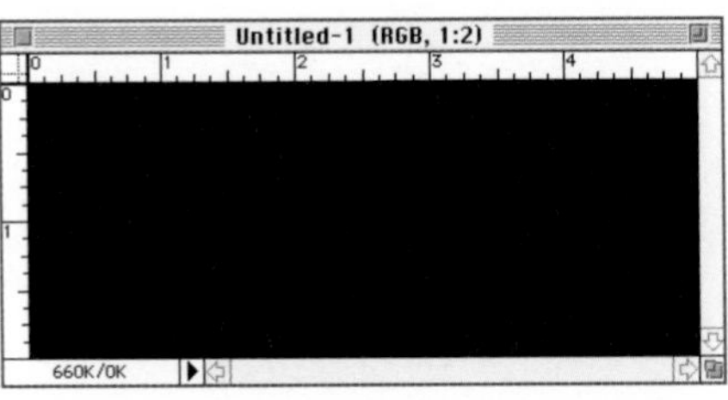

① Create a new file. Fill the image area with black.

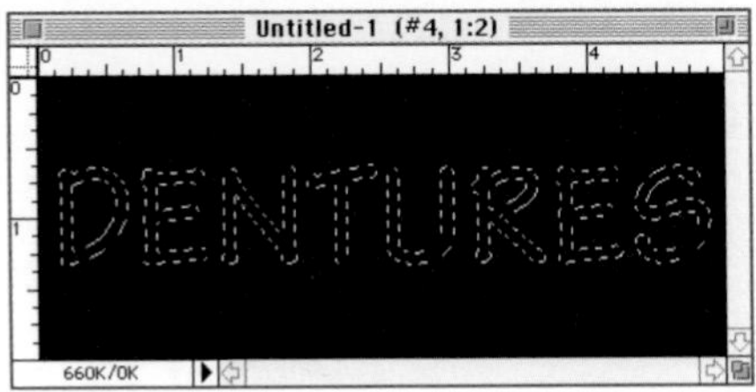

② Create a new channel (#4), set the colors to their defaults (press D), and use the Type tool to enter the text. We used Tekton Bold at 75 points. This technique will also work with complicated fonts like Shelley, but keep in mind that you'll have to play with the settings to get it right.

TIP

If the font you select has hard edges, choose Select ➥ Modify ➥ Smooth (5 pixels). If that doesn't round your text enough, then just Smooth it again until it has a good round contour. Photoshop automatically defloats the selection when you Smooth it, so if you Smooth the text, don't press Command-J in Step 3.

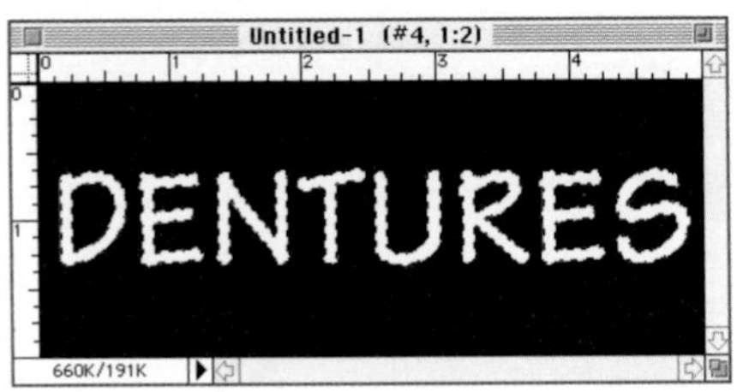

③ Press Command-J to defloat the type. Press Delete to fill the text with white.

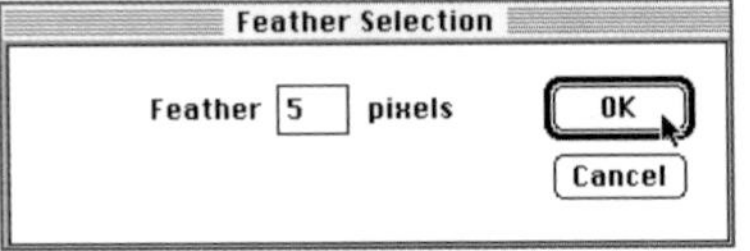

④ Return to the composite channel (Command-0). The text selection should still be active. Choose Select ➥ Feather (5 pixels).

TOOLBOX

GE Plastic Wrap

KPT Gradient Designer 2.1

⑤ Change the foreground color to a color for the gel. We used 100% Magenta. Press Option-Delete to fill the text selection. Deselect the text (Command-D).

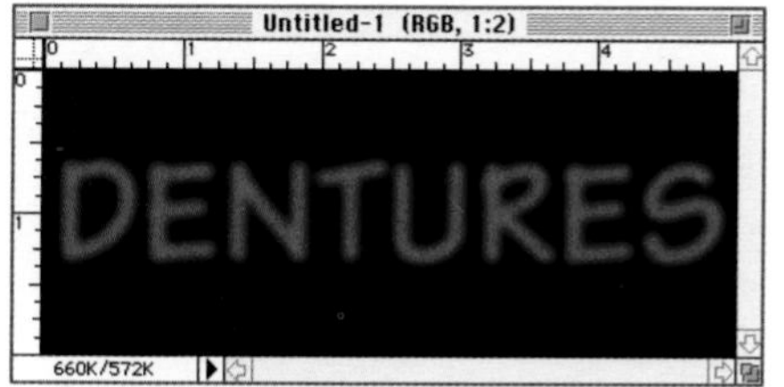

⑥ To add a gloss to the text, we're going to use the GE Plastic Wrap filter. This filter produces very different results depending upon the size of area that is selected. Therefore, we are going to apply the filter to each letter one at a time. First, load the text selection (Channel #4).

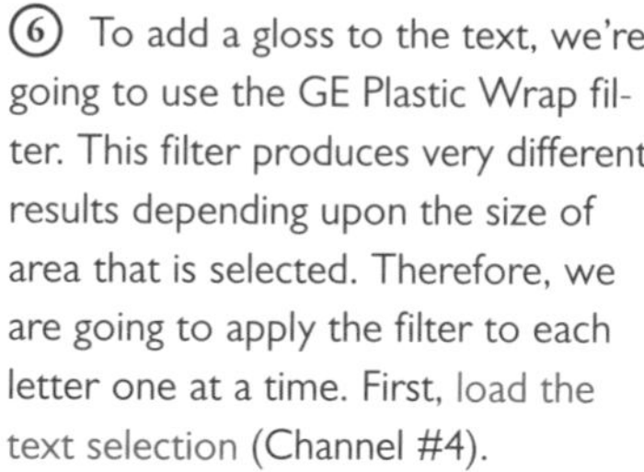

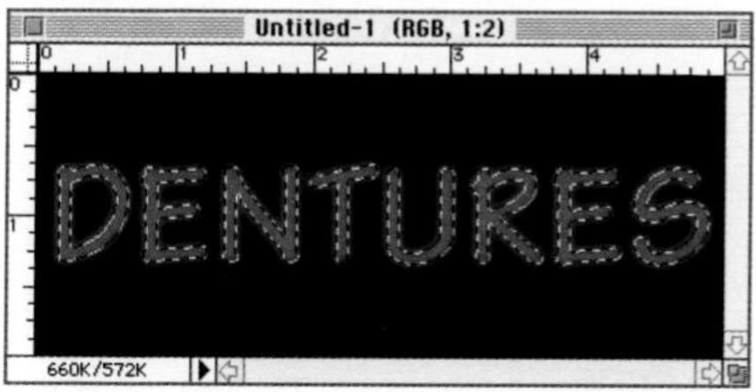

⑦ Select the Lasso tool, and hold down the Shift and Command keys while you draw around the letter you want to select. The selection you draw can be as sloppy as you want as long as you don't run over any of the other selection lines. After you complete the loop around the letter and let go of the mouse button, only that letter will be selected.

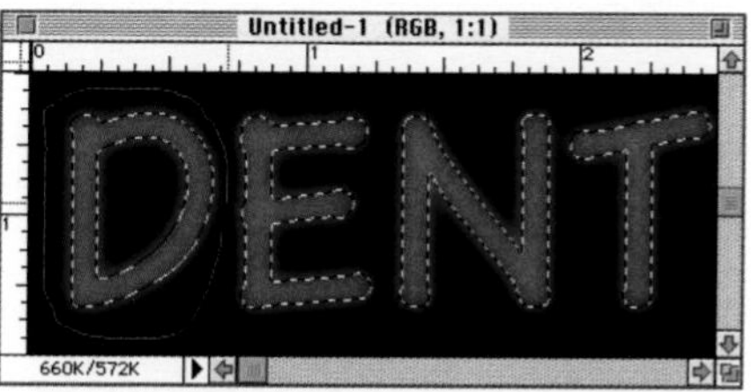

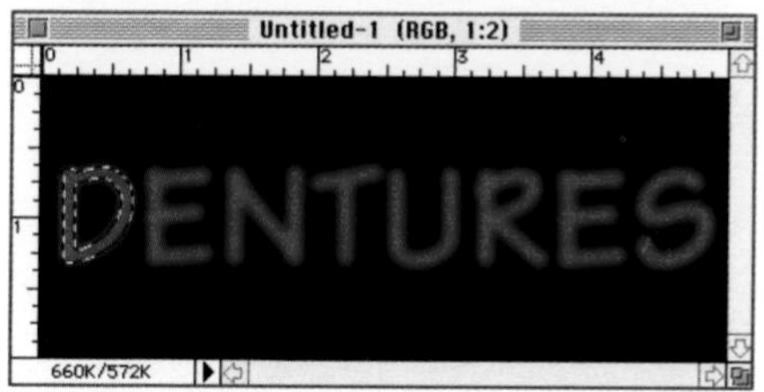

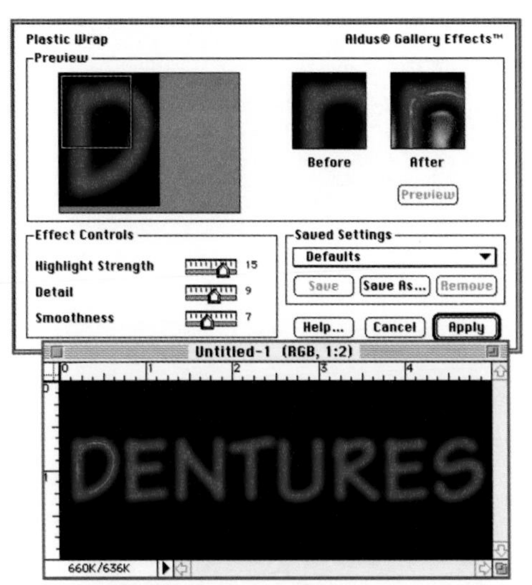

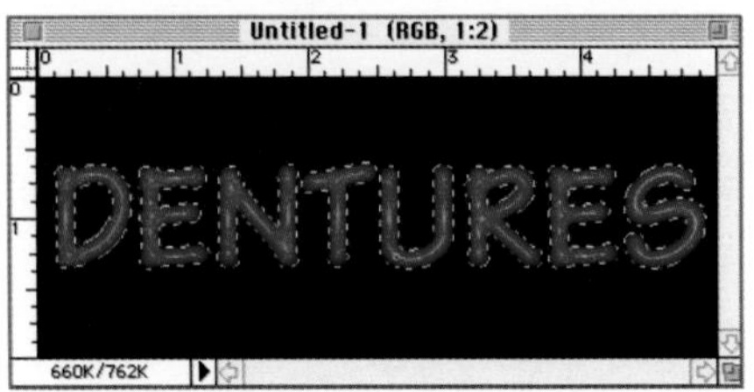

⑧ Now, choose Filter ➥ Gallery Effects: Classic Art 3 ➥ GE Plastic Wrap. Use these settings: Highlight Strength: 15, Detail: 9, Smoothness: 7. Use the preview to test the best settings for your text and to find something that looks like this figure.

⑨ For each letter load the text selection (Channel #4), then do Step 7. After each new letter is selected, press Command-F to apply the GE Plastic Wrap filter with the same settings.

⑩ To make a selection for the text, load the text selection (Channel #4). Then choose Select ➥ Modify ➥ Expand. We expanded the selection 4 pixels. You want to expand the selection so that it includes *almost* all of the blurred color, like this.

⑪ With this selection, you can copy the text and paste onto any background you want.

Gel

VARIATIONS

Outlines If you want to create an outline gel text, you can insert these steps between Steps 3 and 4 above to change the solid text to outlines. It will be difficult to get this technique to work if you choose a narrow or complicated font, so keep it simple and let the effect carry your message.

③ Choose Select ➥ Modify ➥ Contract (8 pixels). We used 8 pixels, but use whatever works for your text to create an outline like the one shown in this figure. Then fill the selection with black.

After finishing the steps above we copied the text to a yellow background, Smudged the edges of the text and applied Filter ➥ Sharpen ➥ Unsharp Mask (55%, 3 pixels, 0 levels). Smudging the text will help incorporate the edges with the background.

KPT Gradient Designer

We used the Shelley Andante font for this variation. After completing the steps, we made a new layer, loaded the text selection into the new layer and filled it with white. With the selection still active, we applied Filter ➥ KPT 2.1 ➥ KPT Gradient Designer 2.1. We selected the Tacky Wacky preset, then customized it. Finally, we chose Color from the Layers palette pop-up composite control menu. ■

©CMCD 1995

This effect will turn your dull, boring text into a shiny piece of see-through stuff. The Smudging in Steps 7 through 13 make it look ultra-realistic.

① Open the image you wish to use as a background. For this example, we used this photo from CMCD. The image was cropped down and the resolution changed to 150 dpi (to match the other examples in the book, so you don't get confused)!

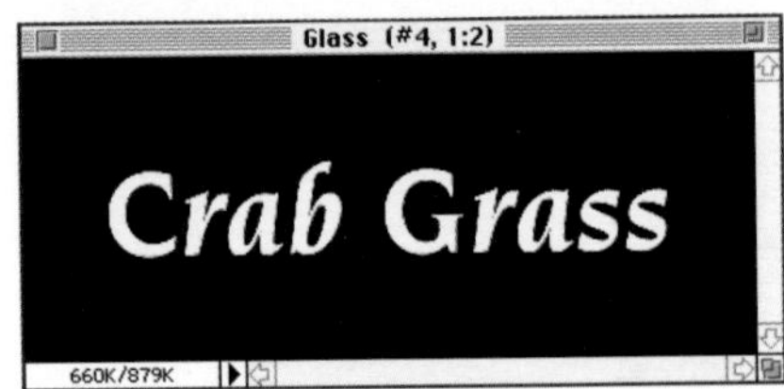

② Create a new channel (Channel #4) and enter your text into it. For this example, we used ITC Novarese Bold Italic at 60 points. (ITC Novarese is the cool font that HSC Software uses for all of the Kai's Power Tool promotions. I bet you've always wondered what typeface that was!) Select ➥ None so you have no active selection.

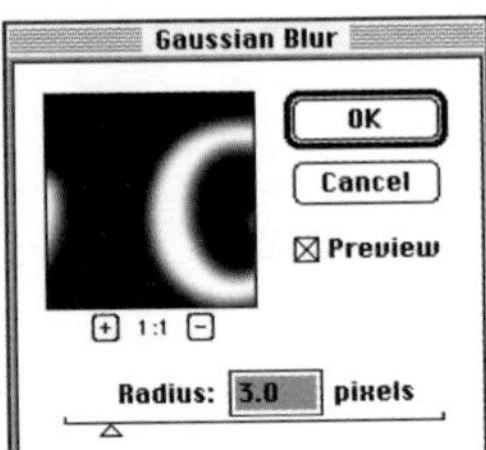

③ Make a duplicate of this channel and name it Blur #1 (to make remembering what the channel is easier). To the Blur #1 channel, apply Filter ➥ Blur ➥ Gaussian Blur with a setting of 3 pixels.

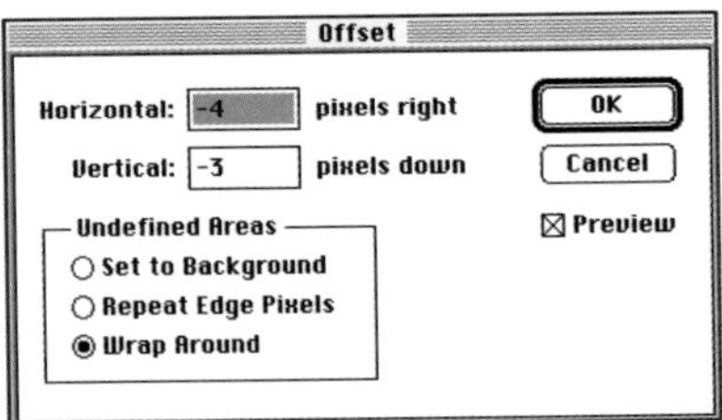

④ Make of duplicate of the Blur #1 channel and rename it Blur #2. Apply Filter ➥ Other ➥ Offset with a setting of -4 pixels right and -3 pixels down.

(5) Now apply Image ➥ Calculations. Both "Source:" options and the "Result:" option should be set to the name of your current document (the default). In Source 1, set Layer: Background and Channel: Blur #1. For Source 2, set Layer: Background, Channel: Blur #2. Set the Blending mode to Difference and the Opacity to 100%. Leave the Invert and Mask boxes unchecked.

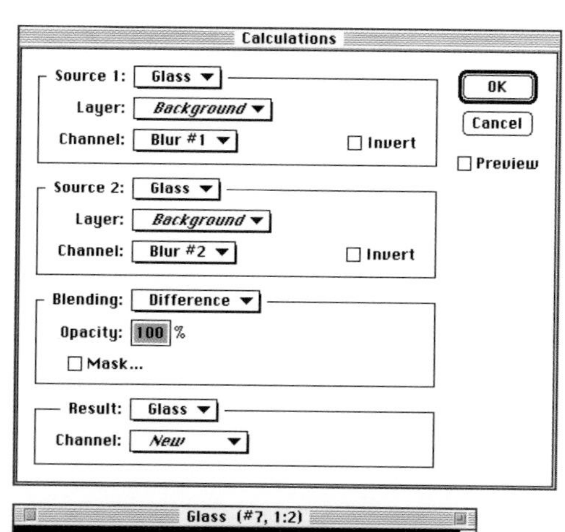

You should get something like this.

(6) Select Image ➥ Map ➥ Invert to reverse the new channel (Channel #7), and apply Image ➥ Adjust ➥ Levels (Command-L). Click on the Auto button to adjust the levels automatically

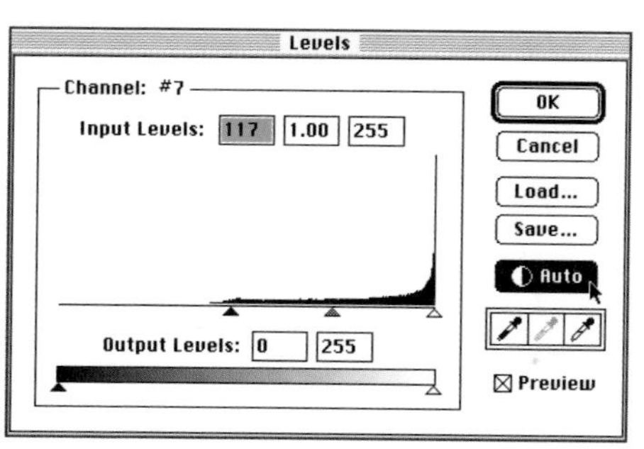

The result should be a more contrasty image.

(7) Now return to the composite channel (Command-0) and get ready for some fun! Load Channel #4 (the channel with the original, unblurred text). In the Paths floating palette, choose Make Path and use a Tolerance setting of 2.0 pixels.

Make Path

Tolerance: 2.0 pixels

OK

Cancel

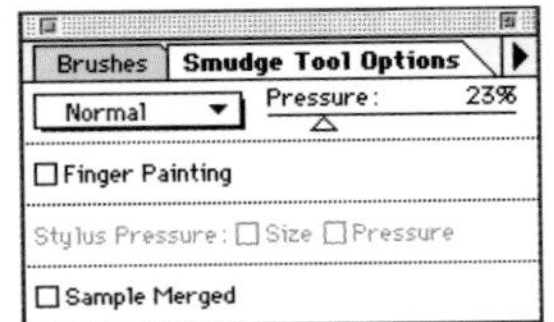

(8) Select the Smudge tool and choose a large feathered brush. In the Options palette, set the pressure of the Smudge tool to 23%.

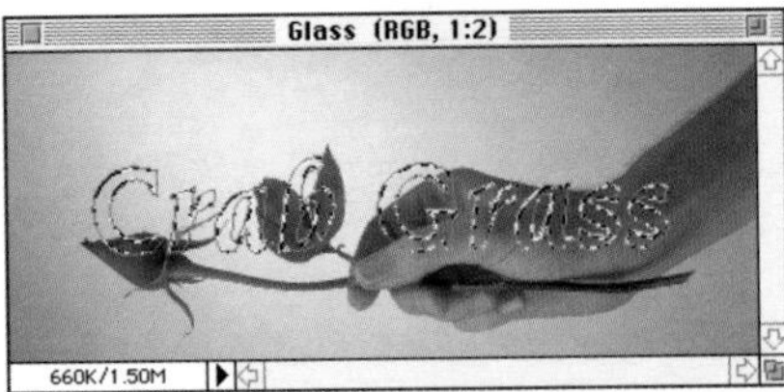

(9) Load Channel #4 again. On your screen, you'll see the path and the selection active (if not, bring the Paths floating palette to the front).

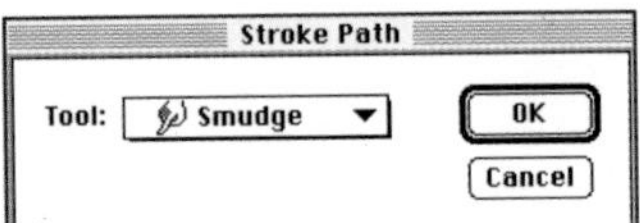

(10) From the Paths floating palette, select Stroke Path and make sure the Smudge tool is selected in the window.

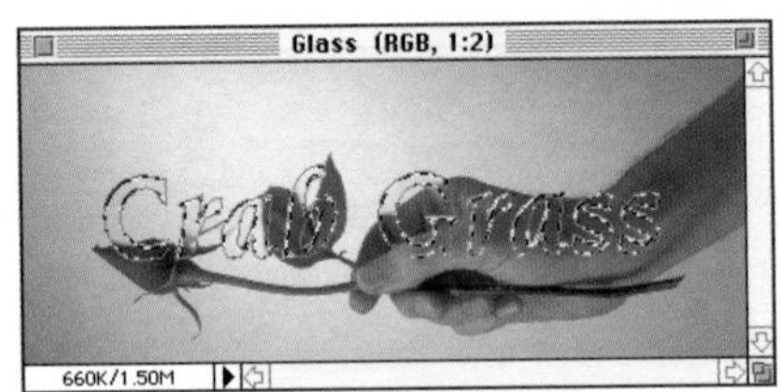

(11) After a few moments, the image *inside* the selection will be smudged somewhat. This was accomplished by loading Channel #4—the blurring only took place inside the selection, not outside.

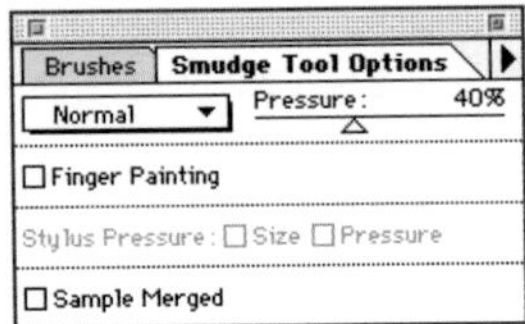

(12) Since glass distorts images more at the outer edges, a little more smudging needs to be done, but closer to the edges. With both the path and Channel #4 still active and the Smudge tool selected, choose a medium-sized feathered brush. Bump the pressure up to 40%.

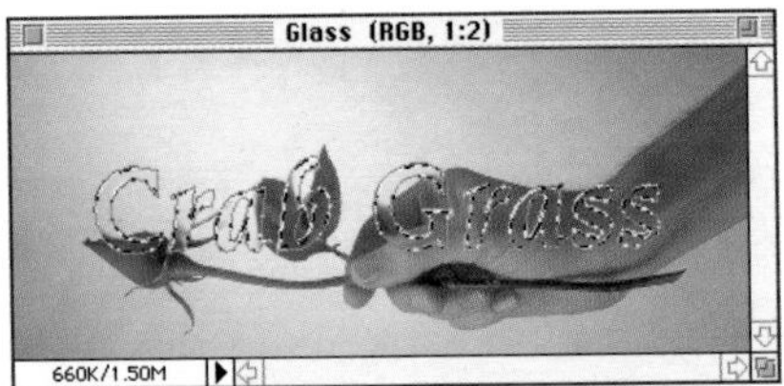

(13) Once again, stroke the path (Paths palette ➥ Stroke Path) with the Smudge tool.

(14) You're finished with the path, so it can be turned off. Simply shift-click on its name in the Paths floating palette. However, keep Channel #4 an active selection.

(15) Now comes the fun part—making it shiny. Bring up the Filter ➡ Render ➡ Lighting Effects dialog box. If you loaded the "GlassLightingStyles" file from the CD then choose it from the preset pop-up menu. If it's not there, just look at the screen shot to get the settings. Also, be sure that the Texture Channel option is set to Channel #7 (or whatever channel was created when the two blurred channels were combined).

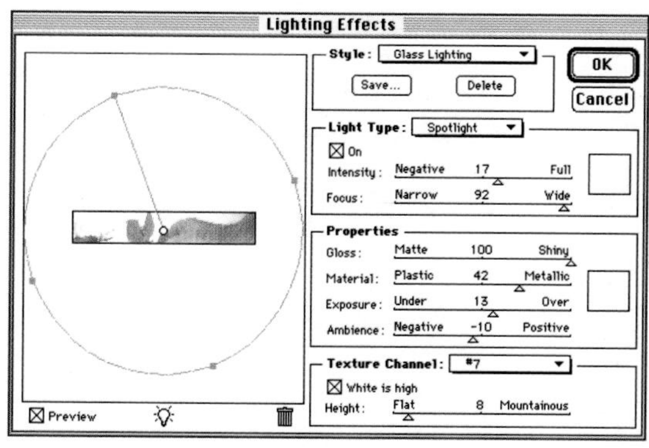

(16) If the preset settings don't give you the ideal result, then go ahead and tweak any of the ones in the Light Type or Properties sections of the dialog box. Try playing with the light direction and size, too. You can also adjust the Height slider to make the text appear more bumpy or flatter. However, don't change the Texture Channel setting. It should be set to the channel that resulted when the two blurred channels were combined. This channel is used to determine where the highlights and shadows will occur on the text. If you change it to a different channel, your text will probably appear really flat with very few highlights, if any! After clicking OK, you should get some nice, bright text.

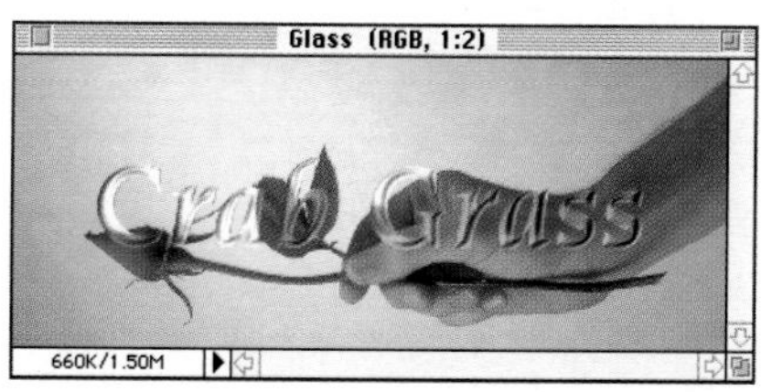

(17) To add an extra gloss to the text, make sure that Channel #4 (the regular text channel) is still loaded. Apply Filter ➡ Sharpen ➡ Unsharp Mask with the settings Amount: 61%, Radius: 2.3 pixels, and Threshold: 0 levels.

This sharpens the image inside the text and nudges the contrast up a smidgen. Be sure to note how the smudging done earlier really adds to the believability factor! ■

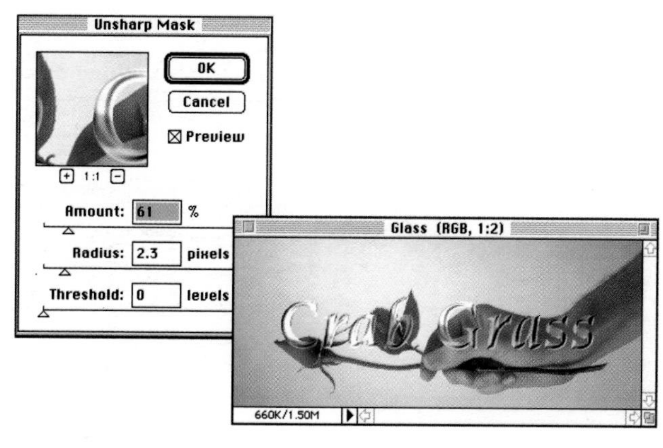

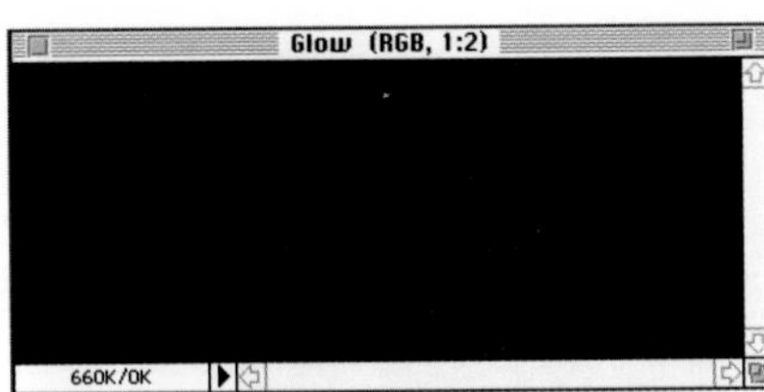

① Create a new file. Change the background color to black. Select ➡ All and press Delete to fill the image with black. Select ➡ None.

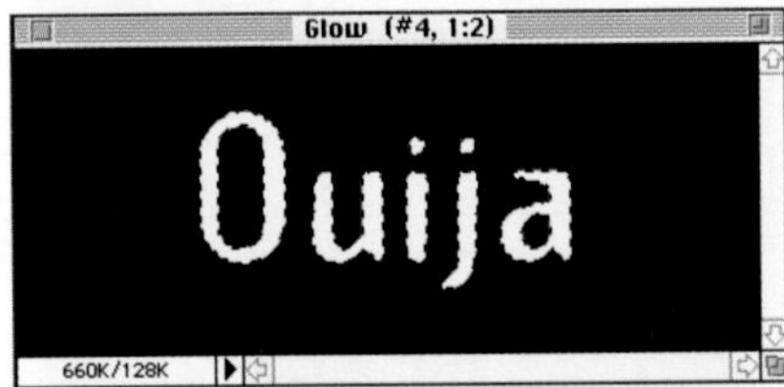

② Create a new channel (Channel #4). Make sure the foreground color is set to white. Type in the text you want to apply the effect to in the new channel. For this example, We used Template Gothic Bold at 90 points.

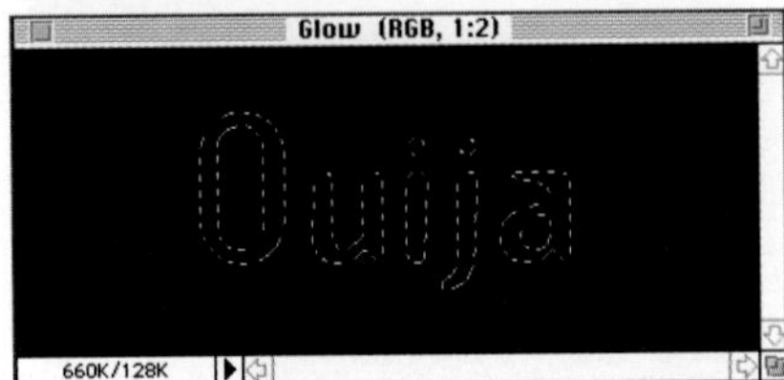

③ Return to the composite channel window. Your text should still be the active selection. If it's not, then choose Select ➡ Load Selection (Channel #4).

Feather Selection

Feather Radius: 10 pixels [OK] [Cancel]

④ Choose Select ➡ Feather and use a setting of 10 pixels. Don't worry if it looks like part of your letters disappear, particularly the skinny lines. They're still there, but the feathering decreased their strength, so Photoshop doesn't show them inside the area of active selection.

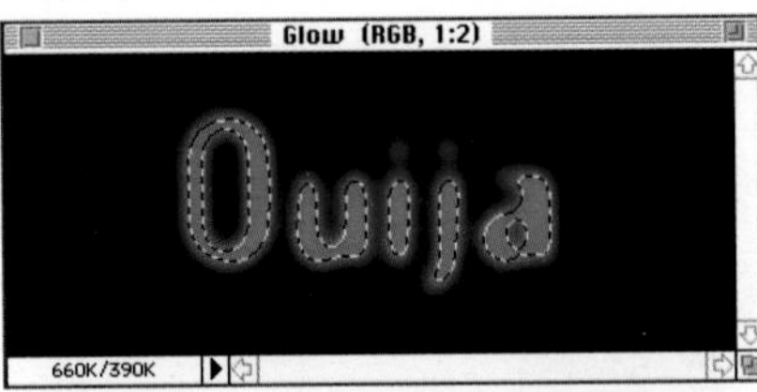

⑤ Change the foreground color to a bright green. Press Option-Delete to fill the selection with the foreground color.

You should get something like this.

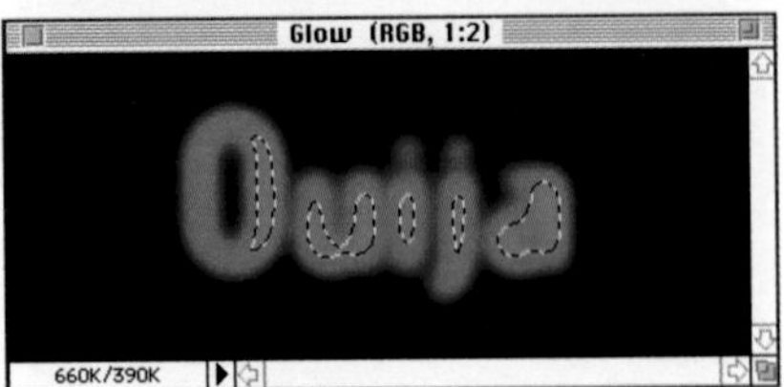

⑥ Once again, choose Select ➡ Feather and use a setting of 10 pixels. This will feather the already feathered selection, creating a really diffused look. Press Option-Delete to fill the selection.

TOOLBOX

KPT Gradient Designer
Alien Skin Glow filter

TIP

If you try combining the two feathering steps by using a setting of 20 pixels for one feathering, the result will be a much less vibrant glow. By using two separate steps, you achieve a more neon-like effect.

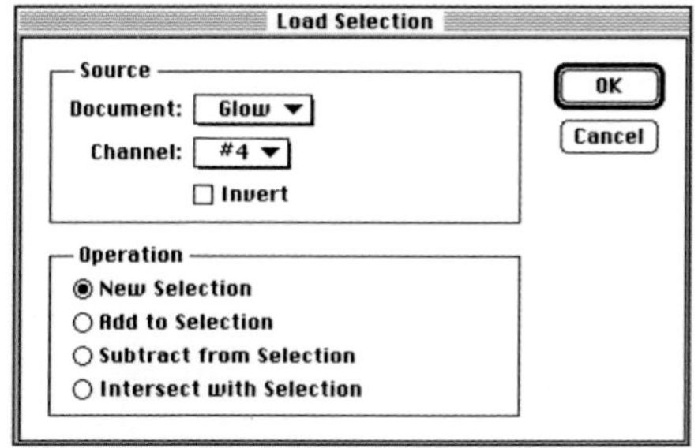

⑦ Now choose Select ➥ Load Selection and load Channel #4.

⑧ Change the foreground color to black and press Option-Delete to fill the selection. Select ➥ None.

VARIATIONS

Blinding Glow

① Follow Steps 1 through 7 above. Choose Select ➥ Feather, and feather the selection just a little—3 pixels.

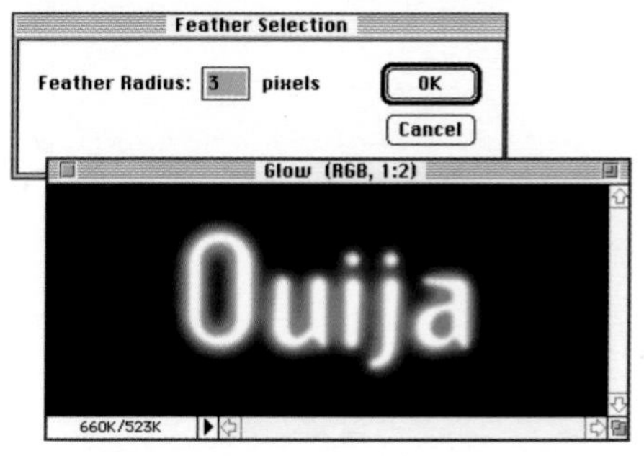

② Change the foreground color to white. Press Option-Delete to fill the selection with white. Wow!

Filled Glow

① Follow Steps 1 through 7 above.

② Set the foreground color to white and the background color to black. Use the Gradient Fill tool and drag from the upper left corner of the word to the lower right corner.

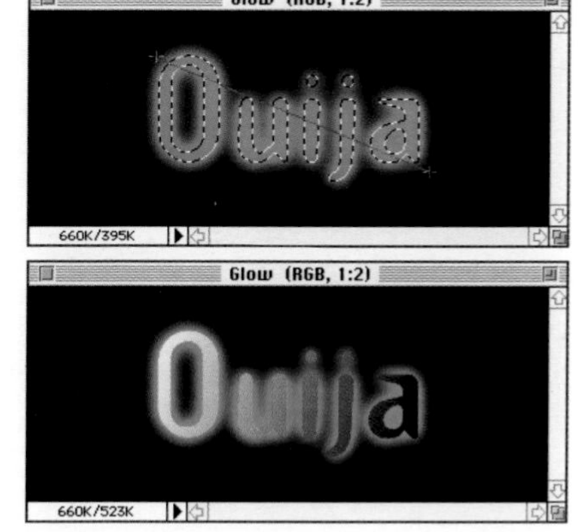

③ Select ➥ None. You should end up with something like this.

Filled Glow with KPT Gradient Designer

This variation is exactly the same as the Filled Glow above, except change Step 2 to:

② Choose Filter ➥ KPT 2.1 ➥ Gradient Designer. Choose **Linear Grayscale Ramp** from the Basic Gradients submenu and set the blend at an angle. Set the repeat option to Triangle A ➥ B ➥ A and click OK.

And here's what you get.

Ghosting

By using a second layer for the text, you can put type with a ghosted effect over an existing photo, like this one from PhotoDisc.

① Open a new file. Create a new layer. Keep both layers visible, so you can see what you're doing, but make sure that Layer 1 is the active layer!

② Create a new channel (Channel #4) and type in your text. We used Folio Extra Bold at 70 points here. Select ➥ None.

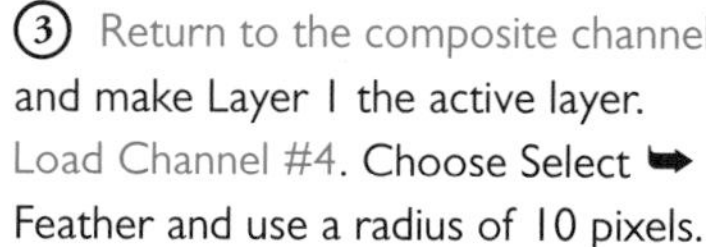

③ Return to the composite channel and make Layer 1 the active layer. Load Channel #4. Choose Select ➥ Feather and use a radius of 10 pixels.

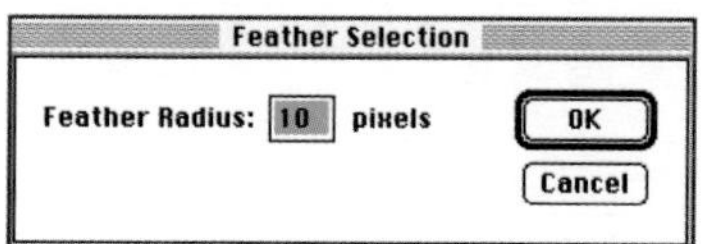

④ Change the foreground color to the color you want to use for the blur. We used a bright red. Press Option-Delete to fill the selection with the foreground color. Press Option-Delete again to intensify the color. Select ➥ None (Command-D).

⑤ If you want to remove color from the selection, then load Channel #4 and choose Edit ➥ Clear.

Aura

① Open a new file with a white background.

② Create a new channel and enter the text.

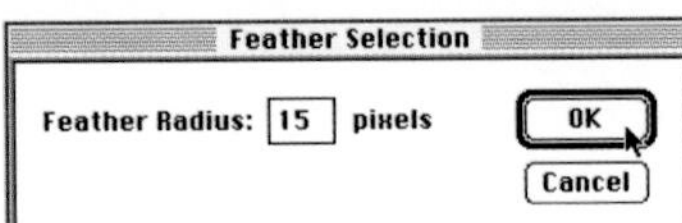

③ Return to the RGB channel. Choose Select ➡ Feather using a setting of 15 pixels.

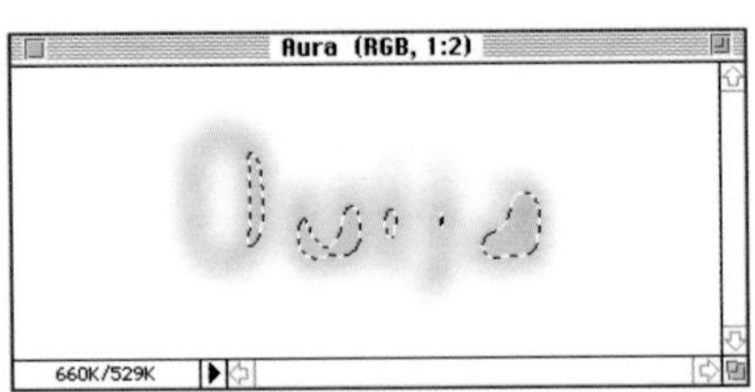

④ Change the foreground color to a medium blue. Press Option-Delete to fill the selection with the foreground color.

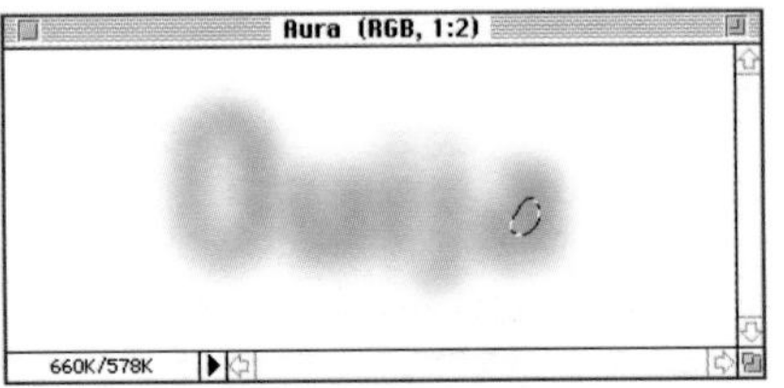

⑤ Again, choose Select ➡ Feather and use a setting of 15 pixels to diffuse the selection even more. Press Option-Delete to fill the selection again.

⑥ Load Channel #4. Change the foreground color to black and fill the selection.

VARIATIONS

Alien Skin's Glow Filter

Here's another easy way to create a glow around your type.

① Open a new file. We used a black background to make the glow stand out (press D, then Option-Delete). Set the foreground color to a color for the text. Enter the text with the Type tool. Press Command-J to defloat the text, and keep the text selection active.

② Change the foreground color to a color for the glow. We used a light blue for a misty look.

③ Choose Filter ➥ Alien Skin ➥ Glow. Set the Glow Color to Foreground. You can vary the settings for the Width (pixels) and the Opacity (%) of the glow. We used 40 pixels of Width and 70% Opacity. Set Opacity Dropoff to Thin. This makes the glow look, well, thin and hazy. If you want a more intense glow, try the Fat option.

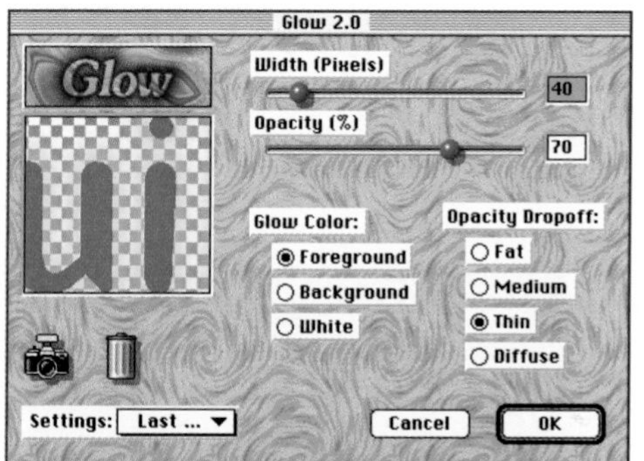

④ Click OK and presto—a super easy glow! ■

Gradient

Filling text with a gradient is a very simple task, but it can produce great effects. As soon as you get to know your away around with masks, the possibilities will seem endless.

Setup As always, the first steps: create a new file, then a new channel (Channel #4), and use the Type tool to enter the text in the new channel (white text on a black background). For these examples, we used SenatorUltra. After entering the text, return to the composite channel (Command-0).

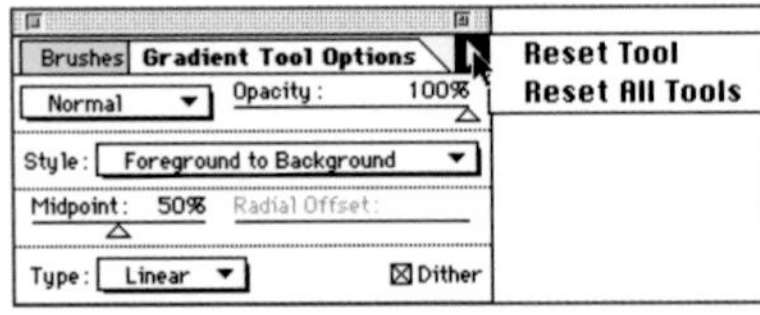

TIP To access the Gradient Tool Options floating palette, double-click on the Gradient tool. Unless otherwise noted, we are assuming that the options are set to the defaults. You can revert to the defaults by choosing **Reset Tool** from the arrow menu in the upper right corner of the palette.

Basic Gradient Here's the basic gradient fill. The gradient tool creates a blend between the foreground color and the background color. Set the colors on the toolbar, then load the text selection (Channel #4). Now, use the Gradient tool, click where you want to start the gradient, and drag to the point where you want it to end. We also gave the text a yellow stroke to set it apart from the background (Edit ➥ Stroke (2 pixels, Center, 100% Opacity, Normal Mode)).

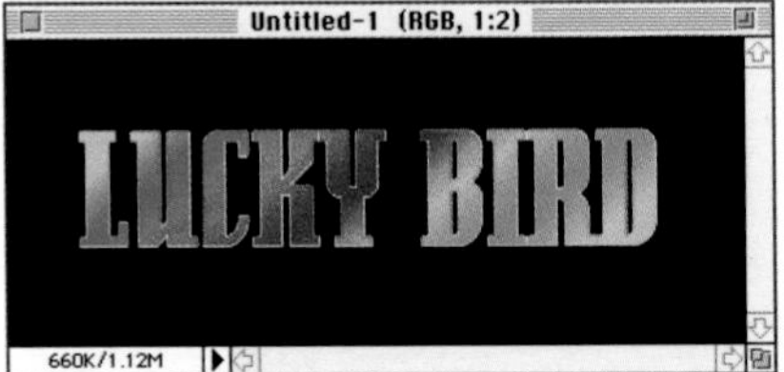

Spectrum The Gradient Tool options floating palette offers some very useful variables. If you want a blend to include all of the colors that lie between the foreground color and the background color on the color spectrum, then choose one of the spectrum options from the Style pop-up menu.

Transparency Grading from a color to transparency is magic for your text. This option allows you to fade type into a background. We used a stock photo from Photosets.

©Fotosets 1995

KPT Gradient Designer Use KPT Gradient Designer for a more complex, but no more difficult, gradient. Sifting through the possibilities could consume hours, but don't forget to come back and read the rest of this section.

KPT Procedural Blend We used KPT Gradient Designer for this one, too. We rendered the type using the Marquee method (page 102), then chose the Procedural Blend option in KPT Gradient Designer. This option will grade the color according to the values already in the type.

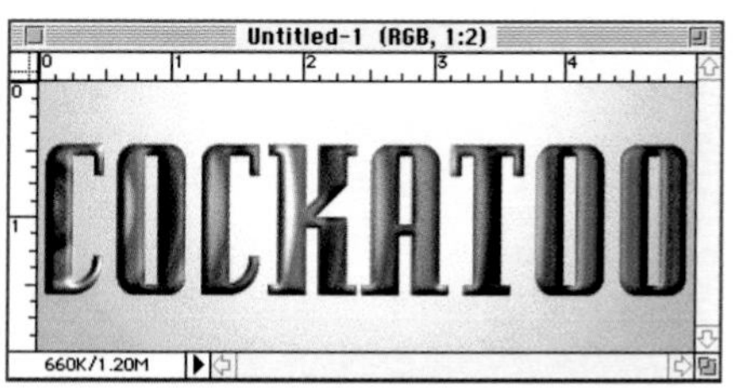

Graded selections

Photographs and other images can be graded into a text selection. First copy an image from another file into the clipboard. Return to the empty file, load the text selection, then switch to Quick Mask mode. Now use the Gradient tool as you did above. The non-red areas in this window represent the areas where the photograph will be seen at full strength. Where there is solid red, the photograph will be completely masked or hidden. Areas in between will gradually fade the photograph. Press Q to exit the Quick Mask mode, and Choose Edit ➥ Paste Into.

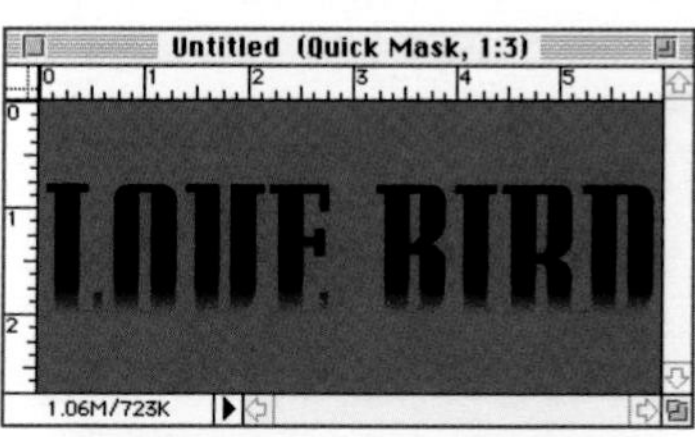

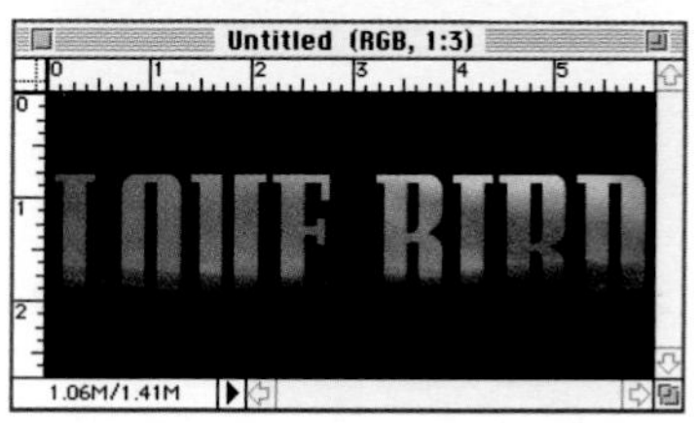

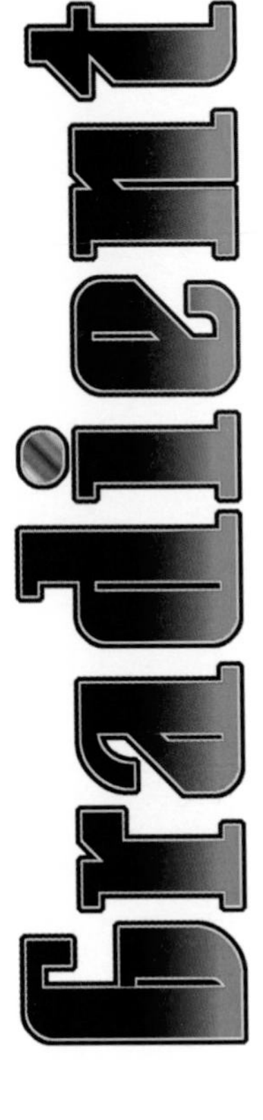

Blending Images You can also use Quick Masks to blend two photographs together into a type selection.

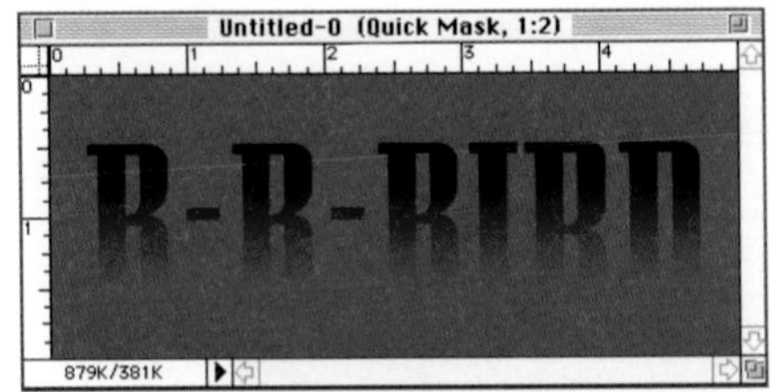

Copy the first image from a separate file into the clipboard. Then, return to the original file, go to the composite channel, and load the type selection. Press Q to enter Quick Mask mode. Use the Gradient Tool, as described above, and drag from just above the bottom of the text to just below the top of the text. You should see something like this.

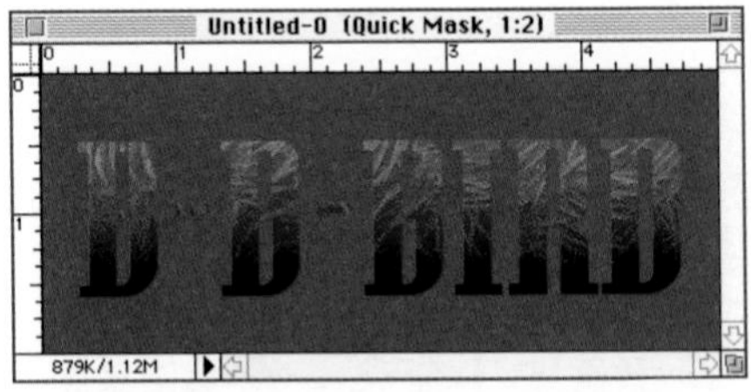

Exit Quick Mask mode (press Q), and choose Edit ➥ Paste Into to paste in the first image.

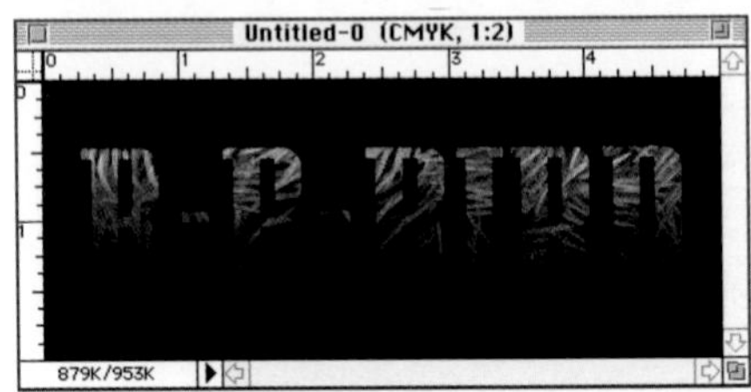

Now, copy the second image from a separate file into the clipboard. Again, return to the original file, go to the composite channel, and load the type selection. Press Q to enter Quick Mask mode. Use the Gradient Tool and drag from just below the top of the text to just above the bottom of the text.

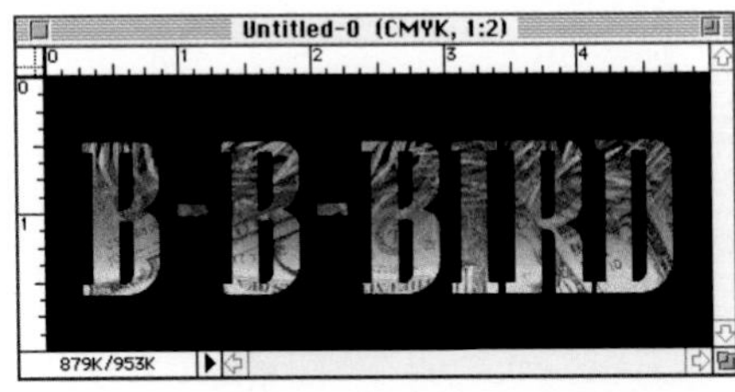

Exit Quick Mask mode (press Q), and choose Edit ➥ Paste Into to paste in the second image. That's it. We added a couple of strokes to separate the text from the background.

Putting it all together This image combines several gradient techniques in a composite of six layers.

Layer #6: the background image was copied to the clipboard, then pasted into a graded mask…

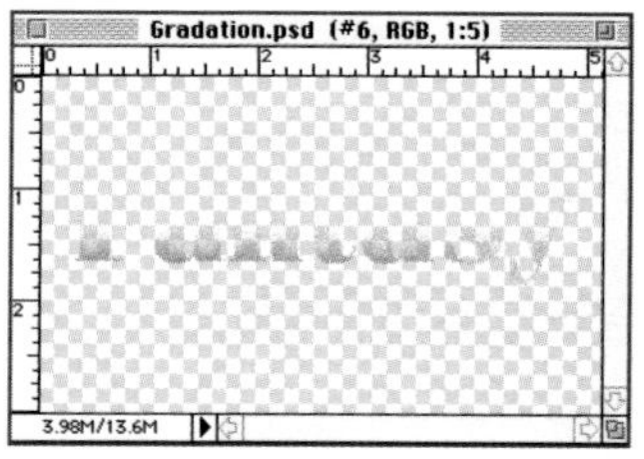

Layer #5: a violet to transparent blend inside the type selection…

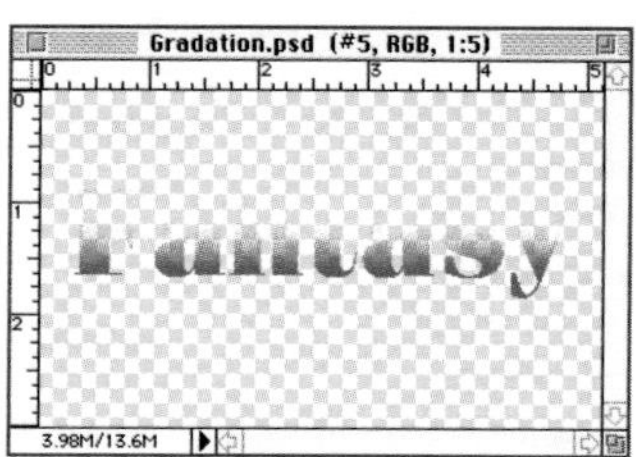

Layer #4: a black to violet blend inside the type selection…

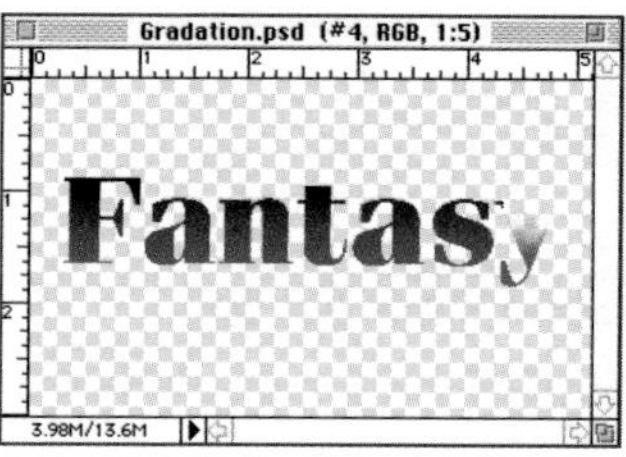

Layer #3: a yellow fill inside the type selection…

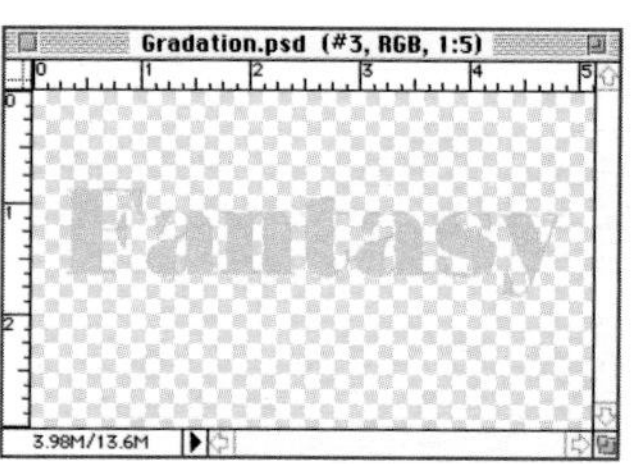

Layer #2: identical to Layer #3 except offset slightly to create a slight shadow…

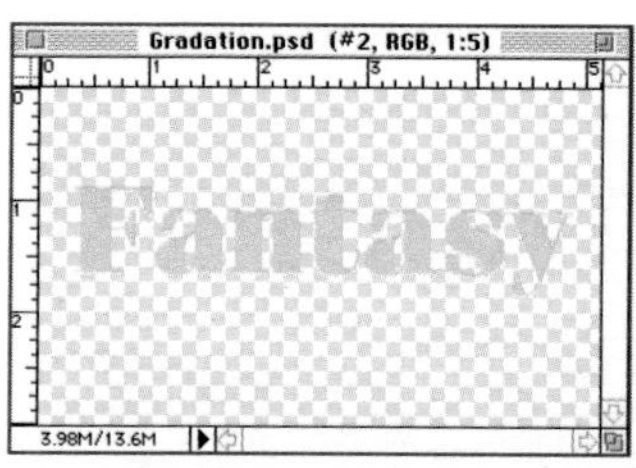

Background Layer: an original background created with KPT Bryce…

The final image after merging the layers (on the right). ■

① Create a new file. Enter the text you want to use. We used Helvetica Black for this example. Here we used two different colors. Choose Select ➥ None.

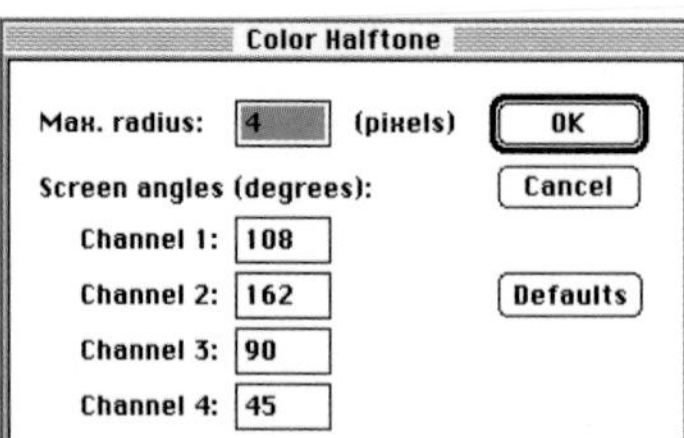

② Apply Filter ➥ Pixelate ➥ Color Halftone. Change the Max. radius to 4 pixels and leave the Screen angles at their defaults.

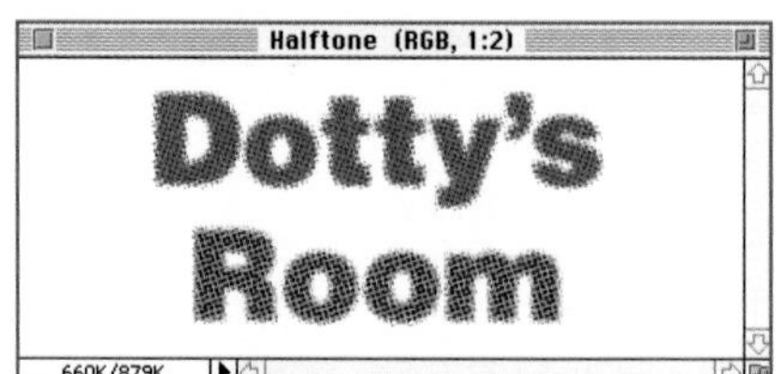

③ You should get something that looks like this.

VARIATIONS

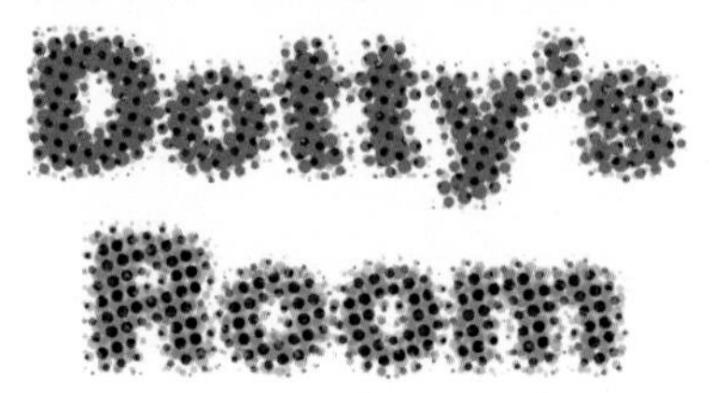

For larger dots, change the Max. radius in the Color Halftone dialog box. Here a setting of 8 pixels was used.

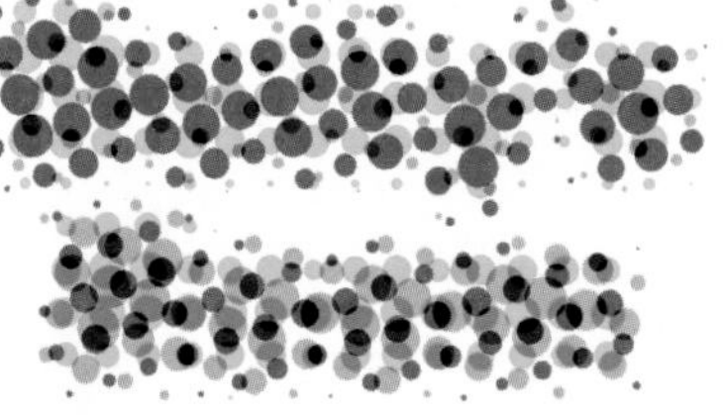

For something more abstract, go crazy with the Max. radius! Try 20 pixels!

You can also create different effects by varying the Screen angles in the Color Halftone dialog box. Here, all Screen angles were set to 0 (the Max. radius was set at 6 pixels.)

A bit of a wavy effect can be achieved by using Screen angles of 0, 15, 30, 45. Again, Max. radius was set for 6 pixels.

Keeping A Defined Edge

① If you want to keep a solid edge on the text, enter the text into a new channel.

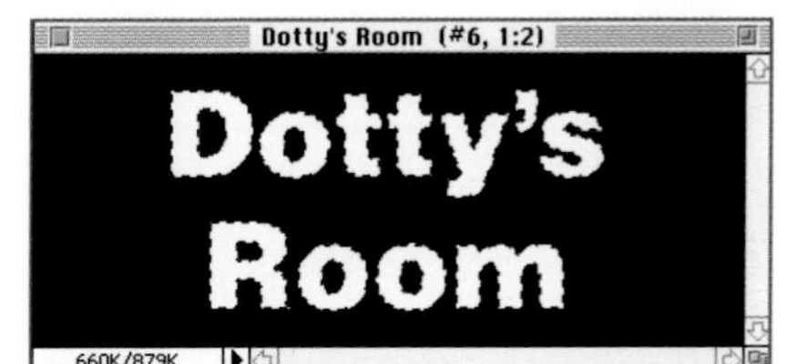

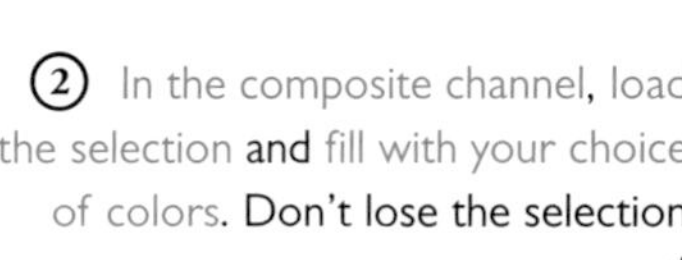

② In the composite channel, load the selection and fill with your choice of colors. Don't lose the selection yet!

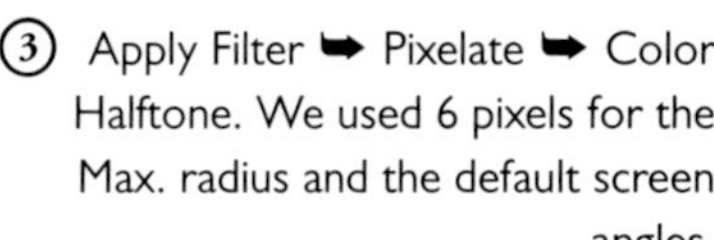

③ Apply Filter ➥ Pixelate ➥ Color Halftone. We used 6 pixels for the Max. radius and the default screen angles.

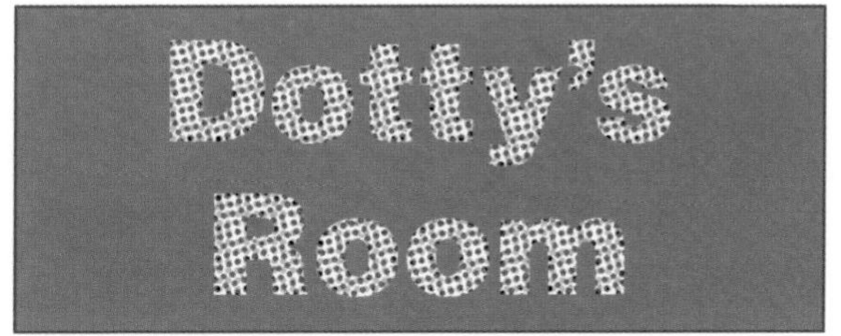

Black and White Halftone

You can also halftone black-and-white images.

① Create a new grayscale file. Type in your text using different values of gray.

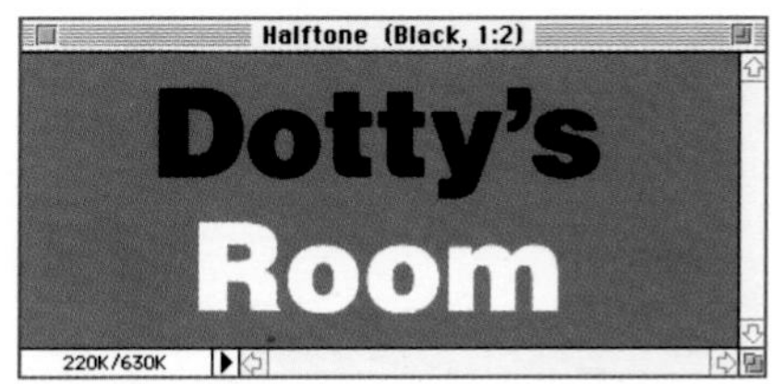

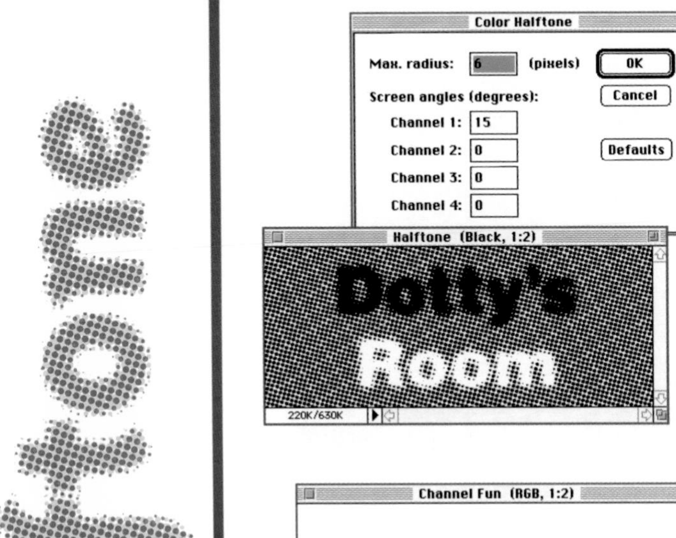

② Select Filter ➥ Pixelate ➥ Color Halftone. Use 6 pixels for the Max. radius and 15 degrees for Channel 1's Screen angle. Since this is a grayscale file, there is only one channel. The other values are ignored.

③ Your final image should look like this.

Fun with Channels

① Create a new image and enter your text. Here, an image was pasted into the text by using the Edit ➥ Paste Into function.

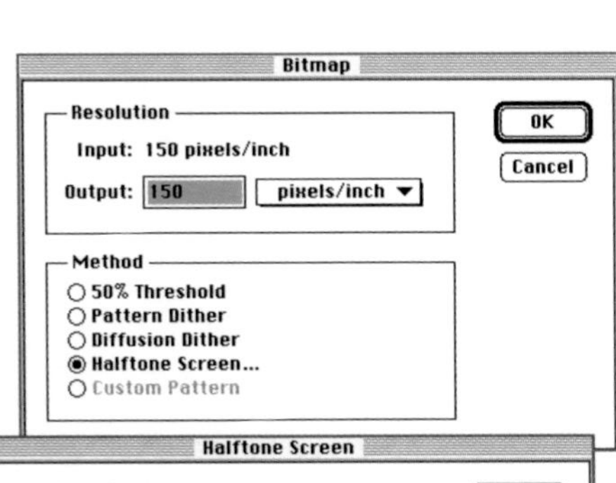

② Use Image ➥ Duplicate to make two copies of the image.

③ With one of the duplicate images, convert it to grayscale (Mode ➥ Grayscale).

④ Next, use Image ➥ Bitmap to convert the grayscale image to a bitmap. In the first dialog box you get, be sure the Output resolution matches the Input resolution. For Method, choose Halftone Screen.

In the second dialog box, use a setting of 20 lines/inch for the Frequency, 30 degrees for the Angle, and Round for Shape.

The image should now look something like this.

⑤ Select ➥ All and copy the image. Return to the original and make the Red Channel the active one. Paste the clipboard image into this channel, replacing what was already there. Return to the composite RGB Channel. You should have something like this.

⑥ Convert the other duplicate of the original image to grayscale. Then convert it to bitmap, but use the following settings. Frequency: 10 lines/inch, Angle: 0, Shape: Round. You should end up with something like what you see in this figure. Choose Select ➥ All to copy the image.

⑦ In the original image, paste the clipboard image into the Blue Channel. Your final image should look like this.

For some added excitement, try distorting one of the channels. Here we used Filter ➥ Distort ➥ Twirl with a setting of 56° on the Green Channel.

Custom Patterns

You can also use a custom pattern for halftoning.

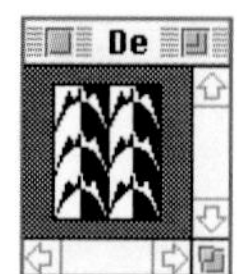

① Before changing the mode to bitmap, open a custom pattern. Keep in mind that smaller sizes tend to work better. Here we used the Deco pattern supplied in Photoshop, opened into a 60 × 75 file.

② Select ➥ All and Edit ➥ Define Pattern to define the pattern.

③ Use Image ➥ Duplicate to make a copy of your original image. Then change the mode of the duplicate to Grayscale (Mode ➥ Grayscale).

④ Choose Mode ➥ Bitmap and make sure both Input and Output numbers are the same. Select **Custom Pattern** from the Method choices.

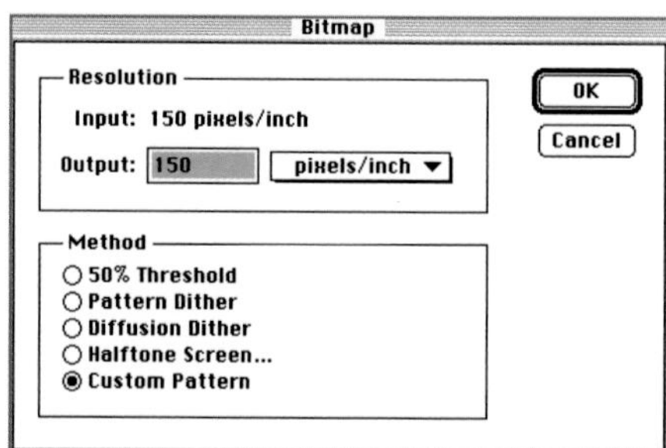

Channel Fun copy (1:2)

Fat Free

28K/28K

This uses your defined pattern for the dot size. The size of the pattern defines the frequency.

⑤ Copy the image and paste it into a channel in your original file. We pasted into the Green Channel for this example. ■

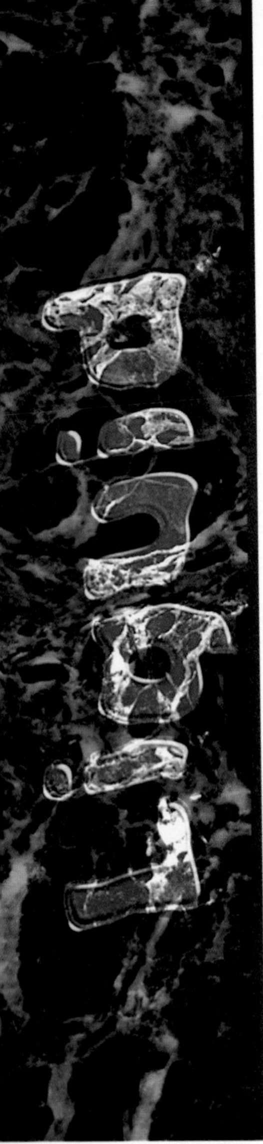

TOOLBOX

LiquidCurve file
LiquidLighting file
GE Spatter
GE Stamp

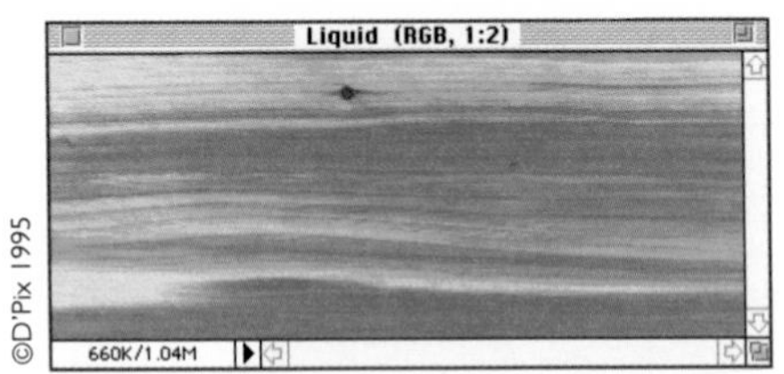

©D'Pix 1995

① Create a new file (it must be an RGB file) or open up an existing image. For this example, we used an image from D'Pix. We changed the resolution to 150 dpi and cropped it down.

② Create a new channel (#4), and use the Type tool to enter text into the channel. This example uses Helvetica Condensed Black at 60 points. Choose Select ➥ None (Command-D).

③ You may be somewhat familiar with this step and the next few that follow it—they're very similar to the beginning steps of Melting text, just in a slightly different order. Use Image ➥ Rotate ➥ 90° CW to rotate the image.

④ Apply Filter ➥ Stylize ➥ Wind with a setting of Wind and Left. Do this twice (press Command-F) so you get a good amount of streakage.

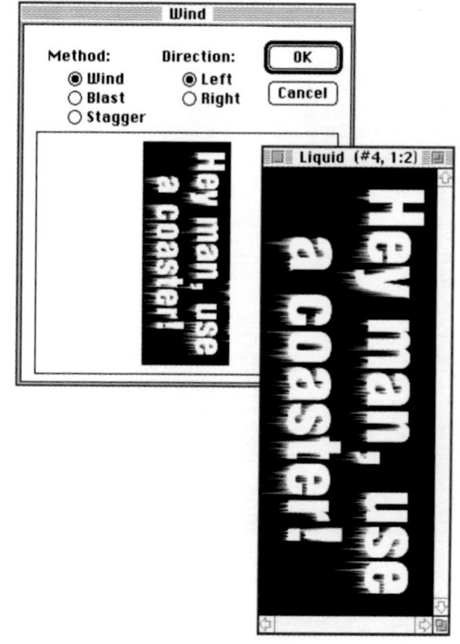

You should have something like this.

⑤ You can now rotate the image back to right side up using Image ➥ Rotate ➥ 90° CCW.

⑥ Apply Filter ➥ Gallery Effects: Classic Art 1 ➥ GE Spatter. Use settings of around 19 for the Radius and 15 for Smoothness. This adds some rough undulation to the text (don't worry…it'll be smoothed out in the next step).

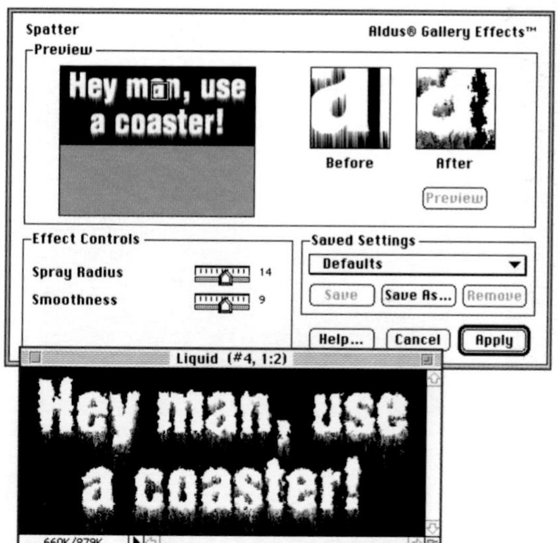

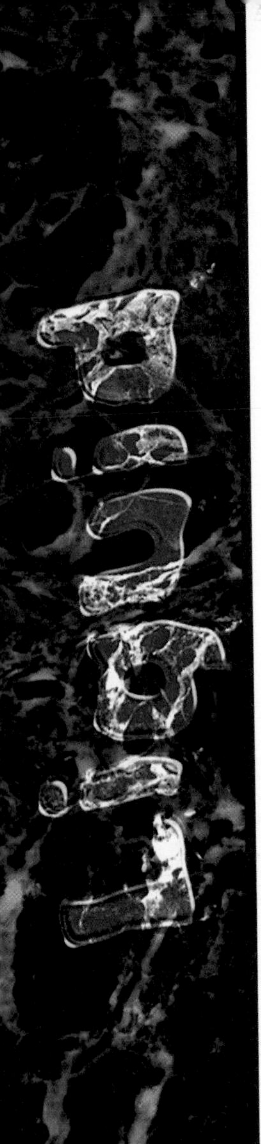

⑦ To smooth out the edges, apply Filter ➥ Gallery Effects: Classic Art 2 ➥ GE Stamp with the setting at 34 for Light/Dark Balance and 11 for Smoothness.

You should end up with something like this.

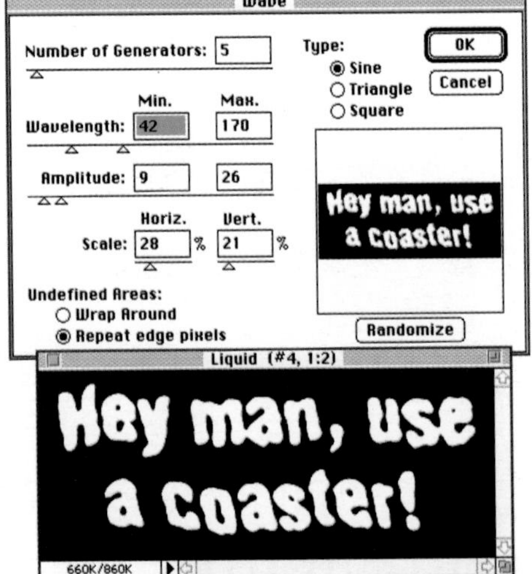

⑧ For more variation in the type, use Filter ➥ Distort ➥ Wave with the following settings: Generators: 5; Wavelength: 42, 170; Amplitude: 9, 26; Horiz.: 28; Vert.: 21; Type: Sine). Click the Randomize button a few times until the preview looks like what you're aiming for.

You should now have some nice, moderately wavy text.

⑨ Duplicate Channel #4 and name it something like "Texture," because that's what it's going to be. In the Texture channel, load Selection #4 and apply Filter ➥ Blur ➥ Gaussian Blur (6 pixels). Because the selection is loaded, the blur only occurs on the inside of the text.

⑩ Bring up the Image ➥ Adjust ➥ Curves dialog box, click the Load button and find the LiquidCurve file.

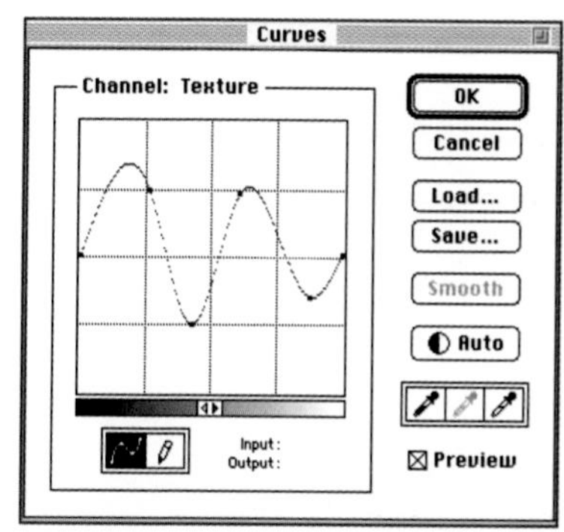

⑪ With Channel #4 still loaded, apply Filter ➥ Stylize ➥ Emboss. Use settings of Angle: -45°, Height: 2 pixels, and Amount: 100%. Your text should now look like it has a bit of a ridge around the outside of the letters.

⑫ Select ➥ None (Command-D) and apply Filter ➥ Blur ➥ Gaussian Blur with a radius of 2 pixels to smooth out any jaggies.

⑬ Now it's time to liquefy the text. Return to the composite Channel and load Channel #4 (the original text channel.) Apply Filter ➥ Render ➥ Lighting Effects and choose the LiquidLightStyles preset from the Style pop-up menu.

This preset uses the Texture channel you created as, well, a texture. This results in highlights and shadows from the various levels of gray in the channel.

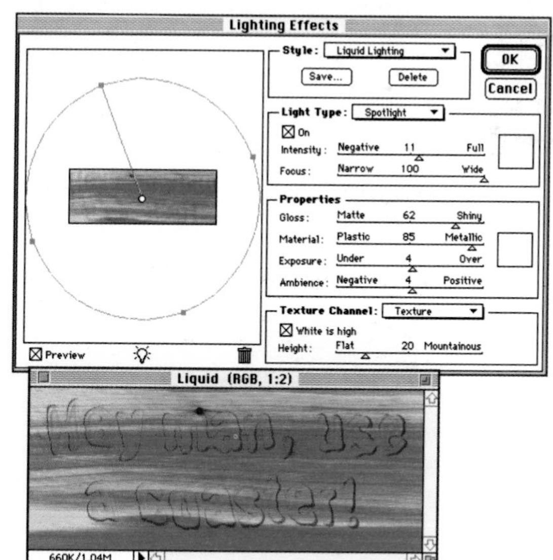

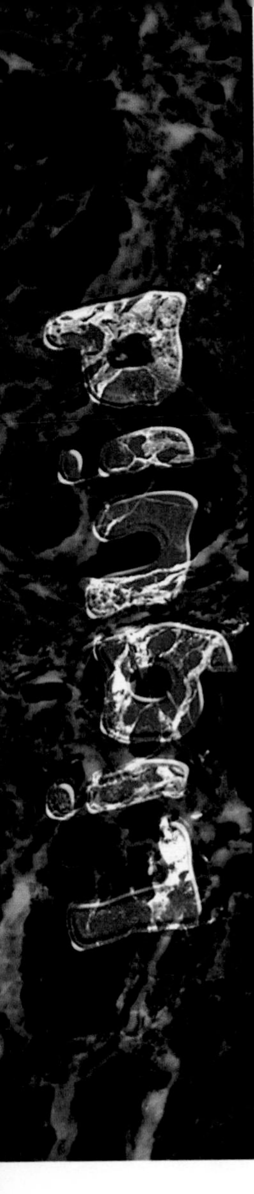

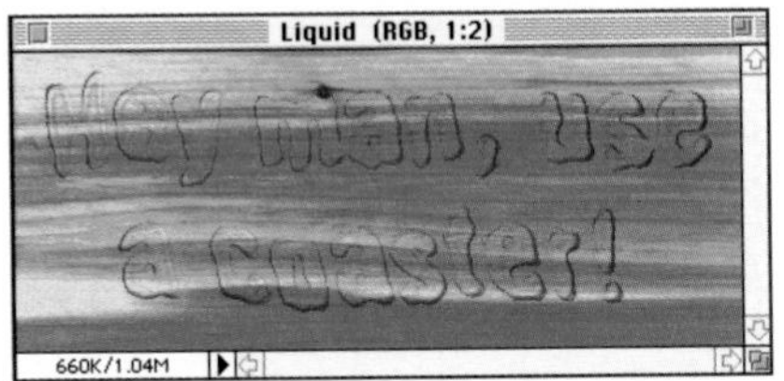

⑭ With Channel #4 still loaded, apply Filter ➡ Sharpen ➡ Unsharp Mask with setting of Amount: 55%, Radius: 3.0 pixels, and Threshold: 0 levels. This will bring up the contrast just a bit to give the illusion of looking through a liquid.

⑮ It may look good, but the highlights still need to be added. In the Texture channel, load Channel #4, choose Select ➡ All, and copy the channel (Command-C). Return to the composite channel and create a new layer (#2). Paste the copied image onto this layer and Select ➡ None (Command-D). You should now have something like this.

⑯ To pull out some highlights, use Image ➡ Adjust-Brightness/Contrast (Command-B) with settings of Brightness: -13 and Contrast: +87.

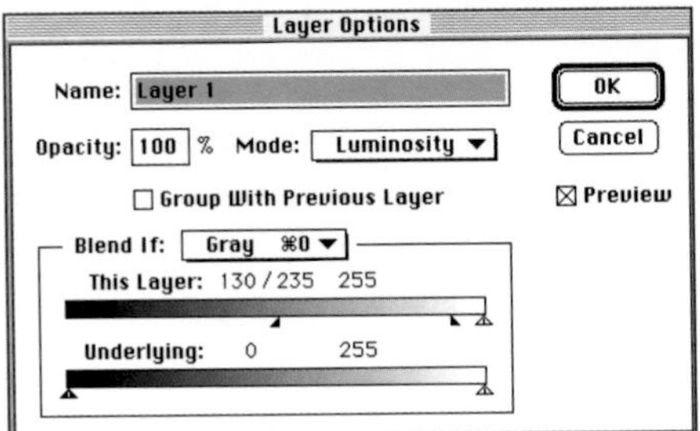

⑰ Double-click on Layer 1 in the Layers floating palette. This brings up the Layer Options dialog box. Set the Mode to Luminosity and adjust the This Layer slider until the numbers read 130/235 and 255 (you can split the arrows by holding down the Option key and moving just half of the slider triangle).

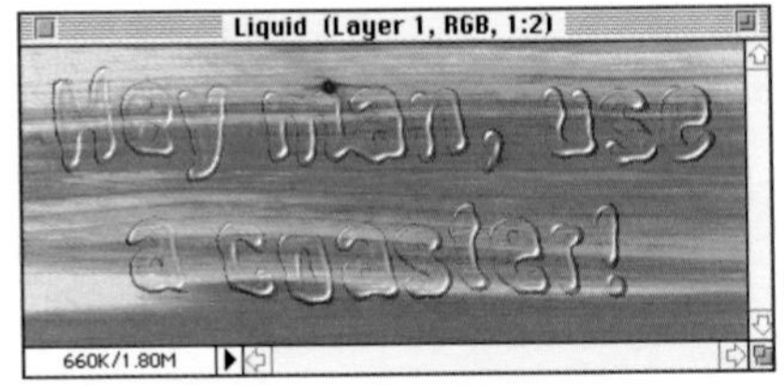

Adjusting this slider determines which values of gray are being used to increase the luminosity. By moving the arrows around you can allow different grays to affect the underlying image.

(18) Finally, take down the Opacity of Layer 1 to around 80%. This softens the intensity of the highlights a bit.

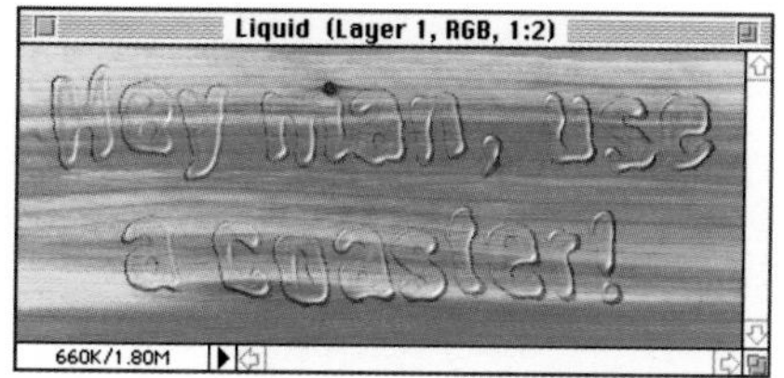

VARIATIONS

If you're looking for something other than clear liquid, try changing the light color in Light Type section of the Lighting Styles dialog box in Step 13. Here, a medium green colored light was used.

If you're looking for an opaque substance, move the Materials slider in the Lighting Effect dialog box from Metallic all the way down to Plastic when you render the text. When you get to Step 16, where you adjust the Brightness and Contrast of Layer 1, use values of 100 for Brightness and 25 for Contrast. For Step 17, change the mode of Layer 1 to Luminosity, but skip the rest of that step. For Step 18, adjust the Opacity level of Layer 1 until the background is just barely visible. We used 76% for this variation. ■

MARQUEE

It doesn't get any easier than this. One of the great new filters available in Photoshop 3.0 does almost all the work for you.

① Open a new file. Change the foreground and background colors to their default settings (press D). Create a new channel (#4). Use the Type tool to enter the text. We used Futura CondExtraBold at 50 points.

② With the selection still active, defloat the selection (Command-J), and choose Filter ➡ Blur ➡ Gaussian Blur (4 pixels).

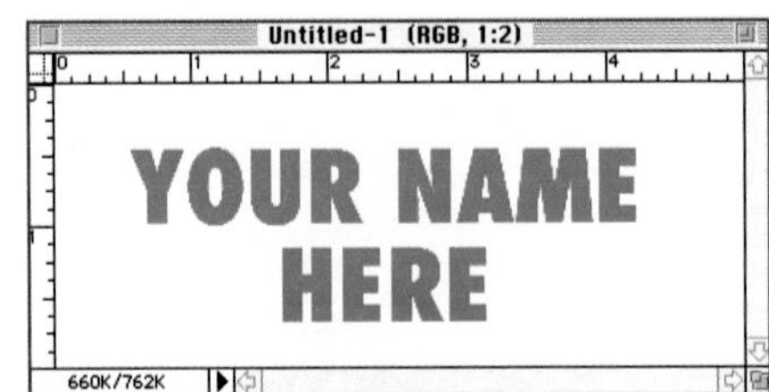

③ Go to the composite channel (Command-0). Change the foreground color to a color for the marquee letters. Press Option-Delete to fill the text with the foreground color.

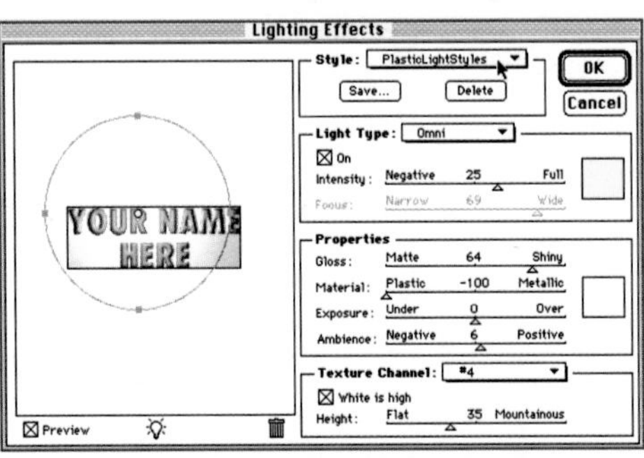

④ Keep that selection active. Choose Filter ➡ Render ➡ Lighting Effects. Choose PlasticLightingStyles (included on the CD) from the pop-up menu. If it doesn't show up in the list, see page 204 to find out how to load it from the CD. You might need to increase the Height setting to get the type as full as you want it.

TIP The text selection should still be active, which means you could copy the text right to the clipboard or use the selection to make a path if you need to drop out the background.

TOOLBOX

PlasticLightingStyles file

VARIATIONS

If you are going to include this text in a composition, you can use the controls in the Lighting Effects dialog box to make the marquee letters appear as if they are being lit by the same light source as other objects in your composition. For this variation, we chose the Soft Direct Lights preset from the pop-up menu.

YOUR NAME HERE

We manipulated the Five Lights Down preset to get this image.

If you deselect the text before applying the Lighting Effects filter, then the light will affect the background too. This text looks a little more like it belongs with its background.

YOUR NAME HERE

Flip to page 148 to find out out how to create more Plastic text. ■

Plastic

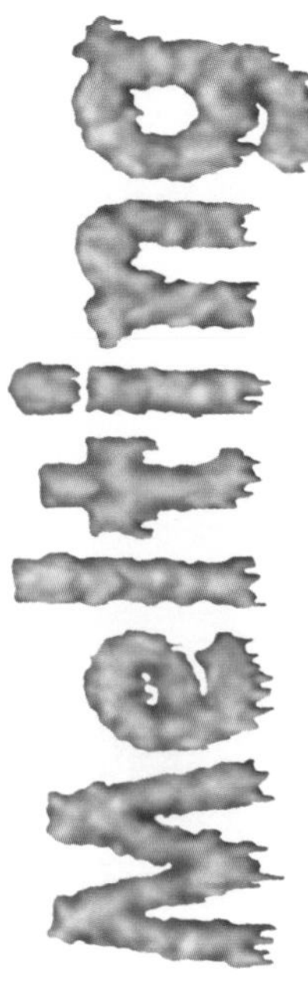

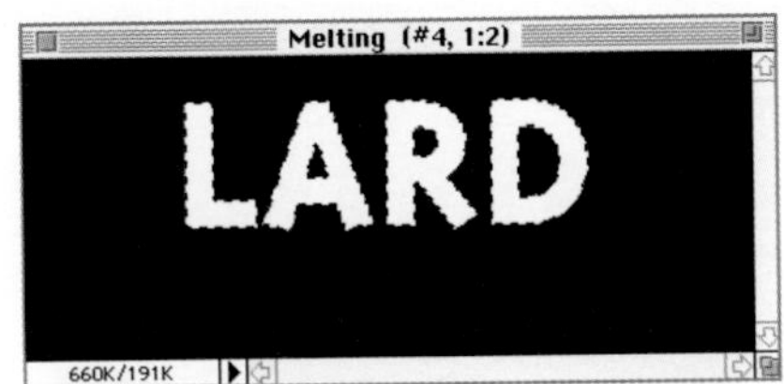

① Create a new document, and create a new channel. Use the Type tool to enter the text into the new channel. This example uses Triplex Extra Bold at 100 points.

② Use Image ➡ Effects ➡ Distort to give your text some dimension. If you don't want much dimension, at least stretch the letters—if your letters are too short, they may turn out to be unrecognizable blobs.

③ Choose Select ➡ None (Command-D), then Image ➡ Map ➡ Invert (Command-I).

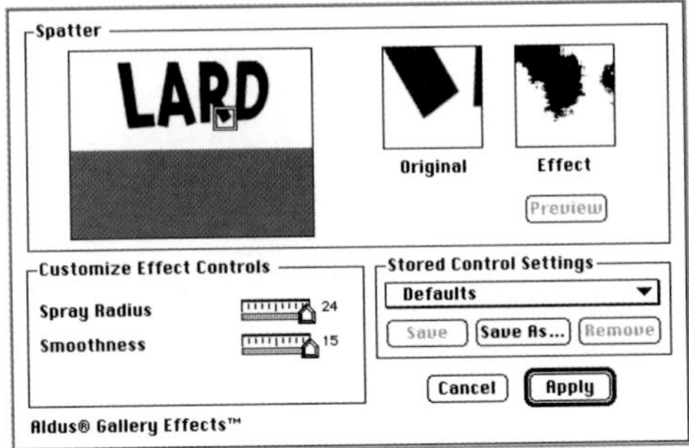

④ Apply Filter ➡ Gallery Effects: Classic Art 1 ➡ GE Spatter. Crank the settings up to 24 for the Radius and 15 for the Smoothness.

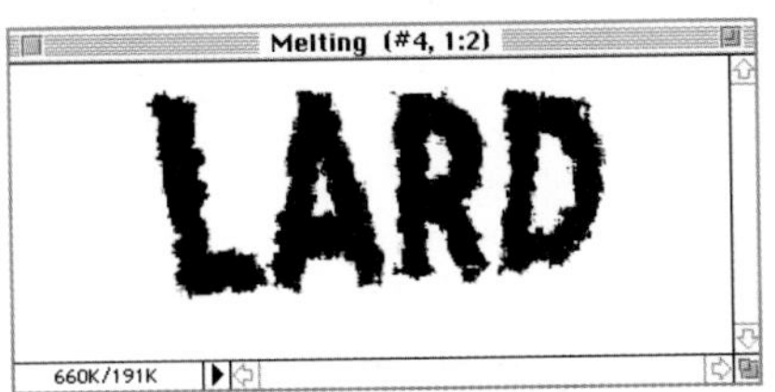

Your type will look pretty rough.

TOOLBOX

GE Spatter
GE Stamp

⑤ Image ➥ Rotate ➥ 90° CW and Image ➥ Map ➥ Invert. Apply Filter ➥ Stylize ➥ Wind, with the settings at Wind and Left, twice.

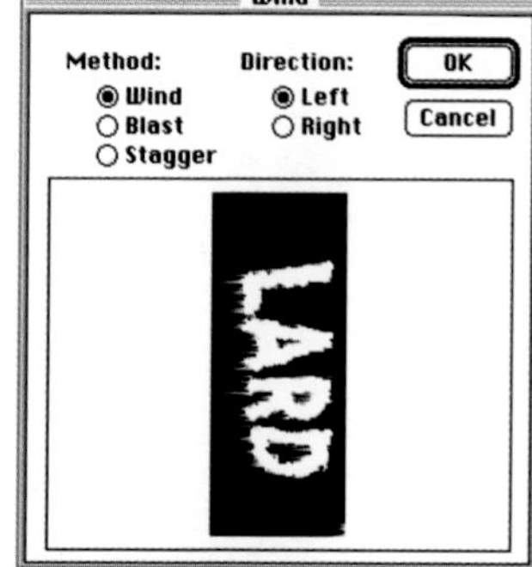

Your image will look like this.

⑥ Image ➥ Map ➥ Invert (Command-I) and Image ➥ Rotate ➥ 90° CCW to get the text back to being right-side up.

⑦ Apply Filter ➥ Gallery Effects: Classic Art 2 ➥ GE Stamp. Set the Light/Dark Balance at 30 and the Smoothness at 13.

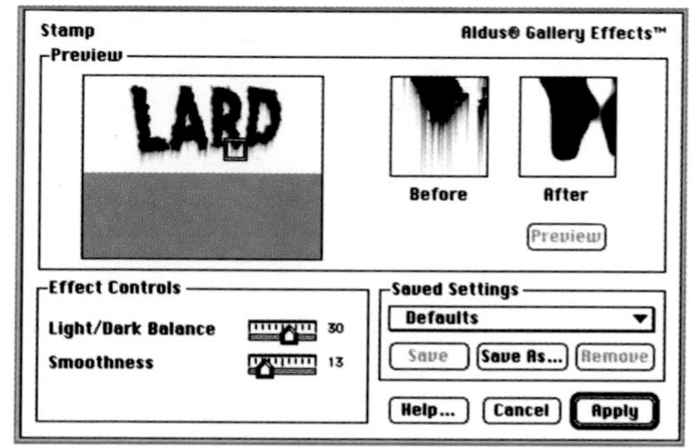

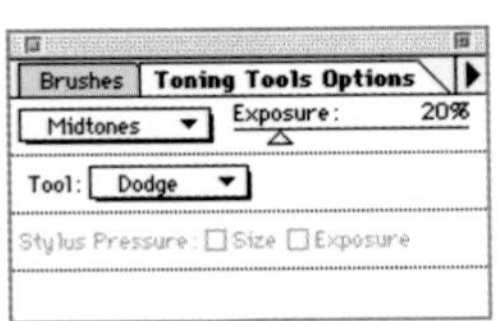

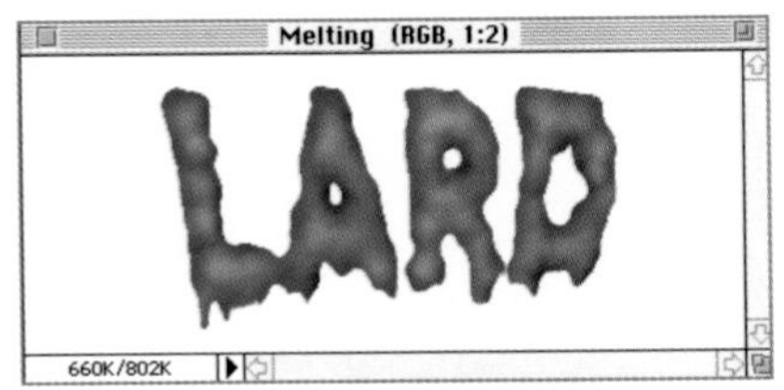

⑧ Image ➥ Map ➥ Invert (Command-I), then return to the composite channel (Command-0). Set the foreground color to a dark brown. Load the selection. Press Option-Delete to fill the selection with the foreground color. Select ➥ None (Command-D).

⑨ To give the type a more oozy quality, use the Dodge and Burn tools to add highlights and shadows. The Dodge tool will add highlights by "under exposing" what's painted with its tool. Burn does the opposite: it adds shadows by painting with "over exposure." Keeping the Exposure level (in the Tool Option pallet) gives greater control over the application. We used a setting of 20% here with the tone values set to Midtone. The same goes for the Burn tool.

To create a blobby effect, apply the Dodge tool several times in the same spot, move a short distance, and repeat. Use varying brush sizes. For this image, the brush size ranged from 25 and 45 pixels. Add shadows with the Burn tool in the same manner. A few streaks of dodging were used to connect the blobs.

Finally, use the Smudge tool, sparingly, to blur the blobs together a bit. That's it, and you didn't even need an oven!

VARIATIONS

Want more or less drippiness? Try varying the settings in Step 7. Here are some different results:

Molasses on a picnic table: Use Light/Dark Balance: 40 and Smoothness: 25.

Ice milk in your hands: Use Light/Dark Balance: 25 and Smoothness: 10.

Snowman in Florida: Use Light/Dark Balance: 20 and Smoothness: 5. ■

You can produce this effect using a variety of combinations of the steps that follow.

① Create a new file. Set the foreground color to the color of type you want. Use the Type tool to enter the text you want to use (For this example, we used Futura-XB at 50 points). Make sure the Italic box is checked. Click OK. When placing the text in the image area, be sure to leave some room to the left (or right depending on the direction you want the text to be moving).

② Deselect the text (Command-D), and apply Filter ➡ Stylize ➡ Wind (Wind, Right).

TIP

To improve the dynamic of the movement use the Smudge tool to lengthen the streaks. This is not necessary, but a few touches can greatly improve this effect. Set the Smudge tool pressure to 50% and use a feathered brush.

③ Now apply Filter ➥ Blur ➥ Motion Blur (10 pixels). You could raise this setting some, but if you go too crazy, Herbie is going to look like he's just standing there shaking.

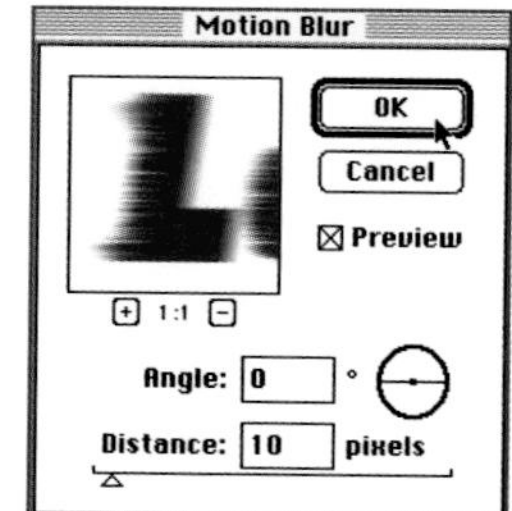

④ One more time, apply Filter ➥ Stylize ➥ Wind (Wind, Right).

⑤ Now, we'll apply Filter ➥ Sharpen ➥ Unsharp Mask (50, 3.5, 2) to sharpen the edges.

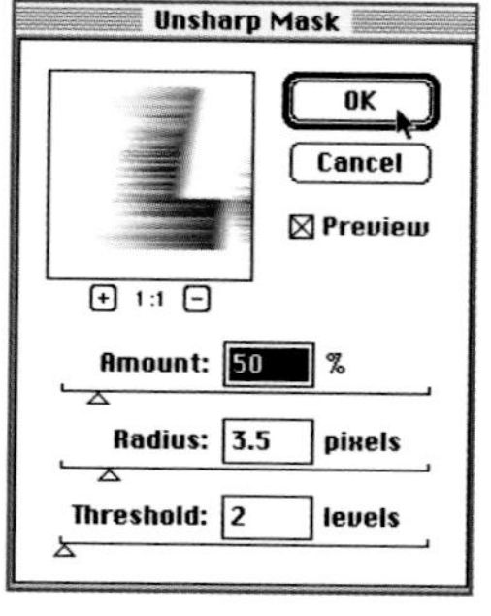

⑥ Next, select Filter ➥ Distort ➥ Shear. You can grab the line in the grid at any point and drag to make it bend. We added one point, then pulled the top and bottom points all the way to the left. Finally, we added another point on the curve to get just the bend we were looking for.

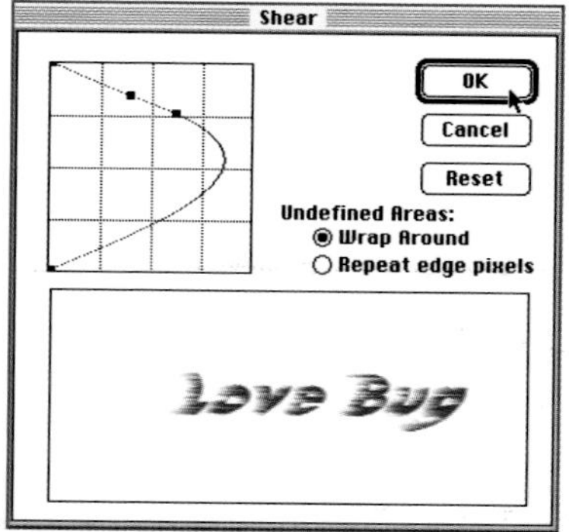

Here's another good place to use the Smudge tool to lengthen and smooth the streaks.

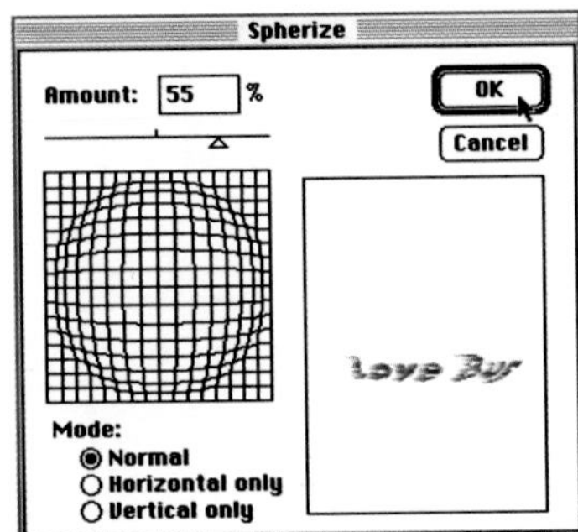

⑦ Finally, choose Filter ➥ Distort ➥ Spherize. Before we chose this filter, we moved the text down a little so the Spherize filter would push it down a little. We set the amount to 55.

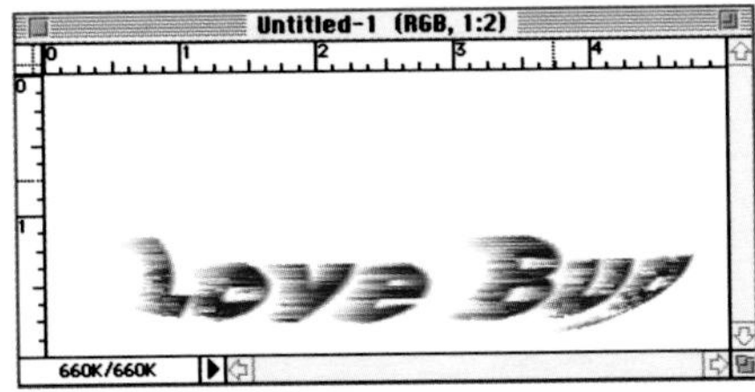

There are many possible combinations of these steps that will yield good results. You could have stopped a few steps ago and decided you had what you were looking for.

VARIATIONS

If you're just trying to put a quick swerve in your type, then enter the text, deselect it and choose Filter ➥ Distort ➥ Shear. Use the mouse to pull the center of the line out and drag the top and bottom back.

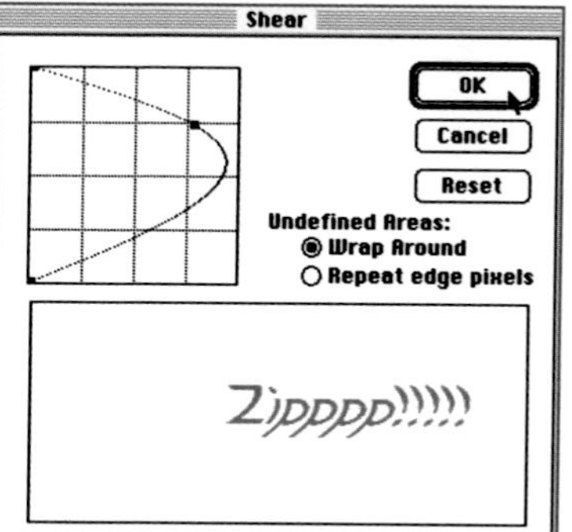

Velocity Filter The easy way: Andromeda Software's Velocity Filter was used for this effect (One-way smear, Intensity: 50, Angle: 0, Height: 50, Width: 90). ■

There are a number of ways to create neon using simple blurring and feathering techniques.

Quick Neon

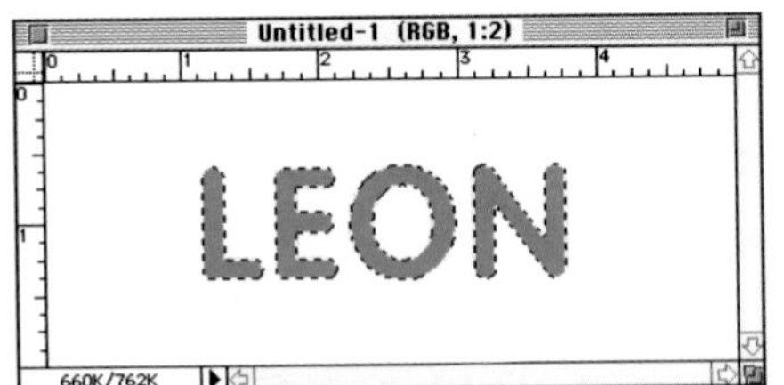

① Create a new file. Change the foreground color to a bright color. Use the Type tool to enter the text. A round-edged font like VAG Rounded Bold (80 points) will work best for this effect. Tekton or Neptune will also work well.

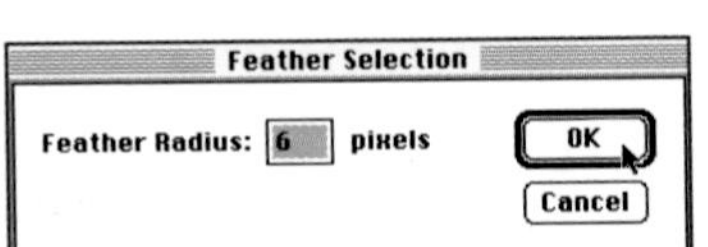

② Choose Select ➡ Inverse, then Select ➡ Feather (6 pixels).

③ Change the foreground color to black (press D). Press Option-Delete to fill the background. That's it—short and simple.

VARIATIONS

This quick technique works well for creating handwritten neon. Create a new channel (Channel #4), then use a hard-edged brush to paint white text on a black background. Return to the composite channel (Command-0), and load the painted text selection (Channel #4). Fill it with a color for the neon and do Steps 2 and 3 above.

CMYK If you are producing an RGB image, then the text may look bright enough already. But if your CMYK neon looks a little dull, try this. After Step 1 save the selection. After Step 4, load the selection, and choose Select ➡ Modify ➡ Contract (6 pixels, or until the selection has moved away from the edges of the text). Choose Select ➡ Feather (1 pixel). Now, choose Image ➡ Adjust ➡ Curves and bend the center of the curve upward slightly, like this. This should help brighten the text.

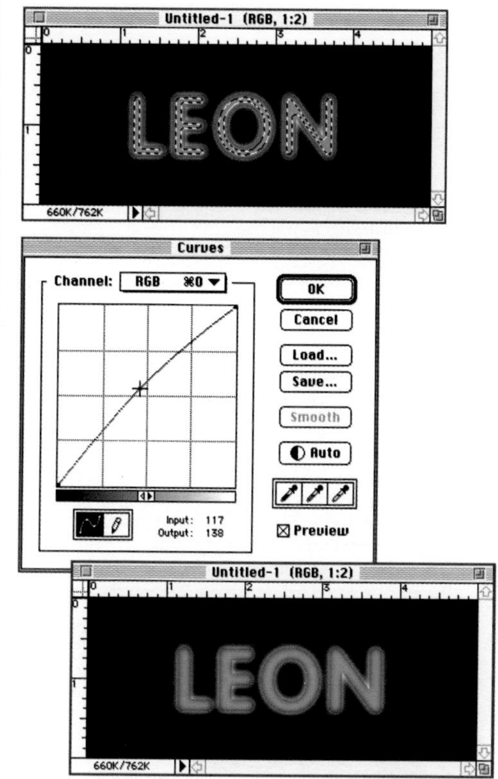

Detailed Neon

① Create a new file (we used a 300 dpi file for this effect). Set the colors to the defaults (press D). Use the Type tool to enter the text. Again, we started with Vag Rounded Bold at 65 points. Save the text selection (Channel #4).

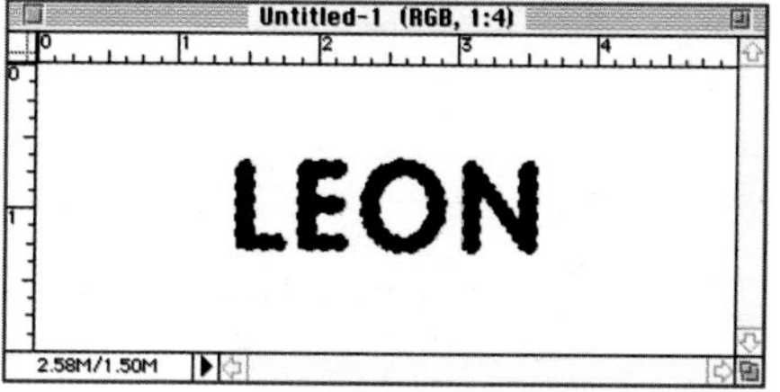

② Choose Select ➡ Modify ➡ Contract (12 pixels). You want a thin selection running all the way through the text. Save this selection to create Channel #5. Press delete and deselect the text (Command-D).

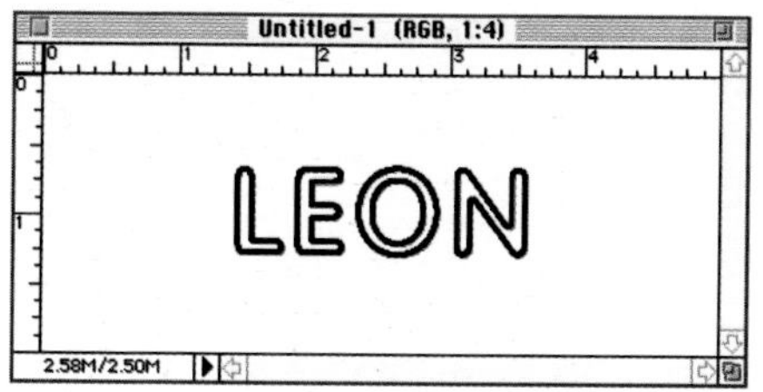

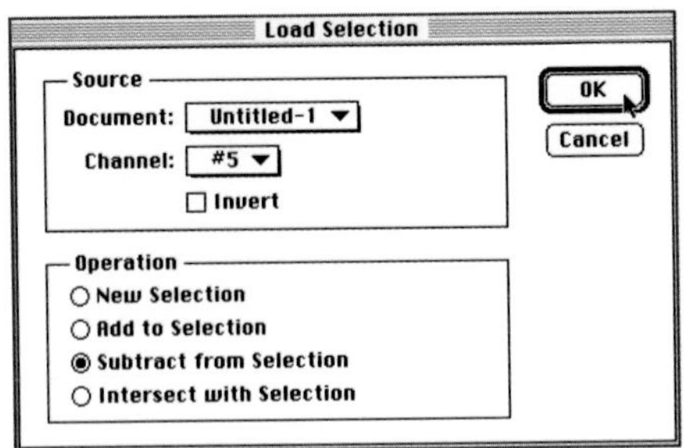

③ Load the original text selection (Channel #4). Now, load the channel saved in Step 3 (Channel #5), and check the Subtract from Selection option. Save this new selection to Channel #6. This saves the selection of what your text looks like now. Deselect the tubes (Command-D).

④ Choose Image ➥ Map ➥ Invert.

⑤ Choose Filter ➥ Blur ➥ Gaussian Blur (5 pixels). This will establish the extent of the near glow.

⑥ Load the selection saved in Step 4 (Channel #6), then choose Filter ➥ Blur ➥ Gaussian Blur. Choose an amount that matches what you see here. We used 8 pixels.

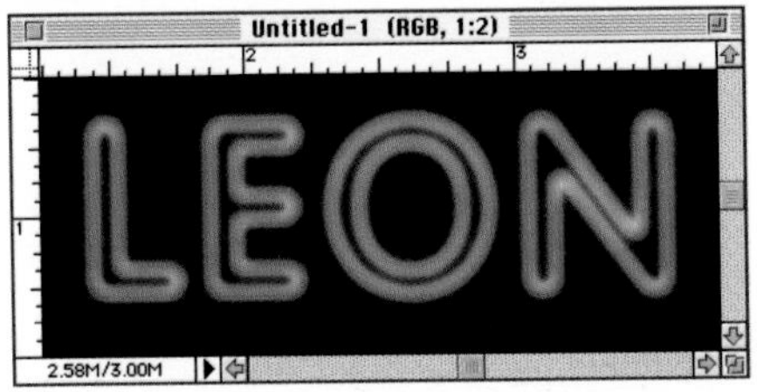

⑦ Choose Image ➥ Adjust ➥ Brightness/Contrast (Brightness: -5, Contrast +10). The settings for your text will probably be different. Find something that looks like what we came up with. Choose Select ➥ None.

TIP

If you plan on printing this file and need a CMYK image, it's a good idea to either switch to CMYK mode or choose Mode ➡ CMYK Preview, now. The RGB mode will produce the brightest neon, but you will be setting yourself up for a big disappointment when you switch to CMYK mode later.

⑧ Choose Image ➡ Adjust ➡ Hue/Saturation. Click on the Colorize checkbox. The preview will immediately glow a bright red. Use the Hue and Saturation sliders to find a color for the neon. Try to strike a balance (with the Saturation slider) between the most intense color and the greatest amount of detail. You want a nice even color in the middle of the tubes. These are the values we used: Hue: 166, Saturation: 60, Lightness: 0.

⑨ Load the tubes selection (Channel #6). Then choose Select ➡ Modify ➡ Contract (4 pixels) to select a narrow line within the tubes. Choose Select ➡ Feather (1 pixel).

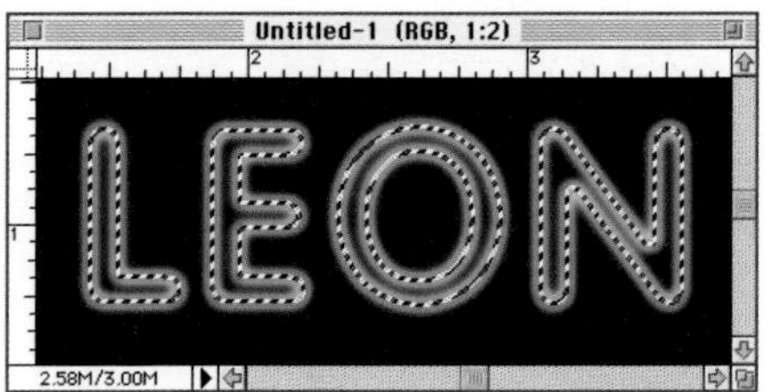

⑩ Choose Image ➡ Adjust ➡ Curves, and bend the composite curve up slightly from the center, like in this figure.

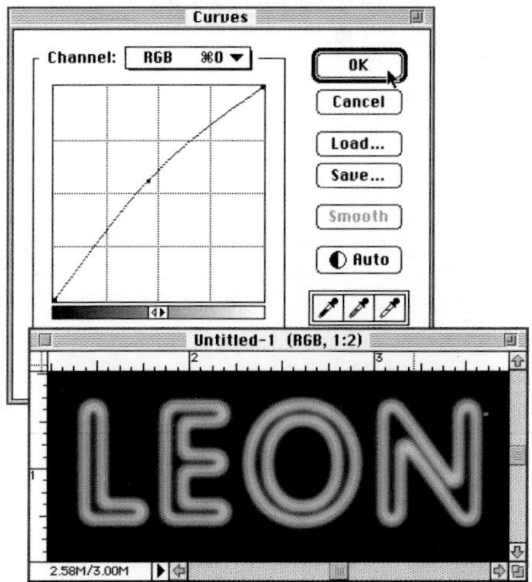

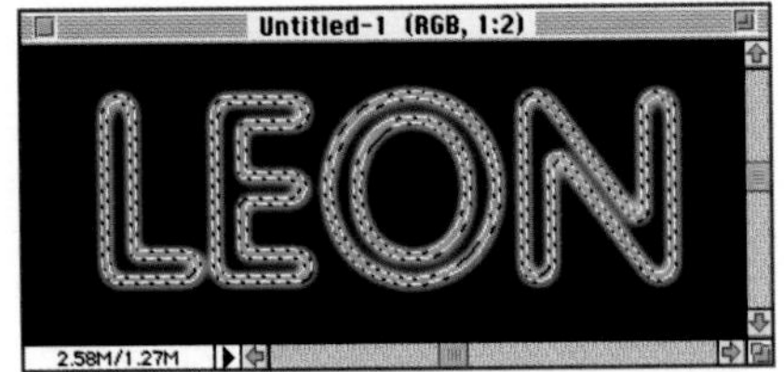

⑪ Now choose Select ➥ Modify ➥ Contract (2 pixels) to select an even narrower line within the tubes. Choose Select ➥ Feather (1 pixel).

⑫ Choose Image ➥ Adjust ➥ Curves. Bend the composite curve up a little more this time.

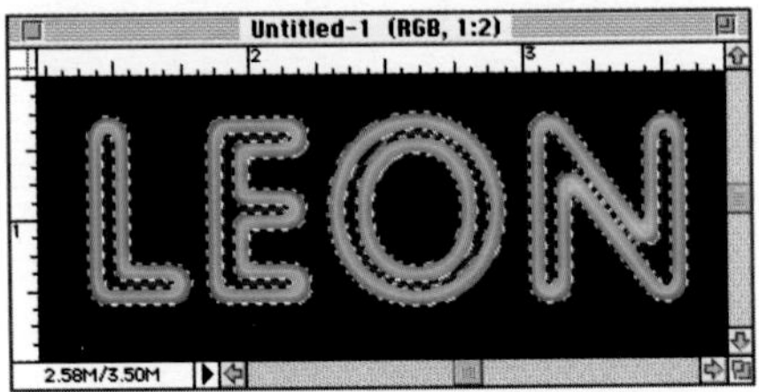

⑬ Load the tubes selection (channel #6), then choose Select ➥ Modify ➥ Expand (4 pixels). The selection should now contain almost all of the glow. Save this selection (Channel #7).

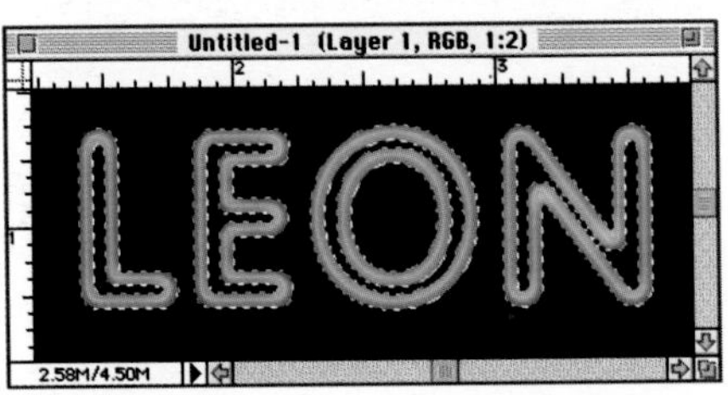

⑭ Cut the type (Command-X), then fill this layer with black. Make a new layer, load the Channel #7 selection and paste (Command-V) it back in on the new layer.

⑮ Go back to the background layer. The selection should still be active. Choose Select ➥ Feather (12 pixels). Choose a color near the color of your text. Fill the selection. In this example, we feathered and filled the selection again.

⑯ Add highlights to the tubes by applying the Plastic Wrap filter included on the CD. Load the tubes selection (Channel #6), and choose Filter ➥ Gallery Effects: Classic Art 3 ➥ Plastic Wrap (Highlight Strength: 6, Detail: 15, Smoothness: 10).

VARIATIONS

Filters can make a quick neon easy.

KPT Gradients on Paths Load the text selection. Choose Select ➥ Feather (3 pixels). Then, apply Filter ➥ KPT ➥ KPT Gradients on Paths. For this example, we used one of the preset gradients: True Blue Tube. Try creating your own.

Gallery Effects: Classic Art 3: GE Neon Press D, then X to make the foreground color white and background color black. Choose a color for the neon. Use the Type tool to enter the text. Save the selection, then deselect the text (Command-D). Press X. The foreground color should be black and the background color should be the color of the text. Choose Filter ➥ Gallery Effects: Classic Art 3 ➥ GE Neon. Finally, we loaded the text selection, feathered it, and filled it with the neon color again. ■

OVERGROWN

① Create a new file. Change the foreground color to a color for the text. Enter the text in the Background layer. Any font will work well for this simple effect, but something with serifs will give the overgrowth some extra limbs to hang from. We used Cheltenham Bold at 50 points.

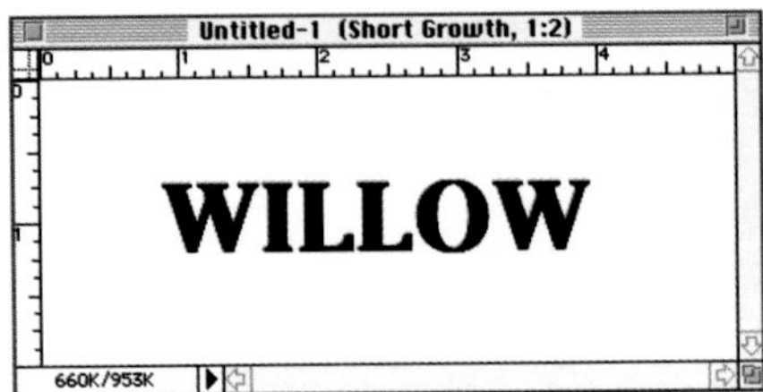

② Save the text selection to create Channel #4. Deselect the text (Command-D) and go to Channel #4. Duplicate Channel #4 and name the new Channel **Short Growth**. Choose Image ➥ Map ➥ Invert (Command-I) to invert this new channel (Short Growth).

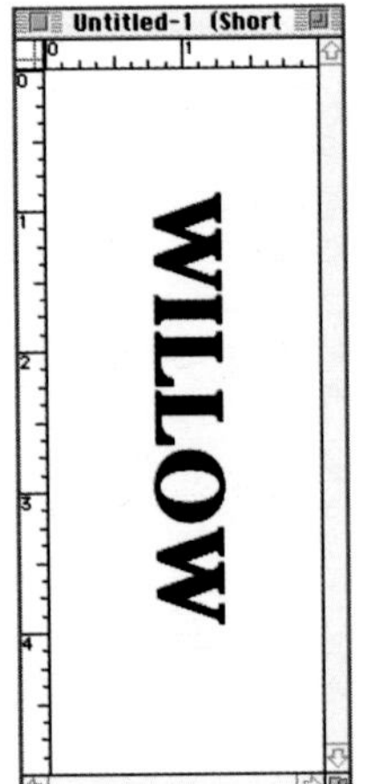

③ Then rotate the entire image 90° clockwise (Image ➥ Rotate ➥ 90° CW).

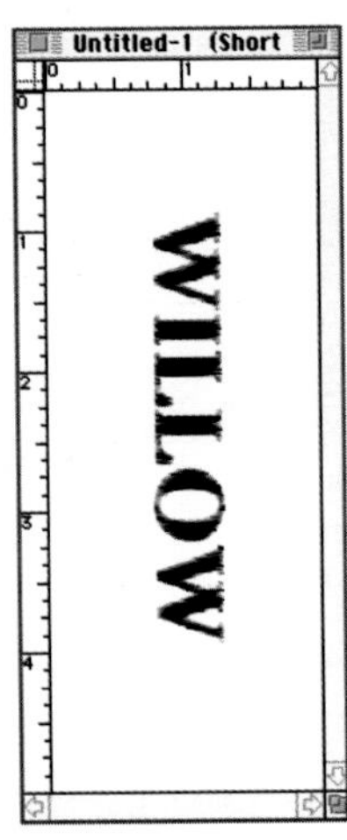

④ Apply Filter ➥ Stylize ➥ Wind (Wind, Right), then press Command-Option-F to bring the Wind filter dialog box back. Switch the direction to Left and click OK to apply it again.

TOOLBOX

KPT Gradient Fractal Explorer 2.1

⑤ Press Command-I to invert Channel #4. Then duplicate the Short Growth channel and name the new channel Long Growth.

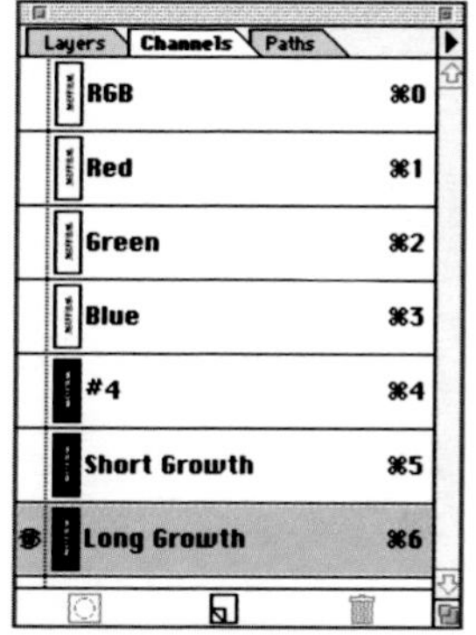

TIP You can press Command-F to apply the last filter you used with exactly the same settings. If you want to apply the filter again, but with different settings, press Command-Option-F and the dialog box from the last filter used will come up.

⑥ Press Command-I to invert the Long Growth channel. To build the overgrowth, we're going to apply the Wind filter 3 times and invert the channel between each application. So, the dance goes like this: Command-F, Command-I, Command-F, Command-I, Command-F, Command-I. Hopefully, you got something that turned out like this.

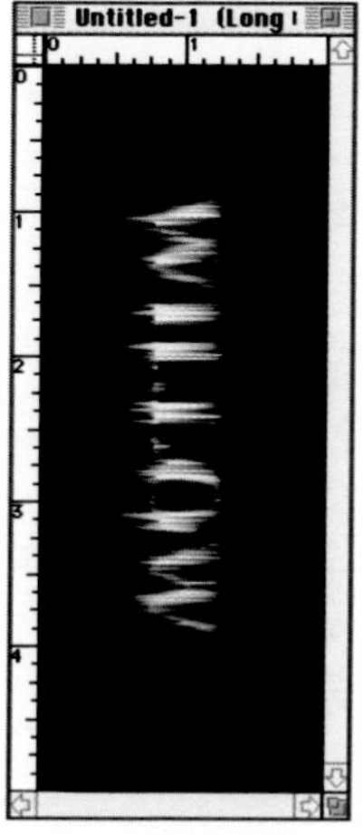

⑦ Choose Image ➡ Rotate ➡ 90° CCW to rotate the entire image back to its original orientation. Then return to the composite channel (Command-0).

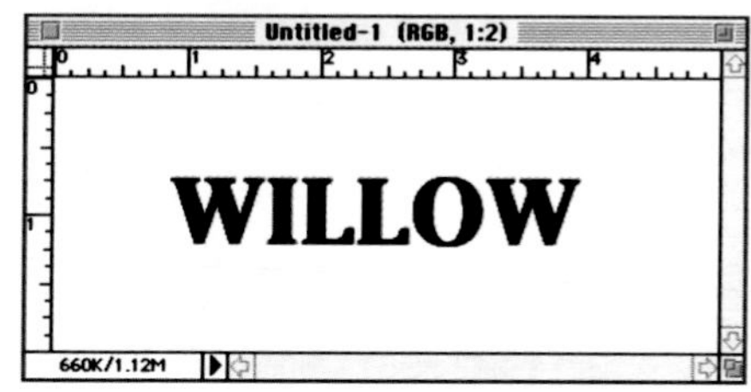

⑧ First, change the foreground color to a color for the overgrowth. Then load the Channel #4 selection. While this selection is still active, choose Select ➡ Load Selection, choose Short Growth from the Channel pop-up menu, and click on the Subtract from Selection option. Press Option-Delete to fill the new selection with the foreground color.

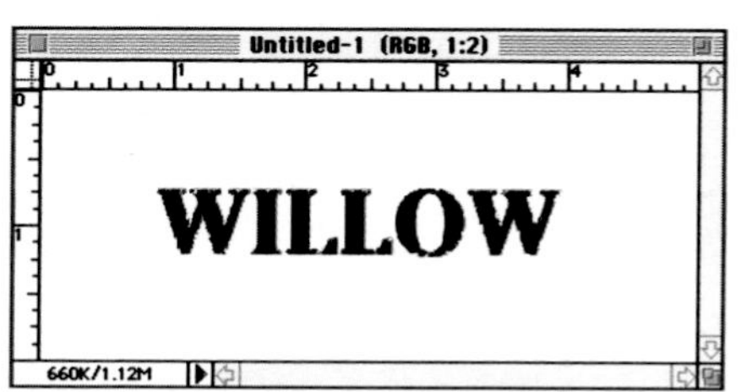

OVERGROWN

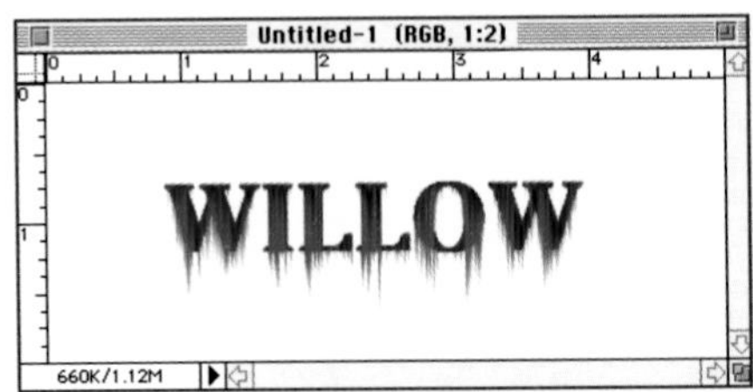

⑨ Now, load the Long Growth channel selection, and press Option-Delete again to fill the new selection with the same color.

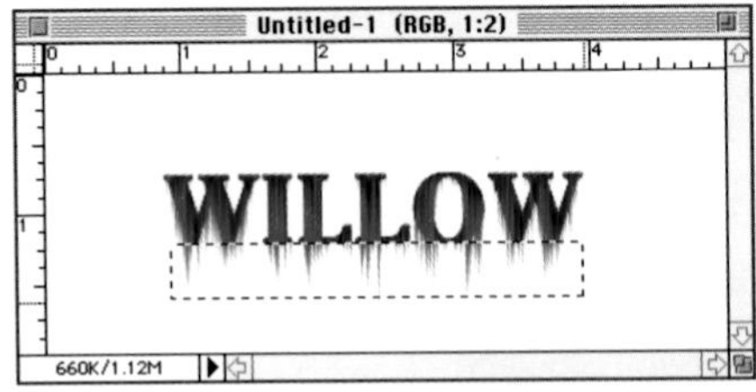

⑩ To add some final touches to the drooping overgrowth, first use the rectangular Selection tool to draw a rectangle around the extra growth beneath the text.

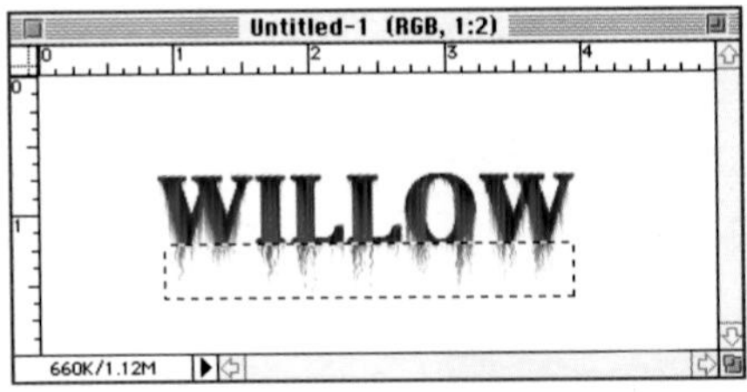

⑪ Apply Filter ➥ Distort ➥ Ripple (100, Medium).

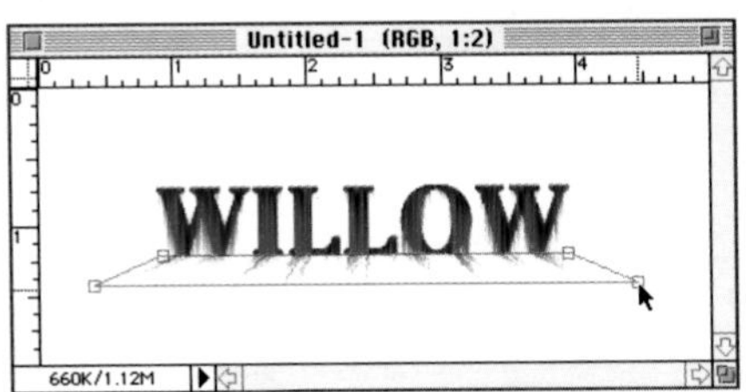

⑫ Then choose Image ➥ Effects ➥ Perspective. Grab the lower right corner of the Perspective frame and drag it to the right. The lower left corner will move in the opposite direction at the same rate. Once you've spread the overgrowth to your liking, click in the selection to set the perspective. Choose Select ➥ None (Command-D) and you're done.

VARIATIONS

For our tribute to peace, love, and hair we used KPT Gradient Fractal Explorer 2.1 to fill the text selection. In Step 2, after saving the selection but before deselecting the text, choose Filter ➥ KPT ➥ KPT Gradient Designer 2.1. Also, once we filled the Long Growth selection in Step 9, we shifted the selection to the right (hold down the Option and Command keys and press the right arrow) and filled it with a different color.

PEACE

You can make steam with this effect, too. We started with black text on a black background. In Step 3, we rotated the image 90° CCW instead of 90° CW. (And made sure to rotate back 90° CW in Step 7.) Then in Step 6 we applied Filter ➥ Stylize ➥ Diffuse (Normal) and Filter ➥ Distort ➥ Ripple (100, Medium). In Steps 8 and 9, we used white as the foreground color for filling the selections. Finally, we converted the entire image to Grayscale mode (Mode ➥ Grayscale), then Duotone mode (Mode ➥ Duotone). The two colors we used were black and Trumatch 38-a5. ■

These techniques will show you how to create text that takes on the characteristics of the surface its painted on. The same techniques will allow you to create some other cool effects.

Painted type

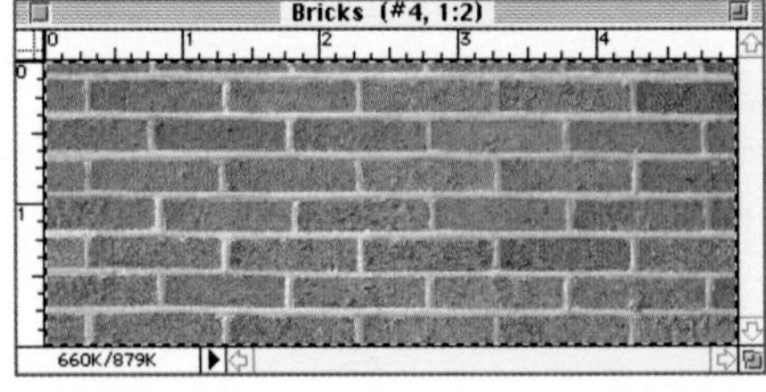

©D'Pix 1995

① Create a new file, or open a file containing the background you want to put your text on. For this example, we used a stock photo of a brick wall from D'Pix.

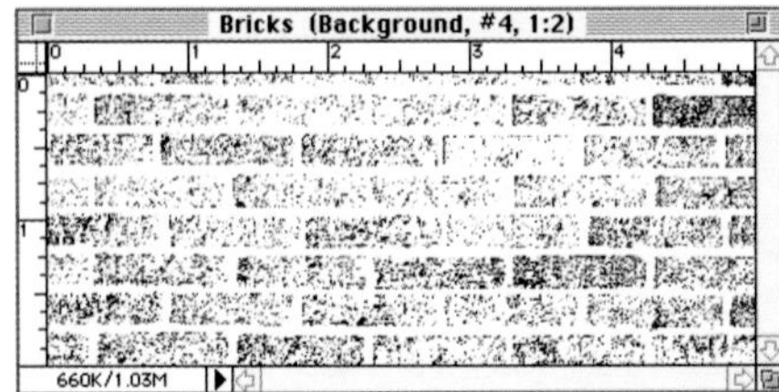

② Select the entire image (Command-A), and copy (Command-C) it to the clipboard. Create a new channel (Channel #4), then paste in the clipboard (Command-V).

Bricks (Background, #4, 1:2)

660K/1.03M

③ The light areas of this channel represent the areas of the surface that will accept the most paint. You probably will have to increase the amount of white in this channel. Choose Image ➡ Adjust ➡ Levels. Grab the right (white) Input slider and drag it to the left until the image has a good amount of white in it. Take a look at what we came up with.

④ Create another new channel (Channel #5), and use the Type tool to enter the text into this channel. We chose the EraserDust font (50 points). Deselect the text (Command-D).

TOOLBOX

GE Texturizer
GE Note Paper

⑤ Return to the composite channel (Command-0) containing your background. Make a new Layer (Layer 1). Load the text channel selection (Channel #5). Then choose Select ➡ Load Selection, and choose the bricks channel (#4). Be sure to check the **Intersect with Selection** option.

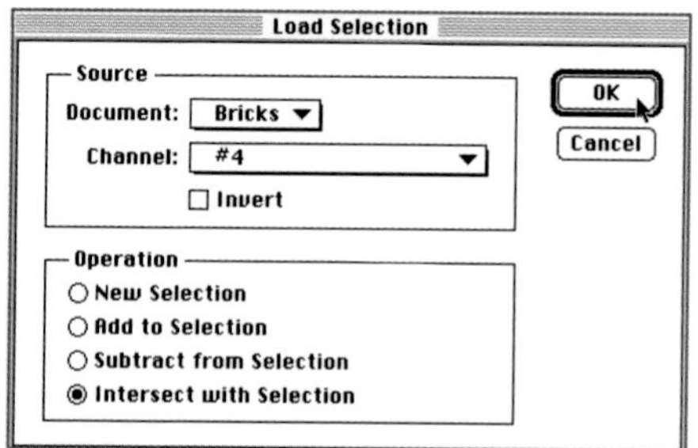

⑥ Choose Select ➡ Feather (1 pixel). Choose a foreground color for the text, and press Option-Delete to fill the text. To bring out more of the bricks lower the Opacity of the new layer to 95%. Presto! Fresh paint without the mess.

TIP If the paint is too faint, then you didn't give the texture channel enough white in Step 3. If it's too saturated then you gave it too much.

Painting the Paint

If you want to paint this painted text, then skip Steps 4 through 6. Instead, return to the composite channel (Command-0), make a new layer, and load the texture channel selection (Channel #4). Choose Select ➡ Feather (1 pixel), and press Command-H to hide the selection edges. Lower the opacity of the new layer before you begin painting to around 95%. Choose a color for the paint, and then grab the Airbrush tool (use a feathered brush with about 50% opacity). Now you can paint on the surface without completely obliterating it.

Any texture will work.

Background: © D'Pix 1995

Gallery Effects: Classic Art 2: GE Texturizer filter contains four textures that you can paint on. For this example we used the burlap texture.

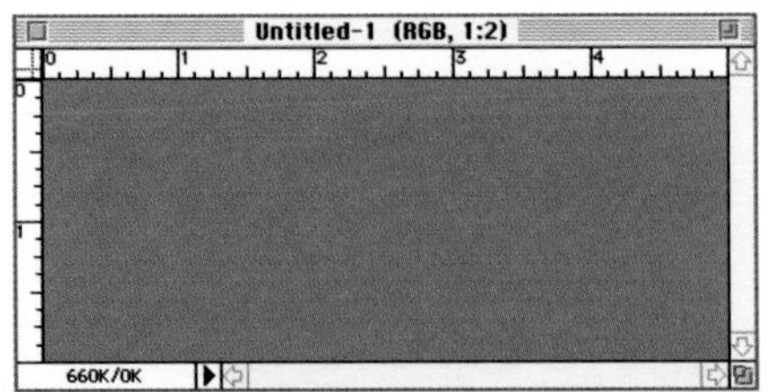

① Create a new file. Choose a foreground color for the burlap. Fill the image area with the foreground color.

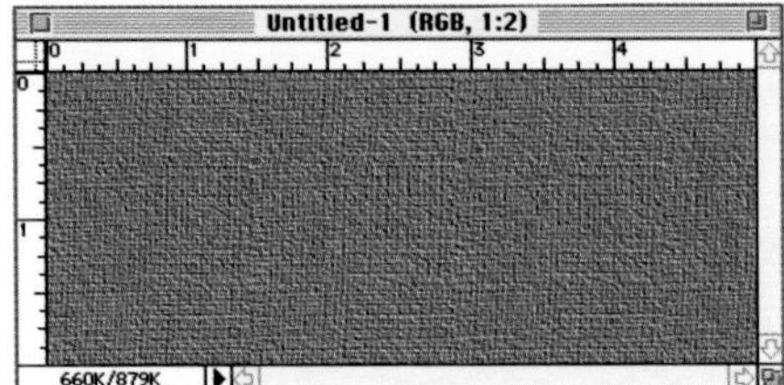

② Choose Filter ➡ Gallery Effects: Classic Art 2: GE Texturizer. Click on the Texture Controls button. Choose Burlap from the Type pop-up menu. Set the scaling to 175% and the Relief to 10.

TIP If you want to paint the text yourself using the Airbrush tool, skip Steps 3 and 4, paint the text, and the rest of us will meet you at Step 5.

③ Create a new channel (Channel #4), and use the Type tool to enter the text into this channel. For this example, we used BrushStrokeFast at 70 pts.

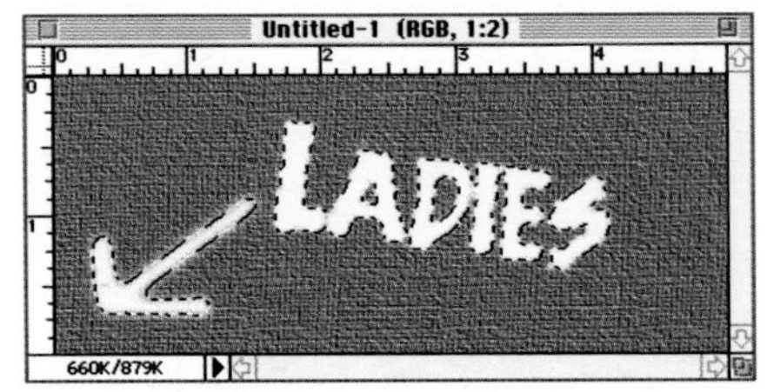

④ Return to the composite channel (Command-0) containing the burlap background. Load the text channel selection (Channel #4), and choose Select ➡ Feather (2 pixels). Choose a foreground color for the text, and press Option-Delete to fill the text.

⑤ Keep the text selection active, and reapply the Texturizer filter (Command-option-F) to get the texture to show through. To exaggerate the texture, we applied the Texturizer filter again.

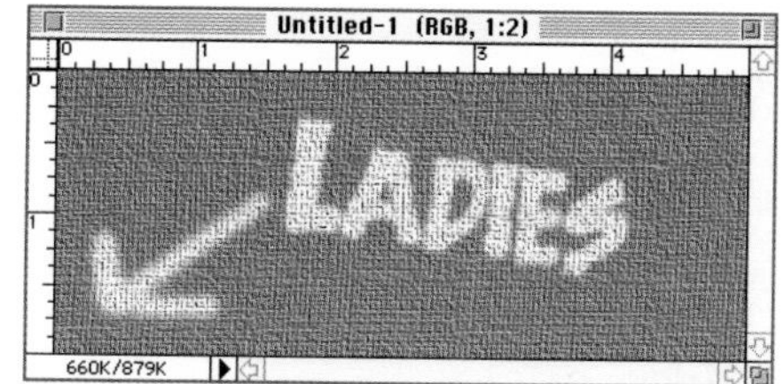

GE Note Paper For this example we created a texture using the GE Note Paper filter and used the Painting the Paint method described above.

Painting with Photographs

The same techniques we've already discussed can be used to "paint" text with a photograph. Here are three ways to do this.

① The first step is the same for all three. Open the file containing the photograph you want to paint with. This image comes from D'Pix.

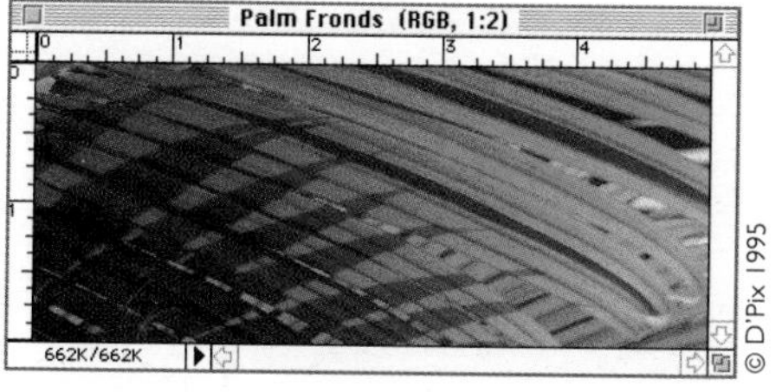

© D'Pix 1995

Use the Type tool to create the type:

② Create a new channel (Channel #4), and use the Type tool to enter the text in the new channel. Choose Filter ➡ Blur Gaussian Blur (3 pixels) so the text will have soft edges.

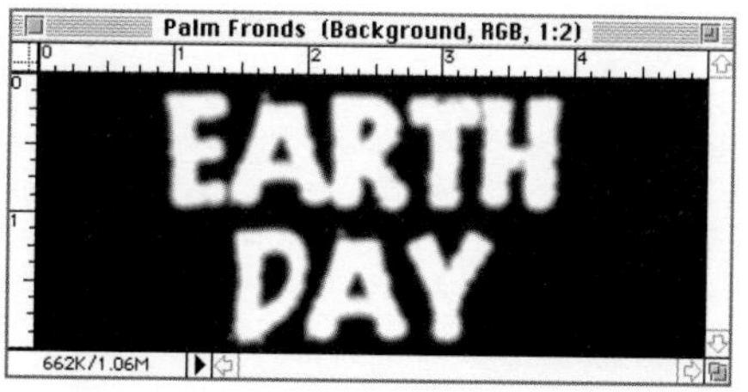

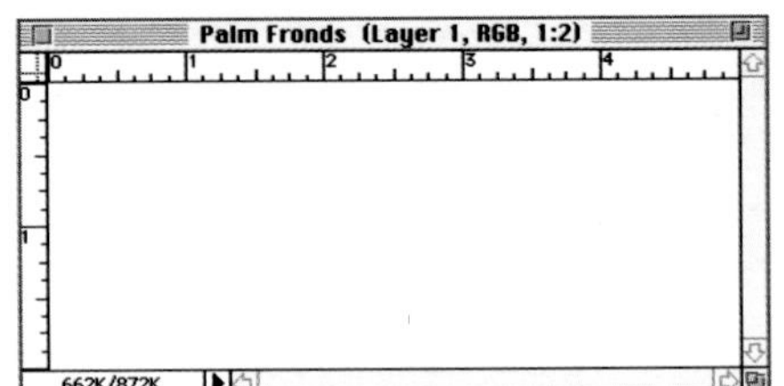

③ Return to the composite channel (Command-0), and make a new layer (Layer #1). Paste in an image for the background that you will paint over, or fill the image area with a color.

④ Load the text channel selection (Channel #4). Simply press delete to reveal the photograph.

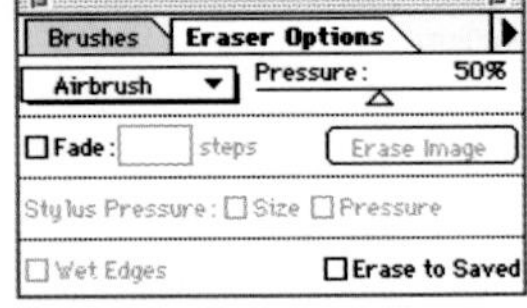

Use the Type tool to create boundaries for painting:

Do Steps 1 through 3 above. Double-click on the Eraser tool to select it and to open the Eraser tool floating palette. Choose a soft brush and use the Airbrush option from the pop-up menu. (Use the Opacity slider to vary the intensity of the paint.) Load the text channel selection (Channel #4), and hide the selection edges (Command-H). Start "painting" within the text. There is no need to be careful because while the selection is active you can only affect the area within it.

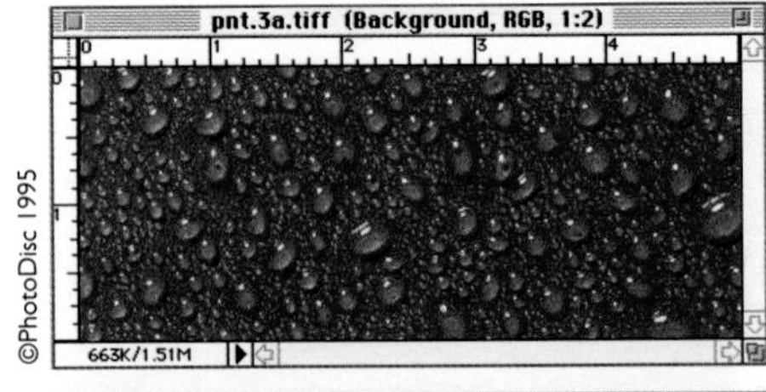

©PhotoDisc 1995

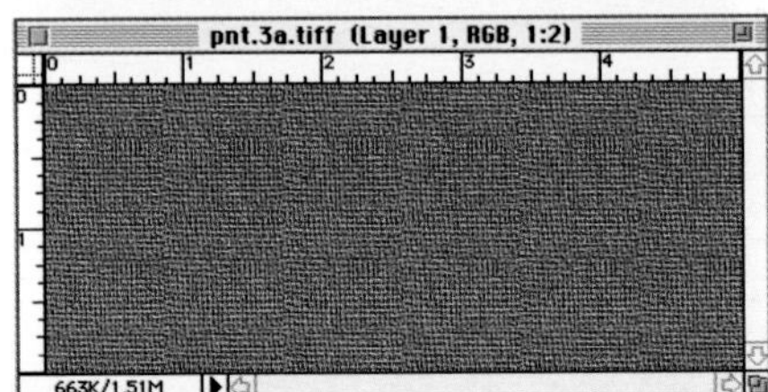

If you want to mask the type inside the brush strokes, then choose Select ➥ Inverse after loading the text selection. Now, you will only be able to paint outside the text selection.

Try filling the top layer with white.

To use the Airbrush tool to paint the type: Do Steps 1 and 3 on page 125. Double-click on the Eraser tool to select it and to open the Eraser tool floating palette. Choose the Airbrush option from the pop-up menu. We raised the Opacity to around 75%. Now, just click and paint.

©D'Pix, PhotoDisc-1995

VARIATIONS

If you want to add texture to the painted photograph, then load the texture into a new channel. Make sure there is plenty of white in this channel. Use the Levels (Command-L) dialog box if you need to add white. Return to the composite channel and the top layer (Layer #1). Load the texture channel selection. Hide the Edges of the selection (Command-H), and paint away with the Eraser tool. ■

©D'Pix 1995

Where can you find some really amazing patterns and textures? Just about everywhere! Check out the stock photocollections on the CD-ROM for some examples. There are also several commercial filters included that let you control the creation of your own textures and patterns—we've used them on the next few pages. Once you've created a pattern or texture you like, you can use it within your type, or even cut your type out of it. There's no limit to what you can do with these images and filters in Photoshop!

① Create a new file. Create a new channel. Choose the font you wish to use and enter the text, using the Type tool, of course. For this example, we used the font Badger at 92 points. with spacing of -10.

② Open the pattern you want to fill the type with. Here we've used a custom pattern, the Disco Frog Pattern, included as a preset file on the CD-ROM. Select ➡ All and use Edit ➡ Define Pattern to make the entire picture into a pattern.

③ Go back into your file, return to the composite channel and load the selection (Channel #4). Your text should be actively selected.

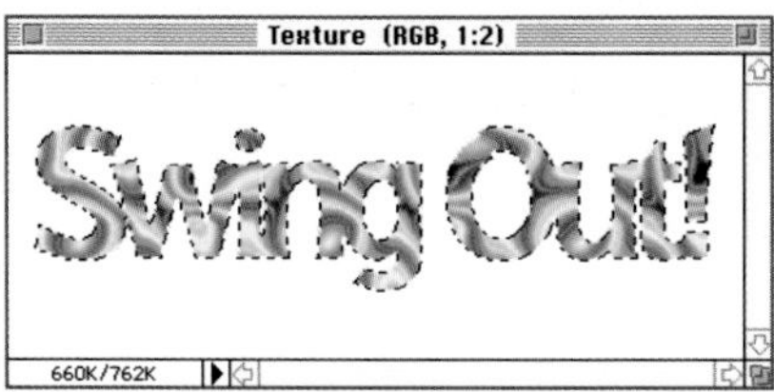

④ Choose Edit ➡ Fill and use the settings of Pattern, 100%, and Normal. This will fill the selection, your text, with the pattern that was defined in Step 3.

⑤ If you'd like a border around your text, choose a foreground color. We chose an obnoxious red for this example. Use Edit ➡ Stroke... with settings of 3 pixels, Outside, 100%, and Normal. This will put a stroke 3 pixels wide on the outside of your selection at 100% opacity.

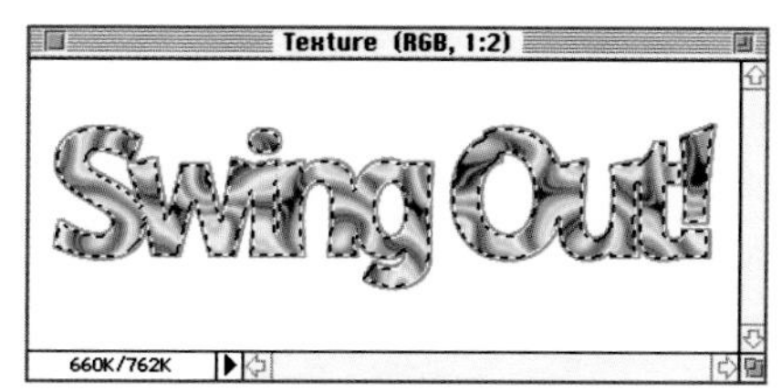

⑥ To stroke on the inside of the text, choose a different foreground color. We used yellow here. Again, choose Edit ➡ Stroke... but use settings of 2 pixels wide, Inside, 100%, and Normal. This will put a white line on the inside of your selection. Violà!

VARIATIONS

Bubbles To create a texture that looks like the Laurence Welk bubble machine just exploded, try this variation. Apply Filter ➡ Xaos Tools ➡ Paint Alchemy and use the "Bubbles Grid" saved style.

Just Plain Weird To create really unusual textures, try Virtus' Alien Skin Textureshop. With this filter you can randomly mutate various parameters to different degrees. The results are truly wild!

To further "funkify" your text, try Filter ➡ Alien Skin ➡ Inner Bevel 2.0 along with Filter-Alien Skin ➡ Glow 2.0.

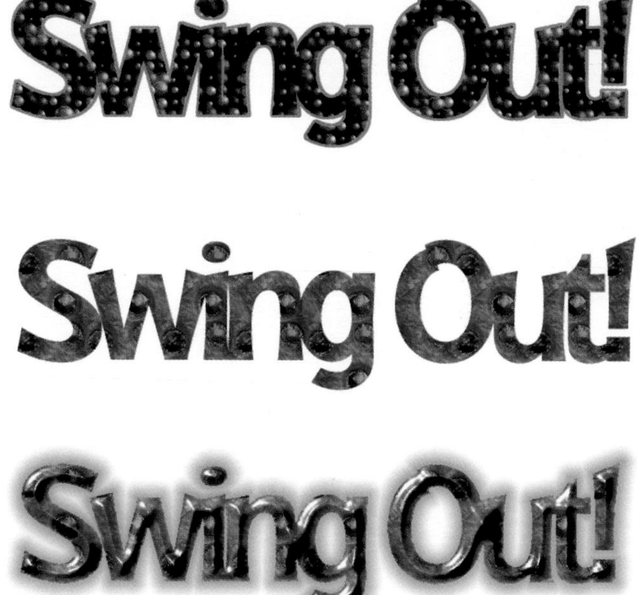

Below are some filters and programs that help you create your own textures.

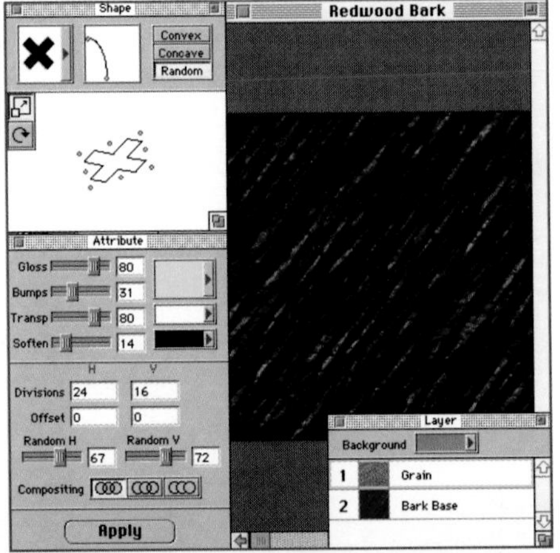

TextureScape TextureScape comes from Specular, the makers of Collage and Infini-D. This is a stand-alone application, rather than a plug-in. Its sole purpose is for creating textures and patterns... and it does it very, very well! If you can't find just the right texture on stock photo CD, take a look at TextureScape!

Here, TextureScape was used to render the bark pattern, then was imported into Photoshop for editing.

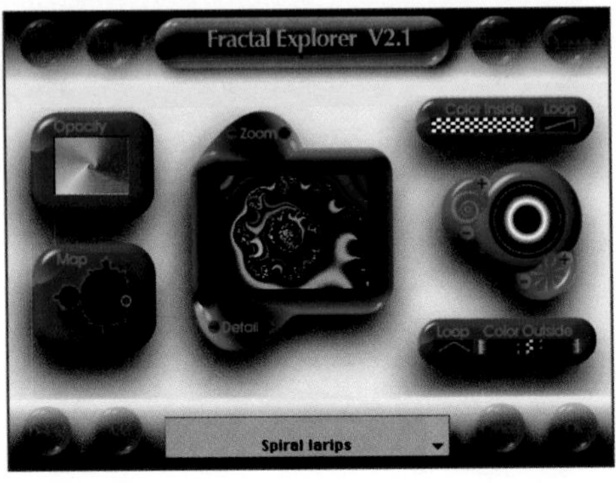

Kai's Power Tools HSC Software offers several KPT filters for creating textures. First, you could use the Fractal Explorer for some pretty wild effects.

Don't forget the almighty Gradient Designer!

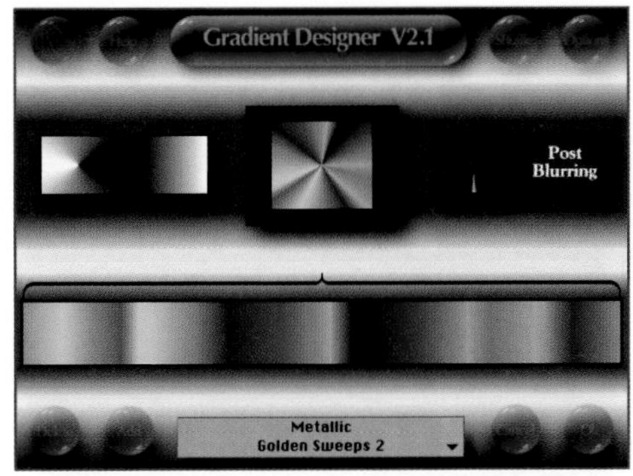

Last, but definitely not least, is Texture Explorer. This is one of the most useful tools for developing textures!

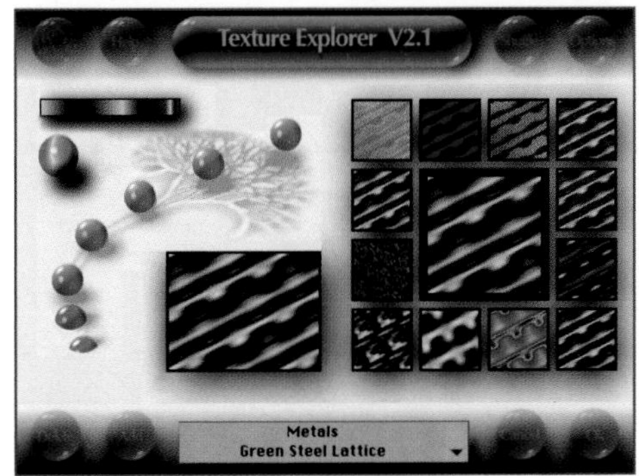

Terrazzo This commercial filter from Xaos Tools was specifically designed to make patterns. The super simple interface makes creating patterns a snap—you can even preview the patterns as you move your cursor around the image!

We started out with this stock photo from Digital Stock.

©Digital Stock 1995

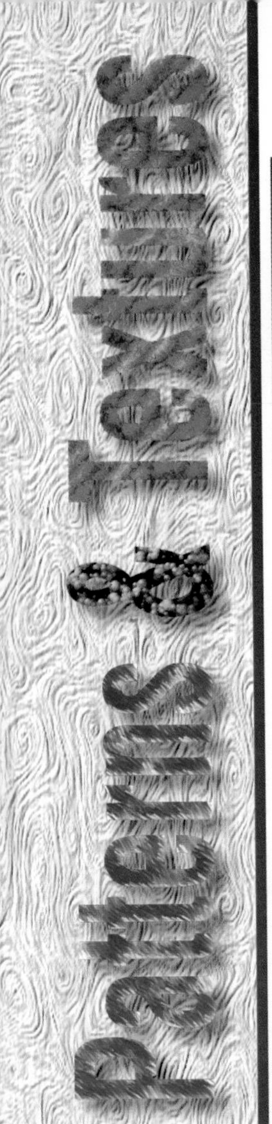

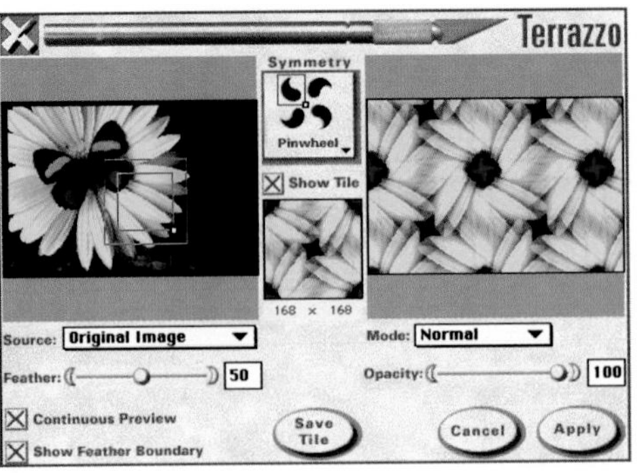

Dragging the tile around the image instantly updates the pattern preview.

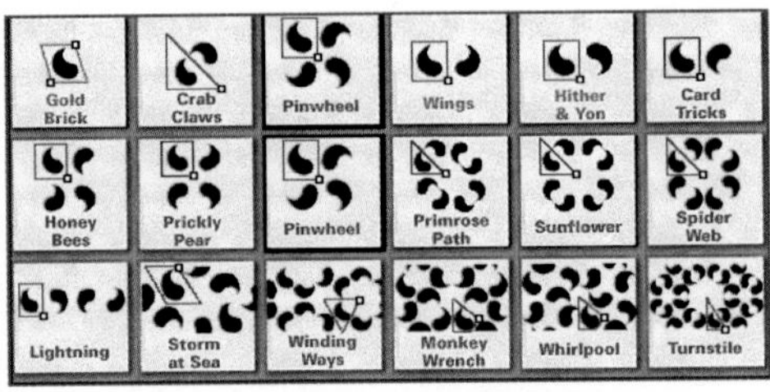

By changing the symmetry, you can create all kinds of patterns.

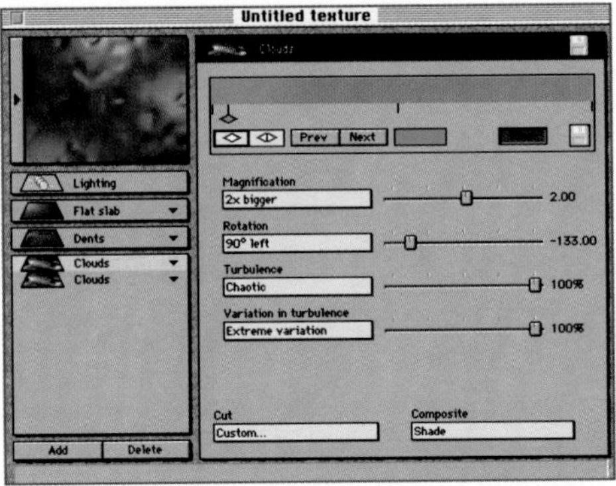

Adobe TextureMaker From the architects of Photoshop comes Adobe TextureMaker. This is another stand-alone program designed for creating custom textures. Being able to control several lighting effects is fantastic!

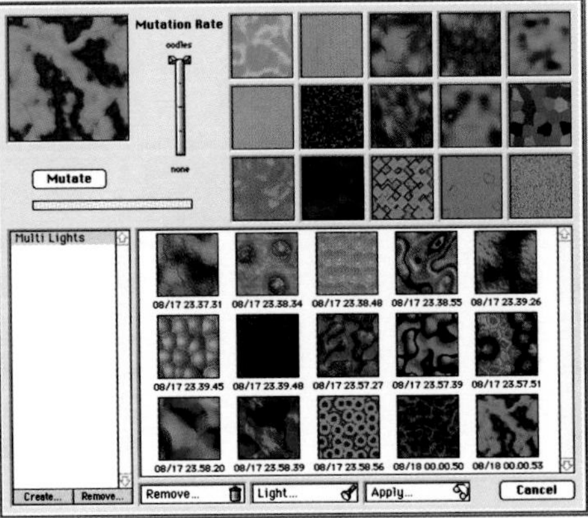

Virtus Alien Skin Textureshop This program has two flavors: a stand-alone application as well as a Photoshop plug-in. By working with the sliders under the Light... and Apply... drawer, you can create some really exciting textures.

MicroFrontier's Pattern Workshop If you like instant gratification, this is the filter for you! Quick and dirty, Pattern Workshop will let you choose from a series of pre-made textures in its library. This is a great plug-in if you need a texture in a hurry.

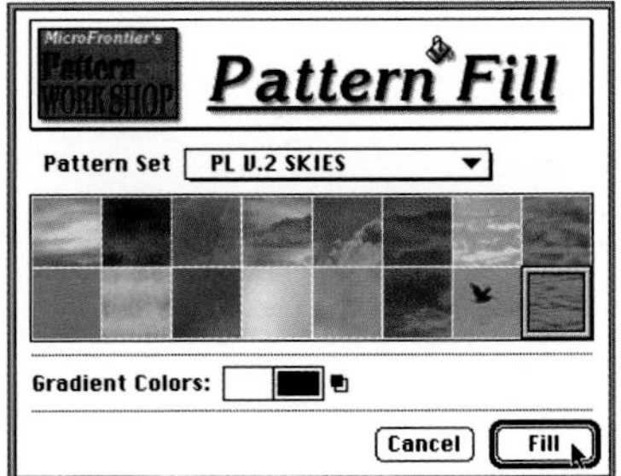

It also comes with a companion filter that lets you edit the patterns. ■

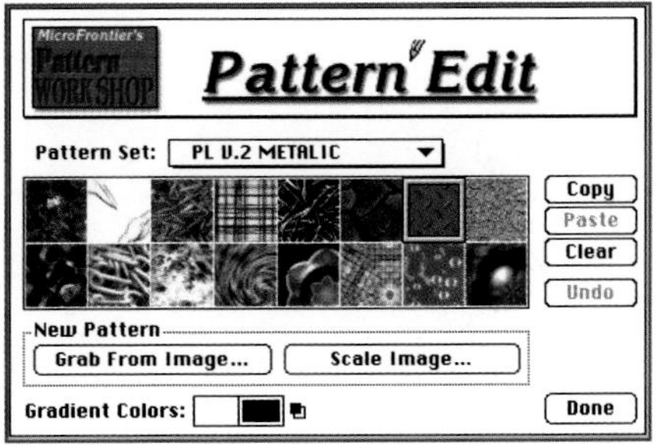

Peel-Away

The KPT Page Curl 2.1 filter makes great curls, but it also has some limitations. The success of this technique is based almost entirely on making the right selections. So, we'll spend some time talking about Selection tools. If you follow these tips you can get this filter to do great work for you.

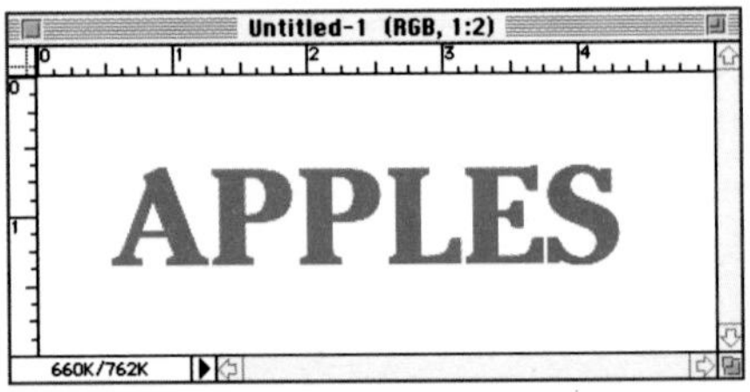

Untitled-1 (RGB, 1:2)

APPLES

660K/762K

① Create a new file, and use the Type tool to enter the text. We used Cheltenham Bold at 70 points for this example. Save the text selection to create Channel #4. We may not need the selection, but it's better to have it on hand just in case.

② The KPT Page Curl filter uses the foreground color as the color it places underneath the peel-away type. So, change the foreground color to a color for the surface. (Note: The color will fill in the entire area within the selection and to the right of the curl.)

Untitled-1 (RGB, 1:1)

APPL

660K/762K

Untitled-1 (RGB, 1:1)

APPL

660K/762K

The easy way To use this filter you must first make a selection. In most cases, you will want to make simple rectangular selections. Inside a rectangular selection, the KPT Page Curl filter will peel the type away from the bottom right. The angle of the top of the flap will follow an imaginary line from the top right corner to the bottom left corner fo the selection rectangle. This selection (made with the rectangular Selection tool) yielded this result (Filter ➡ Distort ➡ KPT Page Curl 2.1).

This is not what we wanted since it looks like the background is peeling up, too. We want the top right corner to be on the right edge of the text, so make a selection like this…

…to get this.

Then you can just grab the Paintbrush tool and paint over the leftover pieces of text.

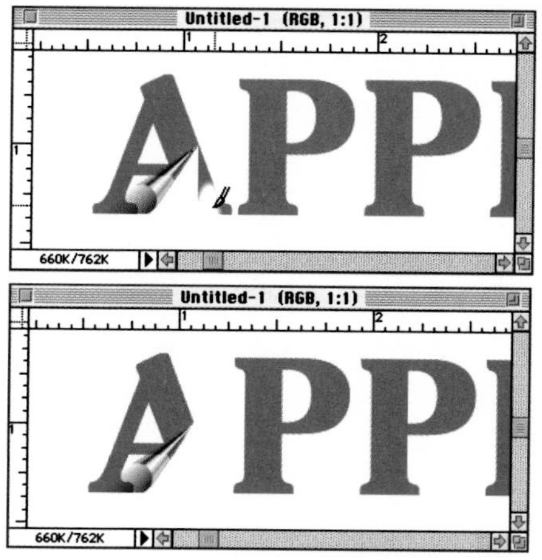

This figure shows the selection we made for the "P".

You could render the entire text with the method above (which is what we did to create this figure), but if you want more control, check out what we did next.

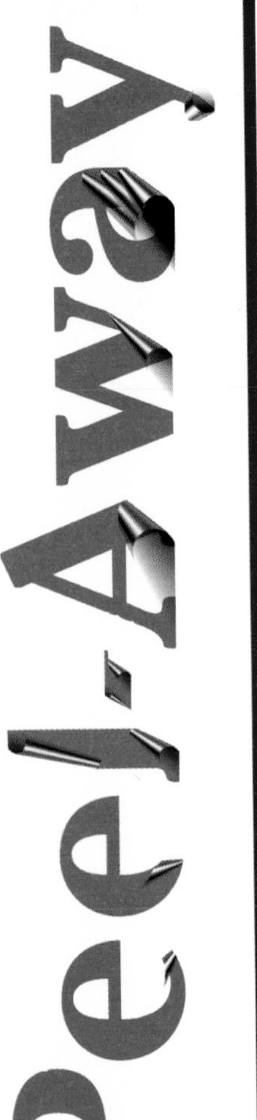

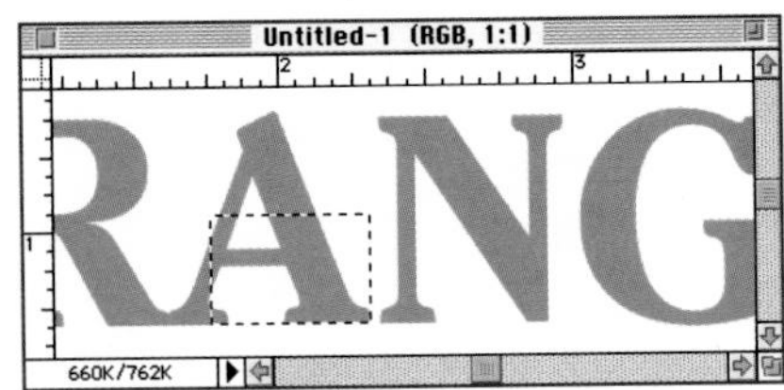

More Control To get more control you're going to have to make some irregular selections. Use the rectangular Selection tool to make this selection.

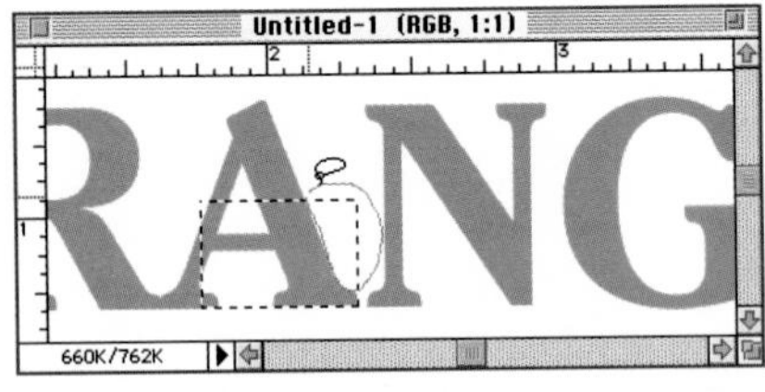

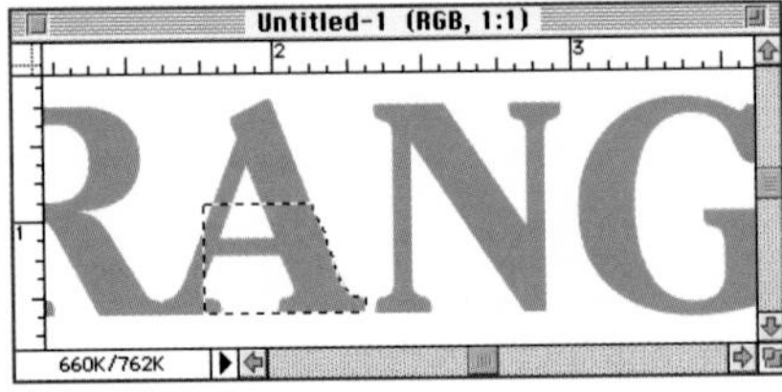

If you have an active selection and hold down the Command key while making a second selection, the new selection area will be subtracted from the active one. Select the Lasso tool. Start outside the active selection and cut into it along the contour of the text, like this.

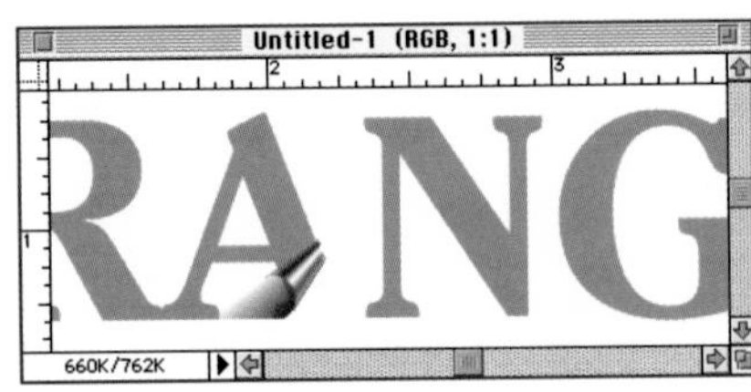

Now, apply Filter ➥ Distort ➥ KPT Page Curl 2.1 to get this.

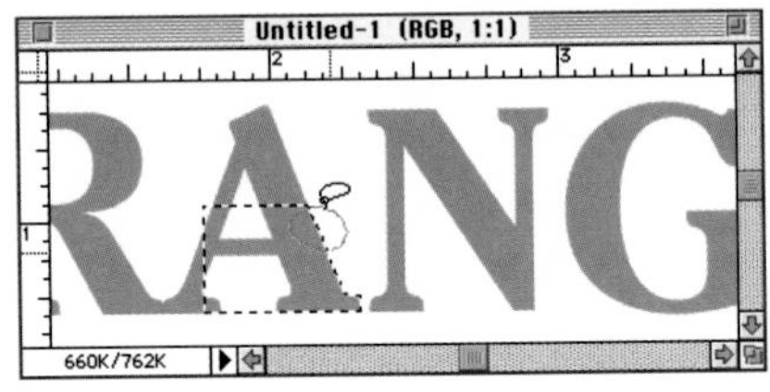

The only problem is the funny edge on the top of the curl. Press Command-Z to undo the curl. Again hold down the Command key, and draw a ring to clip off the corner of the selection, like this.

Apply Filter ➥ Distort ➥ KPT Page Curl 2.1 again to get this.

If you took too much of the selection away and came up with this…

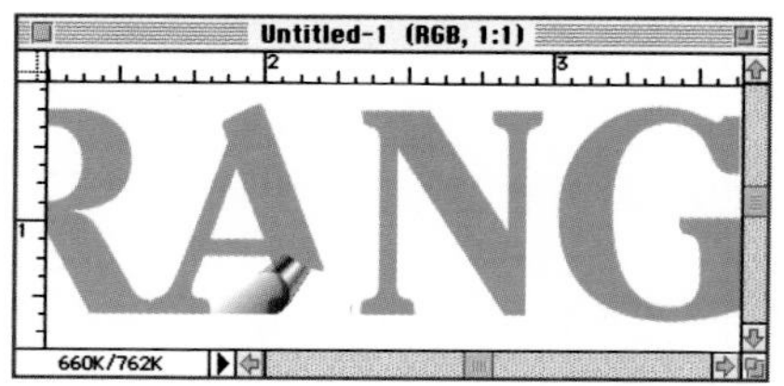

…then you can hold down the Shift key instead of the Command key to add a new selection to the active selection to get this.

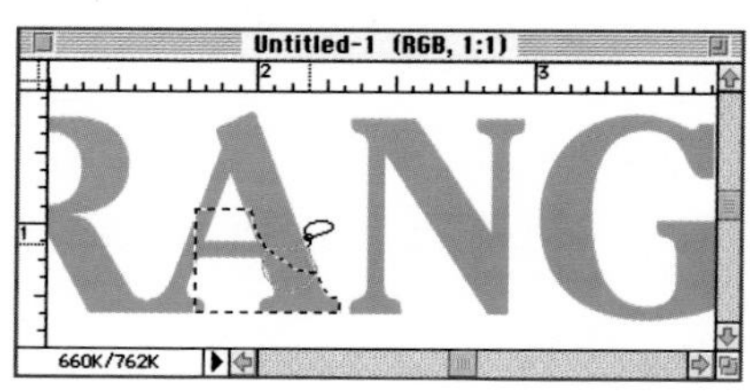

Then apply Filter ➥ Distort ➥ KPT Page Curl 2.1 to get this.

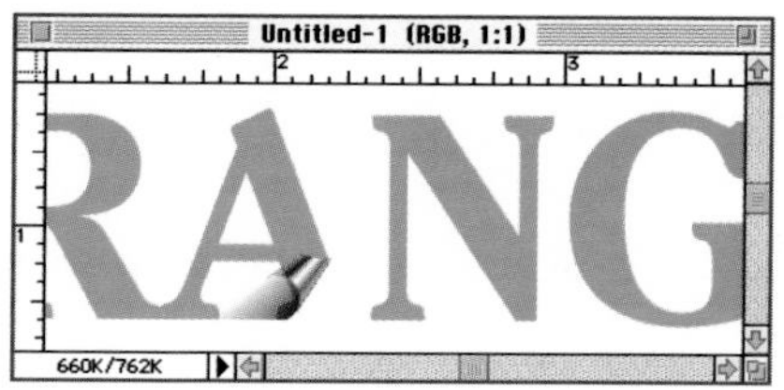

TIP If you want the tops of all the peels to come up to the same point, turn on the Rulers (Command-R) and watch the indicators while you make your selections.

So, build the type one curl at a time. First, make the selection, then apply Filter ➥ Distort ➥ KPT Page Curl 2.1. It's really very simple once you get used to what the KPT Page Curl filter is going to do with your selection. You don't have to be satisfied with one peel per letter, either. Here is our final type.

ORANGES

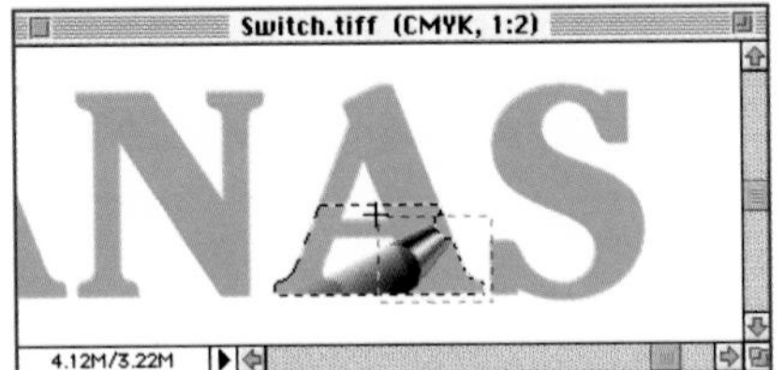

VARIATIONS

Darken the Peel If you want to darken the curl and make it more opaque, then reapply the filter while the selection is still active. Here is the filter applied once, and applied three times to the same selection.

Torn Peels You can use the selection technique described in More Control above to make the text look like it's been torn. When you use the Lasso tool, cut further down into the text.

More Peels First, make the foreground color the same as the type color. Then after applying the Page Curl filter, keep the selection active, and select the rectangular Selection tool. Hold down the Command and Shift keys while drawing a box starting from the lower right and moving to the upper left. But stop before you draw the box over the entire original selection.

Use the Lasso tool as described in More Control to subtract any parts of the selection, and apply Filter ➡ Distort ➡ KPT Page Curl 2.1. Before making the last peel, change the foreground color to the color of the background.

Switch Directions If you want the text to peel up from another direction, the only solution is to rotate (Image ➡ Rotate) or flip (Image ➡ Flip) the image. All the techniques above will still work the same way. When you're finished, just rotate or flip the text back.

Color Underneath If you want the Page Curl filter to insert a color under the areas of the letters that were lifted, then first change the foreground color to that color. Next, load the type selection (Channel #4) you saved in Step 1. Then hold down the Command and Shift keys and draw a selection with the Lasso tool around one of the letters. Now only that letter will be selected. Then use the selection tools as described in More Control to make the proper selection for the letter. You will probably need to subtract from the selection the top half of the letter. In the case of a letter like an "A" you will need to add to the selection the space between the legs of the "A" so the filter has some space to put the curl. ■

Photoshop's Image ➥ Effects features can be used by themselves to quickly add dimension to your type, or they can be a useful aid in layering type onto preexisting surfaces.

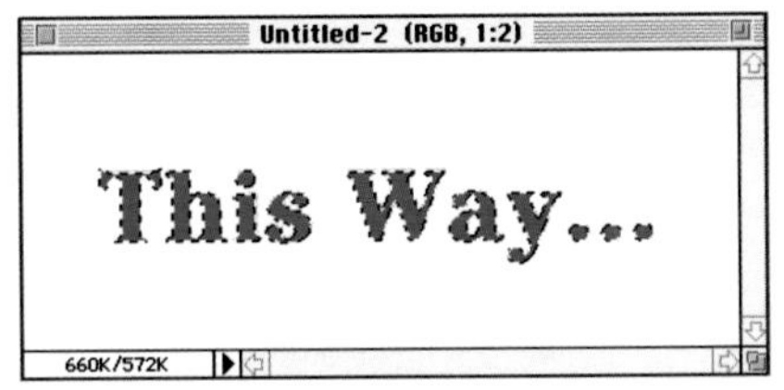

① Here's the way the Perspective feature works. Create a new file, and use the Type tool to enter the text. We began with Cheltenham Bold at 50 points.

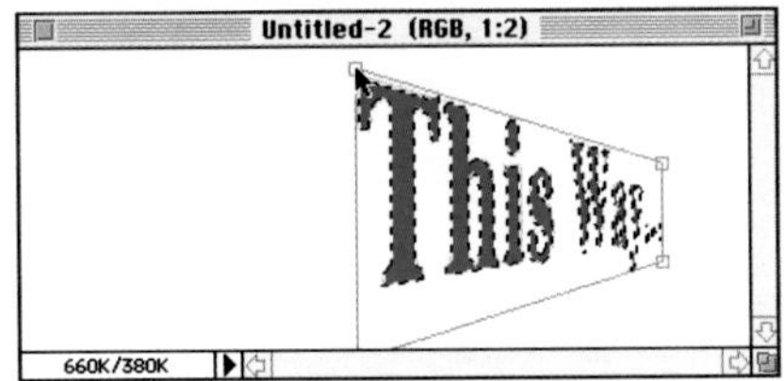

② While the text selection is still active, choose Image ➥ Effects ➥ Perspective. A box will appear around the type. You can use the square tabs on the corners of the box to reshape the box. When you move one of the tabs, another tab (the one that's along the same line as the direction of your movement) moves at the same rate and along the same line, but in the opposite direction. It sounds a little confusing, but as soon as you try it you'll understand. The result is that the text is either compressed or expanded at one end, creating the illusion that it's receding in space.

③ When the mouse pointer is moved over the text, it turns into a gavel. Click the gavel anywhere within the perspective box to set the text as you see it. Click outside the box to cancel the changes. This is what you'll end up with.

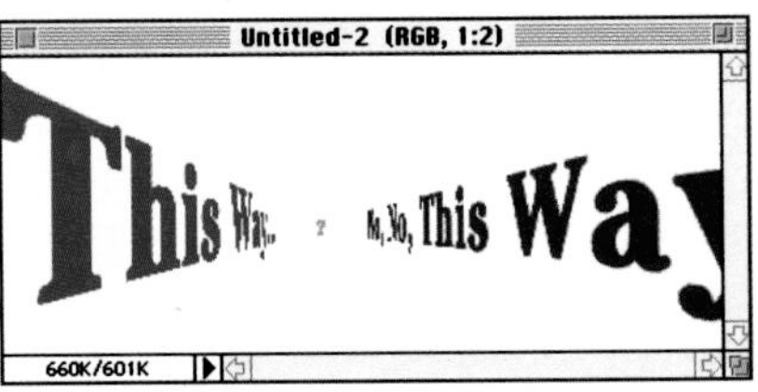

④ You can have the perspective move in any direction you want.

Placing text on a receding surface

① For this example, we opened a stock photo of a mailbox from CMCD. Using the perspective feature helped us put Santa's name on the box.

©CMCD 1995

② Create a new layer (#4) for the type, and use the Type tool to enter the text (15-point Cheltenham Bold). Remember, font size is important to make this look authentic. Also, we used the Eyedropper tool to select a color for the type from the mailbox flag.

③ The quickest way to lay type on a flat, receding surface like this mailbox is not to use the Perspective feature, but rather the Skew feature. Position the type so the first letter is in place, like you see in the previous figure, then choose Image ➥ Effects ➥ Skew. A box will appear identical to the box used in the Perspective feature.

④ Now, if you move one of the corner tabs, the tab you move toward moves away in the *same* direction creating a parallelogram. However, once you release the tab for the first time, the tabs will act independently of all the others. So, first we grabbed the tab on the upper right and moved it upward until the top line of the Skew box was in line with the lines near it on the mailbox.

⑤ Then we moved the lower right tab upward to compress the text and make it appear as if it was receding. Click the gavel within the skew box when you're done.

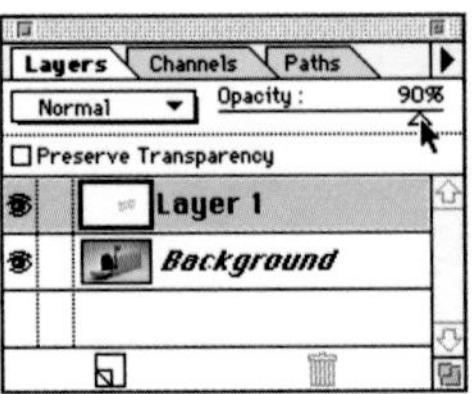

⑥ The next two steps will help blend the text into the side of the mailbox. First, find the Opacity slider on the Layers palette and lower the Opacity if Layer 1 (the Santa Claus layer) to 90% to allow some of the mailbox to blend with the colored type.

⑦ Next, create a layer mask for Layer 1. In the layer mask, choose Filter ➡ Noise ➡ Add noise (Uniform). Before pressing return you can watch the type in the image window change as you adjust the noise Amount, which we set at 80. Click OK, flatten the image, and you're done.

VARIATIONS

The perspective feature was used to create this type, before adding the drop shadow. See page 168 to find out how to create the shadow. ■

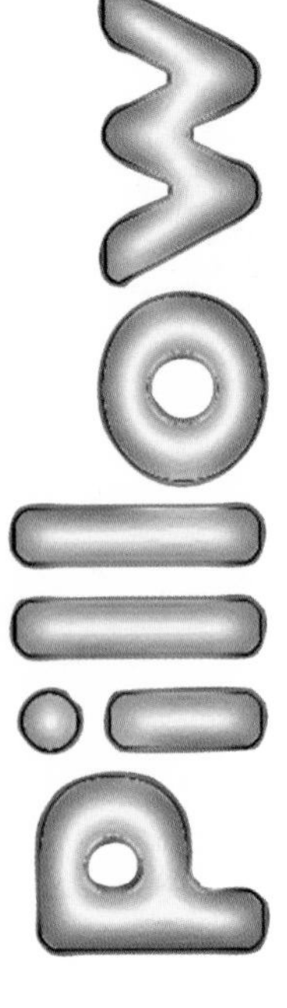

Here is a soft 3D look with a crimp around the edges.

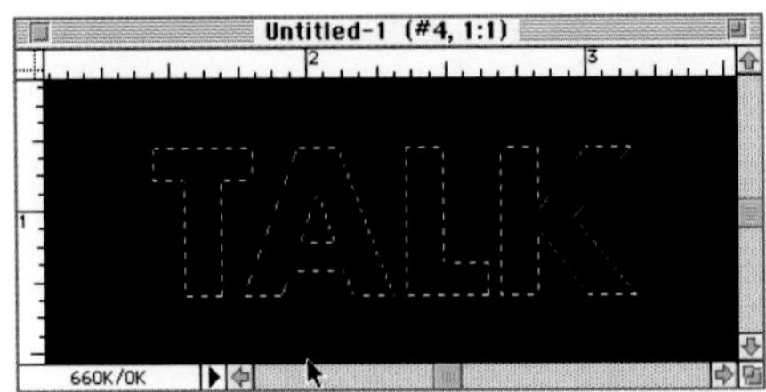

① Open a new file, and create a new channel. Change the foreground color to black and the background color to white (press D). Use the Type tool to enter the text in the new channel. In this example, we used BFutura Bold at 50 points.

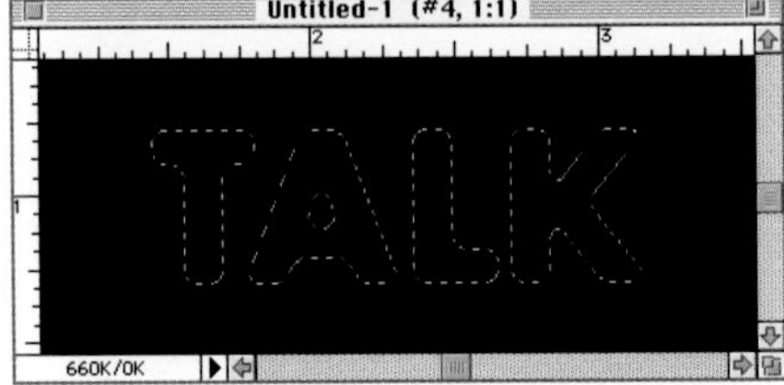

② We began with a typeface that had hard edges, so we chose Select ➥ Modify ➥ Smooth (5 pixels) to round the edges. If you choose a nice rounded typeface to begin with, then you can skip this step.

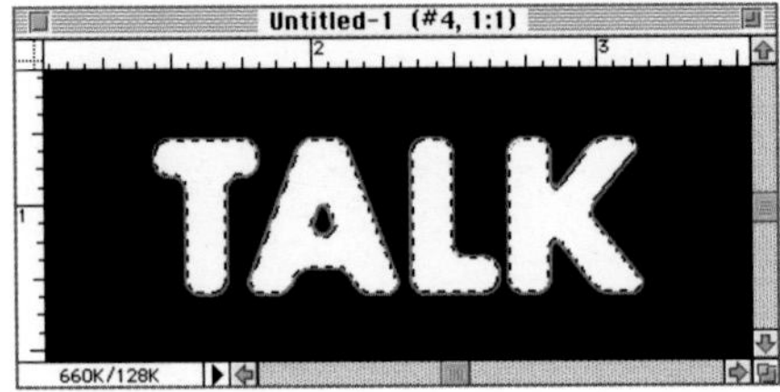

③ Press X to switch the foreground and background colors. Choose Edit ➥ Stroke (2 pixels, Outside, 50% Opacity, Normal). Press Option-Delete to fill the selection with white.

④ Choose Filter ➡ Blur ➡ Gaussian Blur. The amount will depend on the thickness of your text. We chose 8 pixels. Then choose Image ➡ Adjust ➡ Brightness/ Contrast (Command-B) and raise the contrast until you see some black move in around the edges. We raised the contrast to +25.

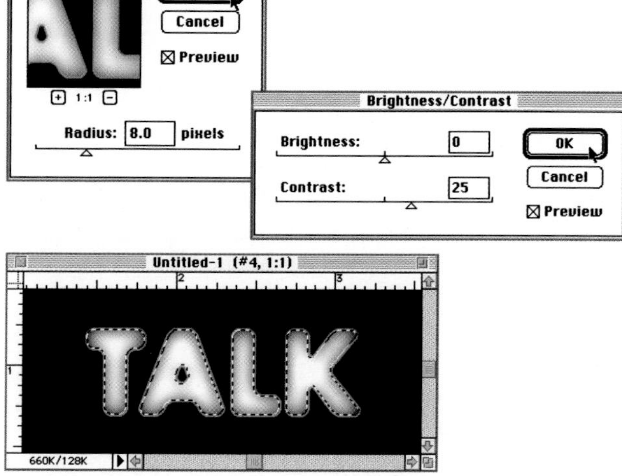

⑤ Choose Image ➡ Adjust ➡ Levels, and slide the Output Levels right (white) slider to the left until the box above it reads about 200.

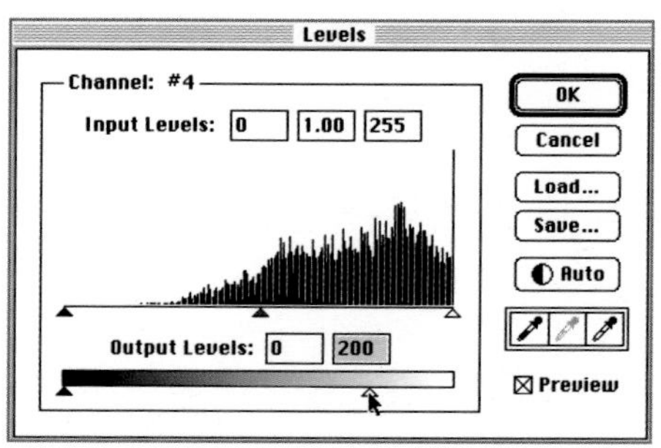

⑥ Now, to fluff the pillow. Choose Filter ➡ Stylize ➡ Find Edges. If the text is too contrasty after applying the Find Edges filter, then you probably raised the contrast too high in step 4. You can use the Levels dialog box (Image ➡ Adjust ➡ Levels) to adjust the values in the text.

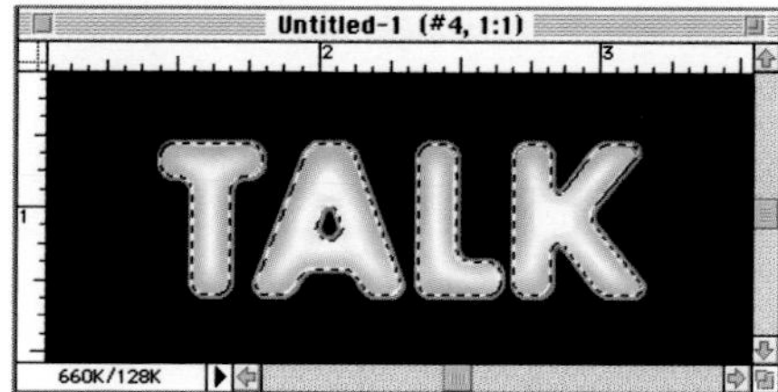

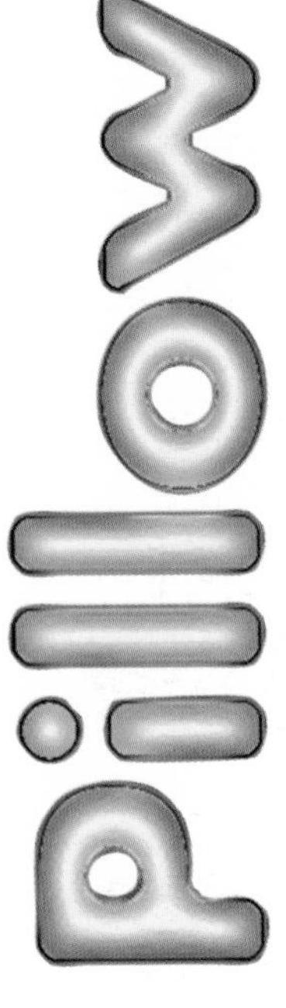

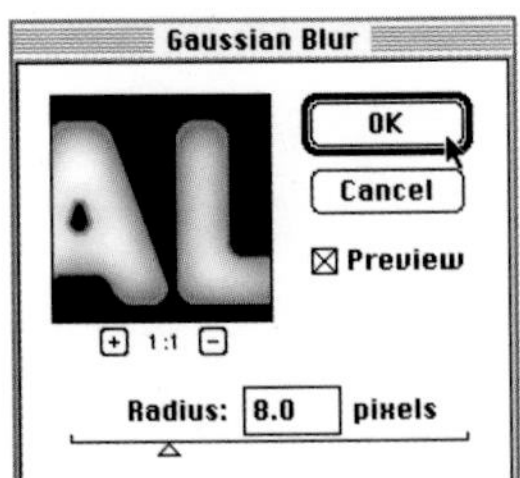

⑦ Return to the RGB channel (Command-0). We filled the background with black to get the shiny text to stand out. Load the selection you created in Step 1 (#4 if you are working in an RGB file).

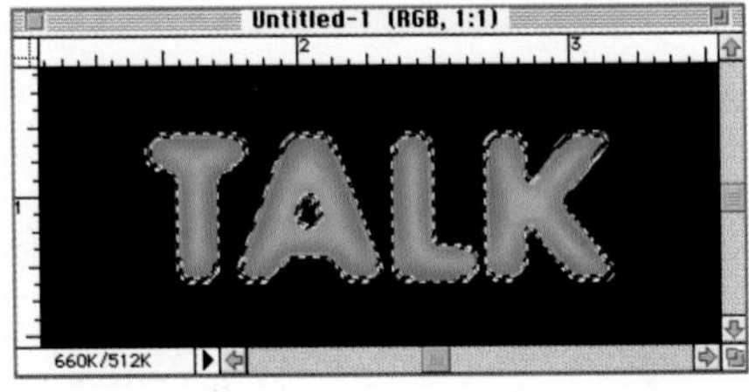

⑧ Change the foreground color to a color for the text. Press Option-Delete to fill the text.

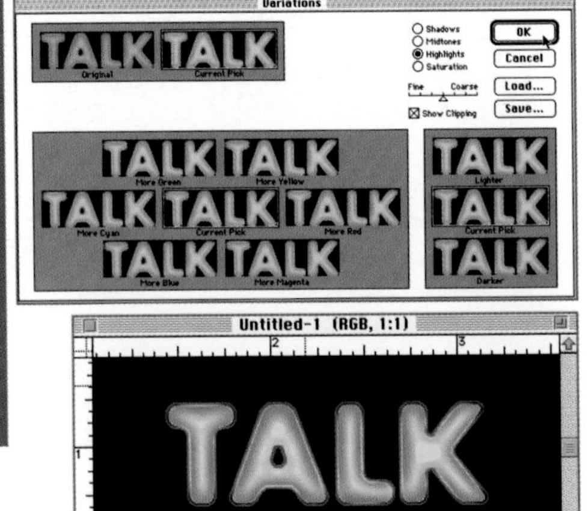

⑨ You may think the text looks a little dull. Choose Image ➥ Adjust ➥ Variations and use the previews to monitor your alterations. Then choose Image ➥ Adjust ➥ Brightness/Contrast and bump the contrast up again to +40. You could also fill the text twice by pressing Option-Delete a second time in Step 8.

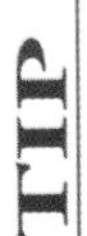

Don't forget that hiding the active selection will give you a better unobstructed view of what your text really looks like. Press Command-H to deselect the text, and press it a second time to reselect.

VARIATIONS

To add a slight glow and softness to the text, after Step 9, with the selection still active, choose Edit ➥ Stroke (2 pixels, outside, 50% opacity, normal).

To add some texture to the text, choose Filter ➥ Stylize ➥ Wind (Wind, Left). Then apply the same filter (Command-Option-F), but change the settings to Wind and Right.

For this variation, we loaded the selection into a new transparent layer and pasted a colorful image into the selection. Then we chose Color from the composite control pop-up menu. ■

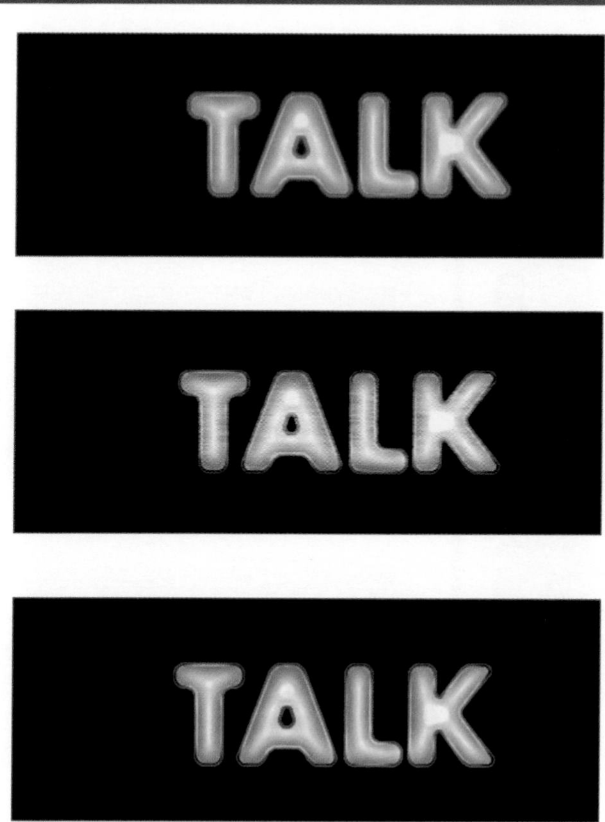

This task takes advantage of Photoshop's Lighting Effects filter. Included on the CD is a lighting styles file that contains the presets for this effect. If you want to use this preset file, consult Appendix A, *What's on the CD-ROM*, to find out where to put it on your hard drive.

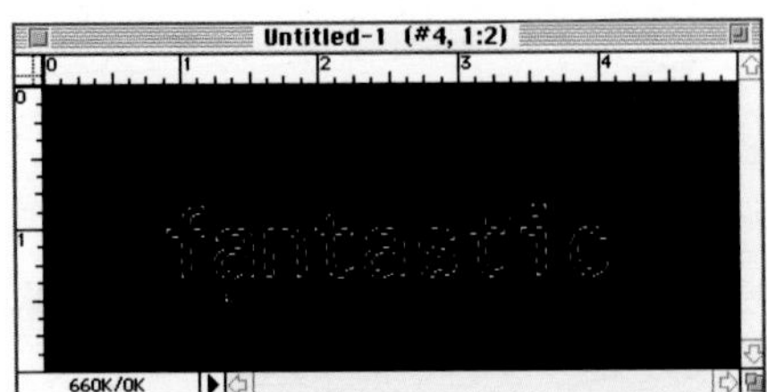

① Open a new RGB file. (It must be an RGB file in order for the Lighting Effects filter to work.) Create a new channel. Press D to change the foreground color to black and the background color to white. Use the Type tool to enter your text. In this example, we used OCRB at 50 points.

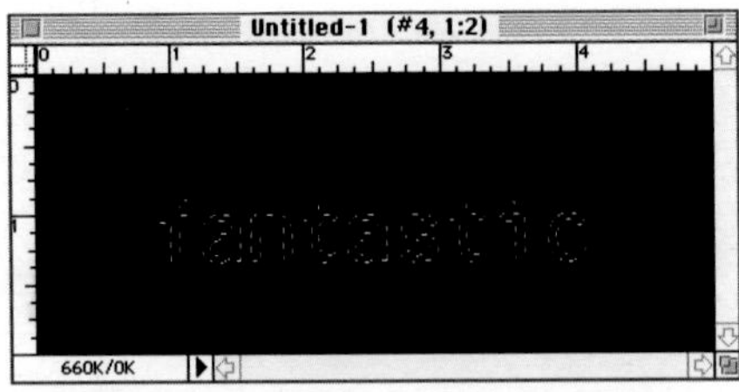

② If you want to give your text some smoother corners choose Select ➥ Modify ➥ Smooth (3 pixels). Save this selection.

③ Fill the text with white by pressing Delete. Deselect the text (Command-D). Choose Filter ➥ Blur ➥ Gaussian Blur (3.5 pixels).

TOOLBOX

PlasticLightStyles file

④ Load the selection of the same channel you are working in. Choose Filter ➡ Blur ➡ Gaussian Blur. Blur the text until you get something resembling what you see in this figure. You should be able to see highlights and dark areas. Deselect the text (Command-D).

⑤ Return to the RGB window (Command-0). Select a foreground color near the complement of the color you wish the text to be. We used a blue for the red-orange text we wanted to make. Fill the image with this color (press Option-Delete).

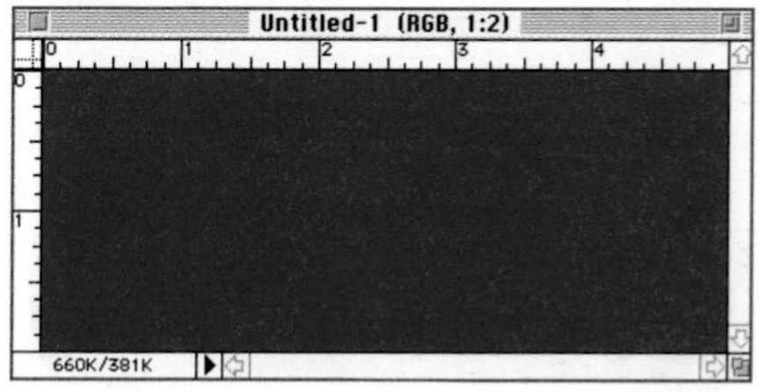

⑥ Choose Filter ➡ Render ➡ Lighting Effects, and choose PlasticLightStyles from the pop-up menu or match the settings seen in this figure. The circular ring surrounding the light source should encompass your text. Click and hold on one of its handles and drag to resize it.

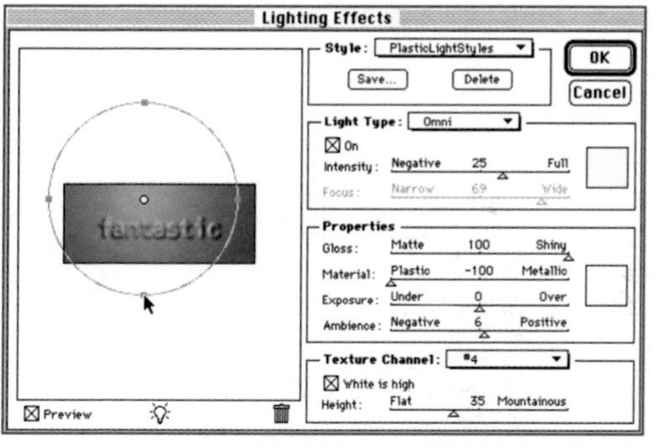

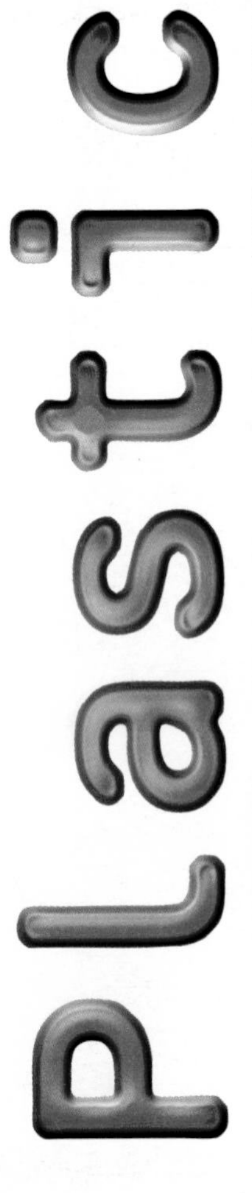

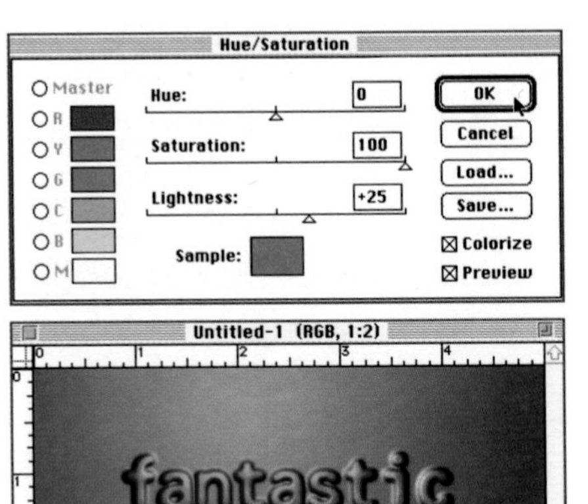

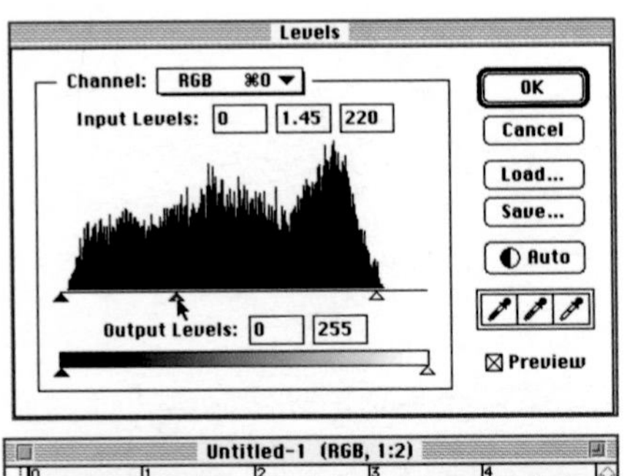

⑦ Load the same selection you did in Step 4. Choose Image ➥ Adjust ➥ Hue/Saturation (Command-U), click the Colorize checkbox, and use the Hue slider to choose the color of your text. We also slid the Lightness slider up to 40. Depending on your color choices you also might want to lower the Saturation.

⑧ You may also want to open the Levels dialog box now (Command-L) and adjust the Input Levels to fine tune the plastic. Moving the right (white) and middle (gray) sliders to the left will help brighten the image.

TIP

To create a clipping path for the text, load the selection saved in Step 2 (#5 if you are working in an RGB image). Choose Select ➥ Modify ➥ Expand. The amount will depend upon the typeface you are using. In this example, we used 6 pixels. You now have a selection you can turn into a path (see Part 2, *Photoshop Basics*, for more info).

VARIATIONS

To bring out more ridges in the plastic (like you see in the "Plastic" vertical tab), before deselecting the text in Step 4, choose Image ➥ Adjust ➥ Brightness/Contrast, and try these settings: Brightness -33, Contrast +13. You are trying to bring out some light and dark areas within the text selection. Continue with the rest of the steps above. We also increased the saturation as a final step.

flamingos

For a quick embossed plastic, you can skip Step 4 and stop after Step 6. For this example, we opened a stock photo from Digital Stock and also skipped everything in Step 5, except returning to the composite channel.

©Digital Stock 1995

The Chrome section contains a variation that uses the steps above to create a chrome look like this. See page 44 for details on creating Chrome type. ■

This type effect is great for making your type look like it pops out of the background. It's a really quick and dirty technique!

① Create a new file or open up an existing image. We used a stock photo from Photo 24 (cropped, obviously) from the CD.

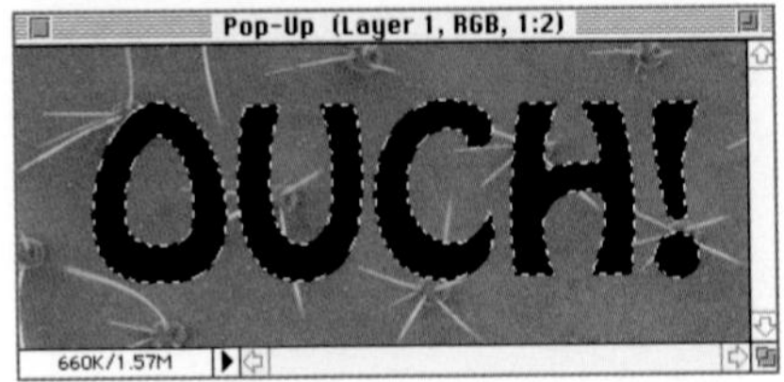

② Create a new layer in the Layers palette. Use the Type tool to enter the text. Be sure that you're in the top layer, *not* the background layer. Also, don't drop the selection just yet. We used the font Hobo at 100 points for this example.

③ Drag the Opacity slider to 1% in the Layers palette. This will make the type transparent. Save the selection.

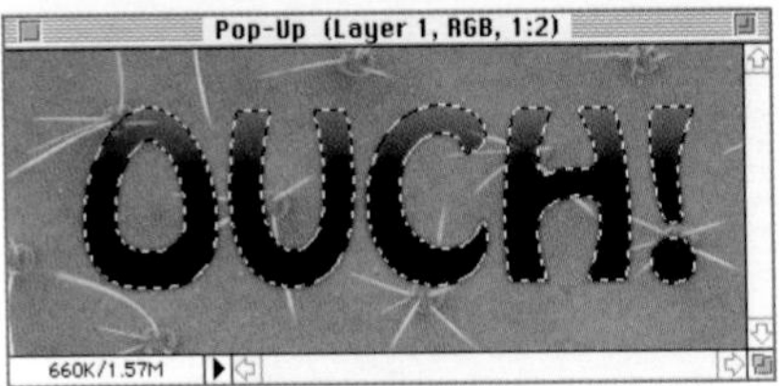

④ Select ➥ Feather and use a setting of 3 pixels. Change to the Gradient tool and set the options to Transparent to Foreground, Linear, and 100% opacity. Drag the gradient tool, top to bottom, about 1/3 the way down the selection. You should get something like this.

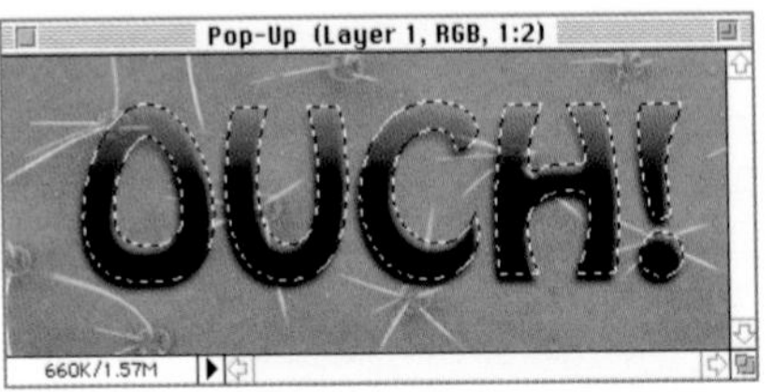

⑤ Now load the saved selection. Change to the Move tool. Hold down the Option and Command keys and move the selection up and to the right until there's a thin line of black on the bottom and left sides of the selection. (Holding down Option and Command allows only the selection to move—not what's in the selection.)

⑥ Press Delete to remove what's in the selection and Select ➥ None. If you need to reposition the shadow, simply use the Move tool. The underlying background is not affected.

To make the text look like it's popping up even more, try this:

After Step 4, use the Images ➥ Effects ➥ Skew command and skew the shadow's bottom to the left. Continue with Step 5. ■

Reflected

©Digital Stock 1995

① Open the file containing the image onto which you want to reflect your type. We chose this calm mountain lake, courtesy of Digital Stock and Mother Nature.

② Create a new layer (#4) for the type, and use the Type tool to enter the text. Move the type into position.

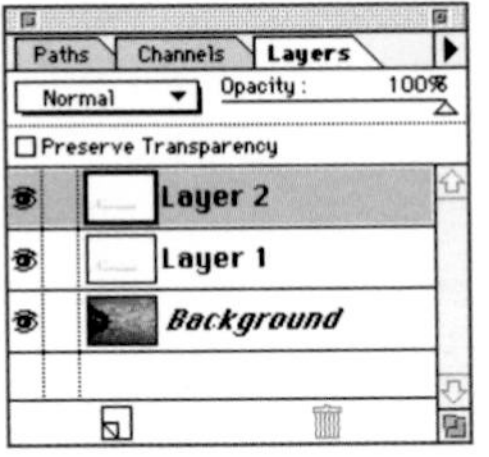

③ While the selection is still active, press Command-J to defloat the type and set it onto the new layer (#4). Then press Command-J again to raise a copy of type into a floating selection. Hold the Option key and click on the new layer icon in the Layers palette. This creates a new layer and automatically puts the floating selection into the new layer.

④ Choose Select ➡ All (Command-A). Choose Image ➡ Flip ➡ Vertical, then drag the flipped type down (while holding the Shift key to make sure it moves straight down) until the bottoms of the letters touch each other.

⑤ Choose Image ➥ Effects ➥ Scale and pull the bottom of the scale box up to squeeze the text vertically. Click the gavel in the center to set the scaling. Save this selection (Channel #4), then deselect the type (Command-D).

⑥ From the Layers composite control pop-up menu, slide the Opacity down to around 45%. This number will vary depending how dark your text is and how dark the surface is. It's that simple to make the reflection. The rest of the steps are for fine tuning.

TIP You may find that switching to either Soft Light mode or Overlay mode works better for your text. If you do switch to one of these modes, keep the Opacity higher.

⑦ Choose **Add Layer Mask** from the Layers palette arrow menu. The Layers palette should now look like this.

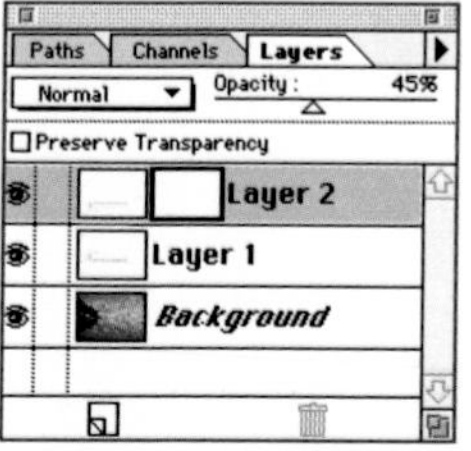

⑧ Now use the rectangular Selection tool to select a rectangle near to the dimensions of the reflected type, like this.

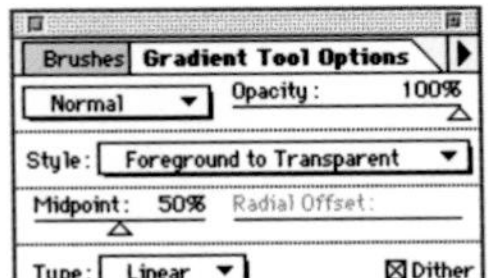

⑨ Double-click on the Gradient tool to select it and to open the Gradient Tool Options palette. Choose the **Foreground to Transparent** option from the style pop-up menu. The gradient Type should be set to Linear. Change the colors to their defaults (press D).

⑩ After you make the gradient, the bottom of the reflection will fade into the surface. Click near the bottom of the rectangular selection and drag towards the top, about two thirds the height of the word. You should now see something like this.

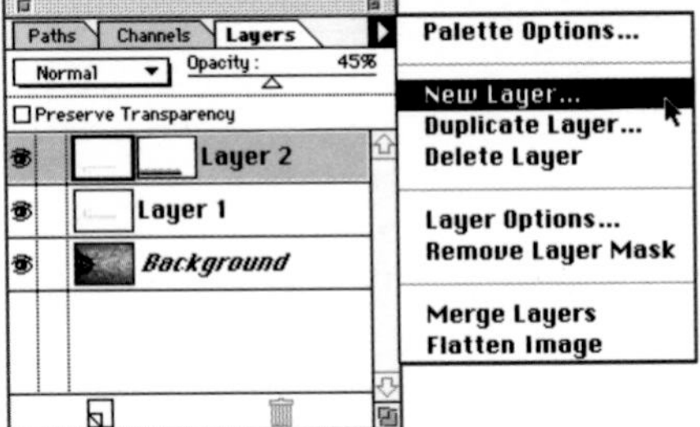

⑪ In the Layers palette, click on the layer containing the reflection (Layer #2) to make it the active layer. Click on the layer mask. Now, press Command-Option-T to select the reflected text. While holding down the option key, choose New Layer from the Layers palette arrow menu. The selection should remain active.

⑫ Make sure the foreground color is set to black (or another dark color). Use the Gradient tool with the same options as you set up in Step 9. Click near the middle of the original text and drag (while holding the Shift key) a short way into the reflected text to create a shadow.

⑬ To distort the text, since ours was underwater, we made the reflection layer (#2) and the top layer (#3) the only visible layers and chose **Merge Layers** from the Layers palette arrow menu. Once the layers were merged, only Layer #2 remained and was set back to Normal.

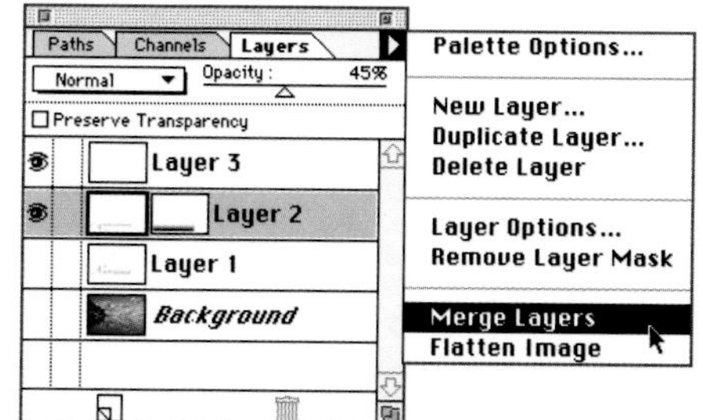

Then we used the Selection tool to select a rectangle around the reflected type. Applying Filter ➡ Distort ➡ Ripple (100, Large) supplied the final touch.

VARIATIONS

Andromeda's filters contain a Reflection filter that will make all of this much easier, but only in certain situations since the area surrounding the type will also be reflected. (If you select the type only, then the filter has no area in which to place the reflection.) The Filter ➡ Andromeda ➡ Reflection dialog box allows you to control 5 characteristics of the reflected type, and gives you a preview.

Wonderland

This checkerboard stock photo from Fotosets already had a slight reflection. We added the type (from the Chrome section, see page 44) and made its reflection match the already existing one. ■

Background: ©Fotosets 1995

Rough Edges

There are countless Photoshop and third-party filters that can be used by themselves or in combinations to add rough edges to your text. On the following pages are demonstrations of what the some of the third-party filters can do. But first, here are a few combinations we came up with by using only Photoshop's built-in set of filters.

Set-up Create a new file, and use the Type tool to enter the text. You could also use any type that you've rendered with another technique and want to embellish. This type is Frutiger Bold at 45 points.

Mosaic

Photoshop Filters Keep the text selection active, and apply Filter ➥ Distort ➥ Ripple (100, Large). While the selection is still active, apply Filter ➥ Distort ➥ Ripple (500, Small).

Mosaic

Deselect the text (Command-D), and apply Filter ➥ Pixelate ➥ Mosaic (6 pixels).

Mosaic

Deselect the text (Command-D), and apply Filter ➥ Pixelate ➥ Fragment.

Mosaic

Deselect the text (Command-D). Now apply Filter ➥ Pixelate ➥ Fragment, then Filter ➥ Distort ➥ Ripple (100, Medium).

TOOLBOX

Paint Alchemy 2.0
Gallery Effects filters

Deselect the text (Command-D). Apply Filter ➡ Pixelate ➡ Fragment, Filter ➡ Distort ➡ Ripple (100, Medium), and Filter ➡ Stylize ➡ Find Edges.

Deselect the text (Command-D). Apply Filter ➡ Pixelate ➡ Mosaic (6 pixels), Filter ➡ Stylize ➡ Find Edges, and Image ➡ Map ➡ Threshold (255).

Defloat the text (Command-F). Apply Filter ➡ Distort ➡ Ripple (300, Medium), and Image ➡ Adjust ➡ Brightness/Contrast (Contrast: +50).

Defloat the text (Command-F). Apply Filter ➡ Distort ➡ Wave (Type: Triangle; 1 generator; Wavelength: 2, 40; Amplitude: 10, 10; Scale: 100, 100; Wrap Around).

Defloat the text (Command-F). Apply Filter ➡ Distort ➡ Wave (Type: Square; 1 generator; Wavelength: 2, 20; Amplitude: 10, 10; Scale: 50, 50; Wrap Around), and Filter ➡ Distort ➡ Ripple (200, medium).

Displace Filter Inside the Adobe Photoshop ➡ Plug-ins folder is a folder named Displacement Maps. In this folder, Adobe has supplied some ready-made displacement maps. Test them all if you've got the time, or consult your Photoshop manual to see how you can make your own.

Deselect the text (Command-D), and apply Filter ➡ Distort ➡ Displace (Horiz.: 7, Vert.: 7, Tile, Repeat edge pixels).

Displace

Horizontal Scale: 7

Vertical Scale: 7

OK

Cancel

Displacement map:
○ Stretch to fit
◉ Tile

Undefined Areas:
○ Wrap Around
◉ Repeat edge pixels

Rough Edges

Mosaic

A dialog box will come up and ask you to find a displacement map. Find the Displacement maps folder mentioned above. For this example, we chose the Crumbles file. You can use the same technique to create all the type variations on this page.

Mosaic

In the Displace dialog box, we entered 10 for both the Horizontal and Vertical settings, and switched to the Stretch to Fit option. Then we chose the Mezzo effect displacement map.

Mosaic

To the figure above, we applied Filter ➥ Stylize ➥ Diffuse (Darken) three times for this result.

Mosaic

The Horizontal and Vertical settings were both set to 7 (Stretch to Fit), and we used the Rectangular displacement map.

Mosaic

We kept the text selection active, but pressed Command-J to defloat it. Then we changed the Horizontal and Vertical settings both to 5. Finally, we used the Schnabble effect displacement map.

PAINT ALCHEMY

Brush | Color | Size | Angle | Transparency

6222 Strokes

Density: 33

Random

Ordered Layering

Paint Layering

Load...

Randomize 447

Brush: Vasili Tip

Positioning

Horizontal Variation: 50

Vertical Variation: 50

Saved Styles:

Style: Vasili

Save | Save As... | Remove...

XAOS TOOLS

ALCHEMY

A A

Preview | Mem...

Cancel | Apply

Paint Alchemy Xaos Tools' Paint Alchemy is a perfect Photoshop plug-in for roughening the edges of text. There is a working version of Paint Alchemy 1.0 on the CD, and a demo version of Paint Alchemy 2.0. We used version 1.0 to create these type treatments. Here is what the interface for Paint Alchemy 1.0 looks like.

And this is the Paint Alchemy 2.0 interface:

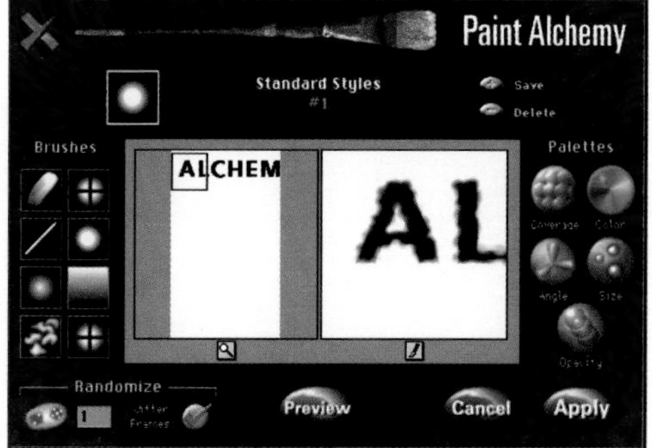

Use the Type tool to enter the text, deselect it (Command-D), then choose Filter ➥ Xaos Tools ➥ Paint Alchemy 1.0 (or Paint Alchemy 2.0). Your options in this interface are endless. If you use the preset styles, you will probably need to make adjustments so that only the edges of your text will be affected. Once you've found an effect you like, click the Randomize button, then the Preview button to see variations of the same settings. Here are some treatments we discovered.

For this one, we chose the preset Vasili, then adjusted the settings to affect only the edges.

Mosaic

This one began with the Cotton Ball preset.

Mosaic

To create this one we started with the Pointillist preset. Then we used Image ➥ Adjust ➥ Brightness/Contrast to increase the contrast.

Mosaic

For the last one here we began with the Screen Mosaic preset.

Mosaic

Gallery Effects Filters

Aldus' Gallery Effects includes three sets of filters full of features to help you roughen the edges of the text. In particular, the Classic Art I set seems to provide a good variety of filters useful for our task.

Here is the Classic Art 1: GE Spatter in action.

Here is Classic Art 1: GE Ripple.

Classic Art 2: GE Rough Pastels with Canvas chosen as the texture.

Classic Art 3: GE Water Paper and some hairy extensions.

A slight fuzz provided by Classic Art 3: GE Conte Crayon. ■

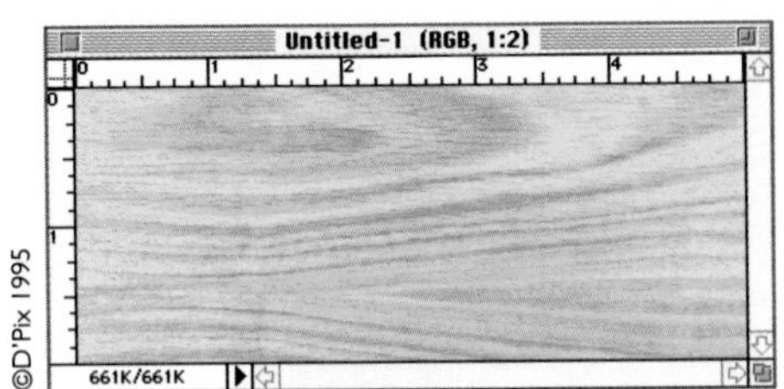

©D'Pix 1995

① Create a new file. We opened a stock photo from D'Pix to use as our background. Create a new channel (Channel #4) and change the foreground color to white, and press Option-Delete to fill the image area with white.

② Enter the text you want to apply the effect to in the new channel. We used Stencil at 50 points.

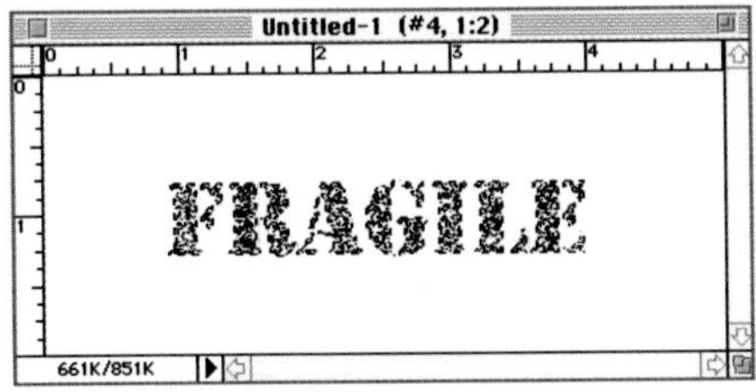

③ While the selection is still active choose Filter ➥ Noise ➥ Add Noise (999, Gaussian, Monochromatic).

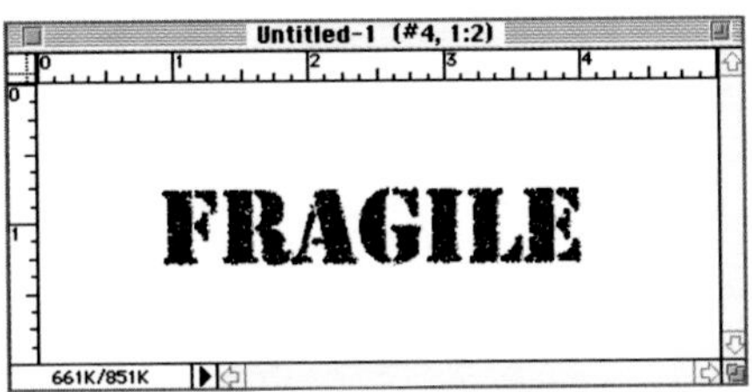

④ Now apply Filter ➥ Stylize ➥ Diffuse (Darken Only). Choose Select ➥ None and reapply the diffuse filter (Command-F).

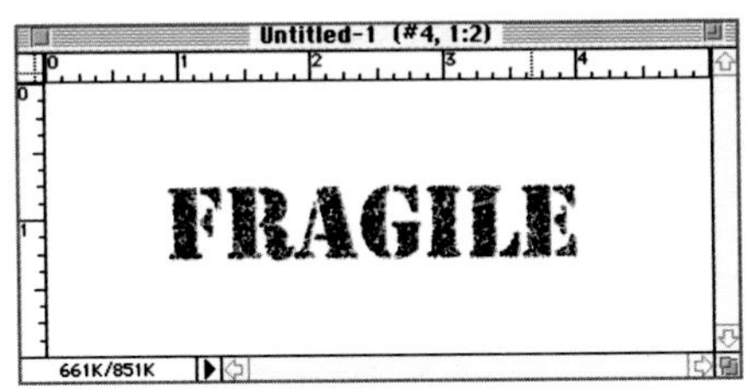

⑤ Apply Filter ➥ Blur ➥ Blur, then choose Image ➥ Adjust ➥ Levels (Input Levels settings: 0, 2.05, 239).

TOOLBOX

Rubber Stamp curve preset file
GE Note Paper

⑥ Now choose Image ➡ Adjust ➡ Curves (Command-M). Click on the Load button and find the Rubber Stamp curve, or bend the curve up just like you see it here. Press Command-I to invert the channel.

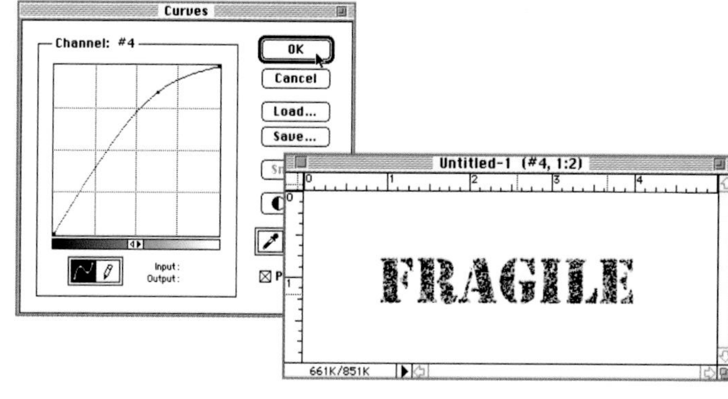

⑦ Return to the composite channel and choose Select ➡ Load Selection (Channel #4). Float the selection (Command-J). Change the foreground color to red and press Option-Delete to fill the selection. Fill it a second time for stronger ink.

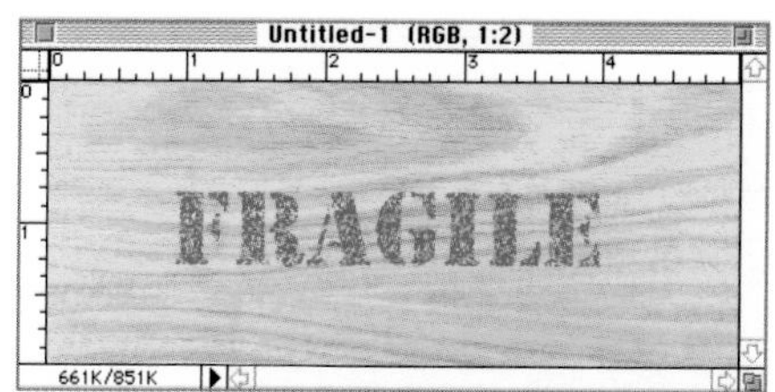

⑧ Now rotate the type selection (Image ➡ Rotate ➡ Free), deselect the text (Command-D) and it's ready to ship.

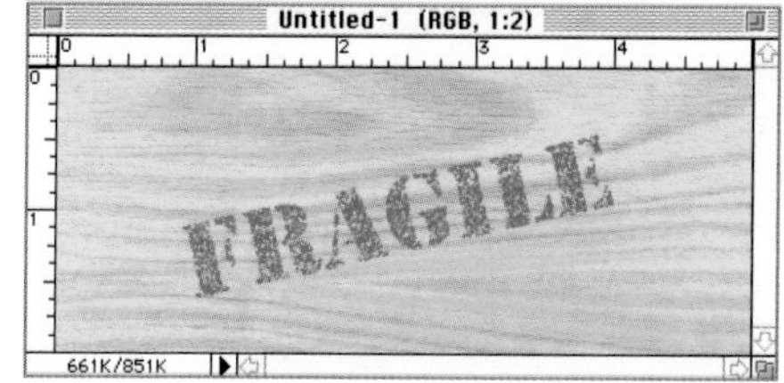

VARIATIONS

Here's another ink-stamped effect. Complete all the steps above, with these exceptions:

Step 4—Skip this step.

Step 5—After blurring the text, choose Filter ➡ Noise ➡ Median (3 pixels). Finish this step, and all the others, too.

To incorporate a paper texture with the ink, we first built the text (using all the steps above except Step 8) in a new file. Then we applied the Gallery Effects: Classic Art 2 ➥ GE Note Paper filter to an empty white channel, returned to the RGB composite channel, and choose Filter ➥ Render ➥ Lighting Effects. We chose the note paper channel (Channel #5 for us) as the Texture Channel and set the Height to 50. We used a white Omni light and moved it far enough away that it wouldn't shine too harshly on the paper surface.

Now see what happens when you apply the Gallery Effects: Classic Art 2 ➥ GE Note Paper filter to the final image with these settings: Image Balance: 25; Graininess: 10; Relief: 13. ■

Shadows

Basic Drop Shadow

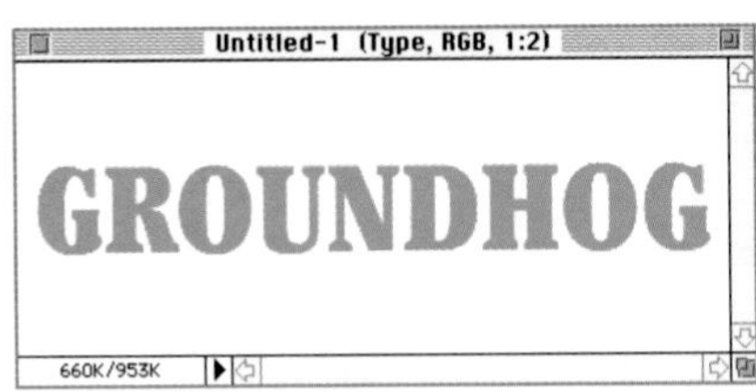

① Create a new file, or open a file containing a background for your type.

② Make a new layer, and name it Type. Choose a color for your type, and use the Type tool to enter the text. We made this groundhog with 60-point ITC Cheltenham UltraCond type. Press Command-J to set the type onto the layer, but keep the text selection active.

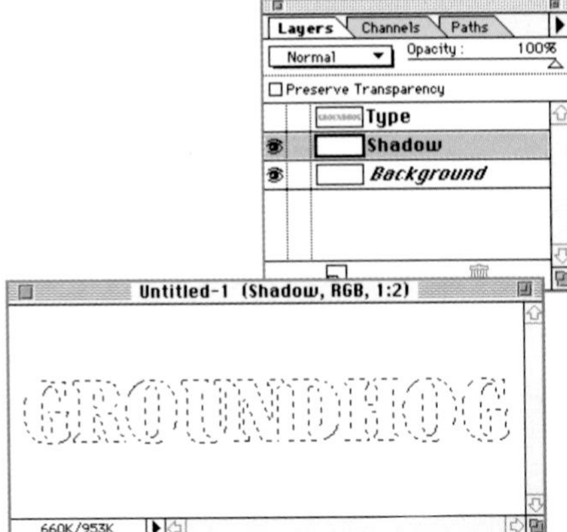

③ Create another new layer, name it Shadow, and drag the layer so it becomes the layer directly below the Type layer. Hide the Type layer so you can see the Shadow layer—just a blank white screen in our case.

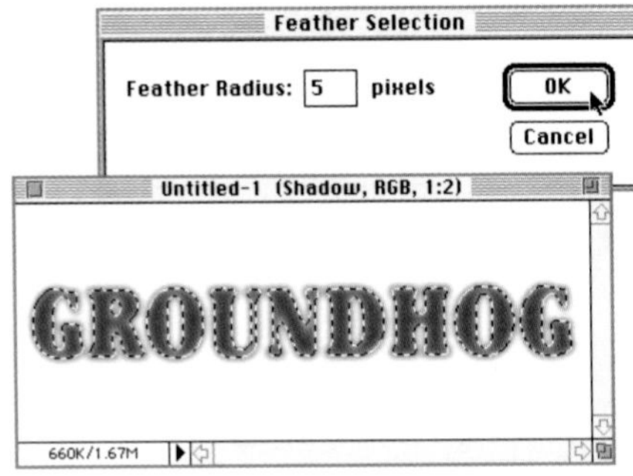

④ The text selection should still be active. Choose Select ➥ Feather (7 pixels). The higher the feather radius, the more diffused the shadow. Choose a foreground color for the shadow color, and fill the selection. Deselect the shadow selection (Command-D).

TIP

Black is the most common color for shadows, but choosing black doesn't mean that the shadow won't have any color. If the shadow is black and you lower the opacity of the layer, the color from the background will show through the shadow.

TOOLBOX

Alien Skin Drop Shadow 2.0 Filter
KPT Gradient Designer

⑤ Make the Type layer visible again, but keep the Shadow layer as the active one. The Layers palette will look like this.

⑥ Use the Move tool to move the shadow out from underneath the text. Then use the Opacity slider on the Layers palette to control how strongly the shadow covers the background. The Shadow layer opacity in this example is 90%. Now you have a basic drop shadow.

Shadows on Images If you are placing the text on top of an image and want a more realistic shadow that takes the background image into account, then do Steps 1 and 2 above and continue with these steps:

③ The text selection should still be active. Select the Move tool. Hold down the Command and Option keys while dragging the selection slightly away from the type. The selection will move, but your type should stay where it is. Choose Select ➥ Feather (7 pixels).

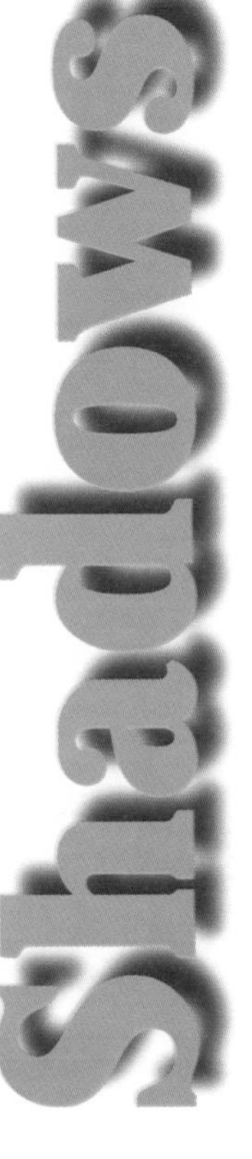

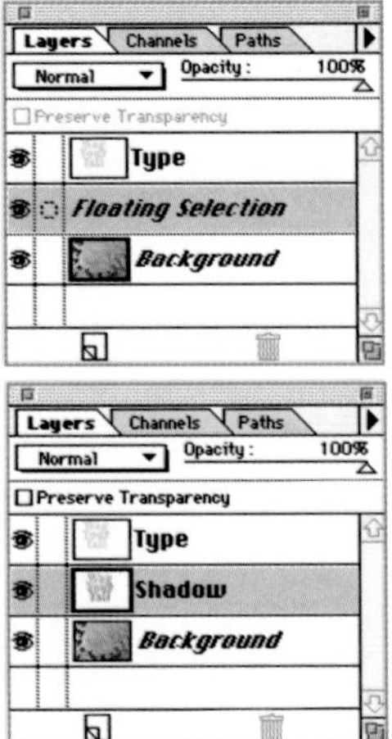

④ Now, make the layer containing the background the active layer. Press Command-J to float a copy of the selected area of the background. Choose **Make Layer** from the Layers palette arrow menu. Name it Shadow. The floating selection will become this new layer.

©Background: Fotosets 1995

⑤ Now that you have the background copied into the Shadows layer (we used a photo from Fotosets here), you can alter it with any of Photoshop's tools. For this example, we chose Image ➥ Adjust ➥ Hue/Saturation (Hue: -115, Saturation: -65, Brightness: -49), and set the Shadow layer mode to Multiply. For a soft shadow set the mode of the Shadow layer to Multiply in the Composite Controls pop-up menu on the Layers palette. Or try colorizing the shadow with the Image ➥ Adjust ➥ Hue/Saturation Colorize option.

VARIATIONS

Adding a Glow Make the Shadow layer the active layer. Press Command-Option-T to select the shadow. Make a new layer. Drag the new layer so that it becomes the layer directly below the Shadow layer. Choose Select ➡ Modify ➡ Border (15 pixels). Set the foreground color to a color for the glow, and press Option-Delete to fill the selection. Press Option-Delete two or three more times to intensify the glow.

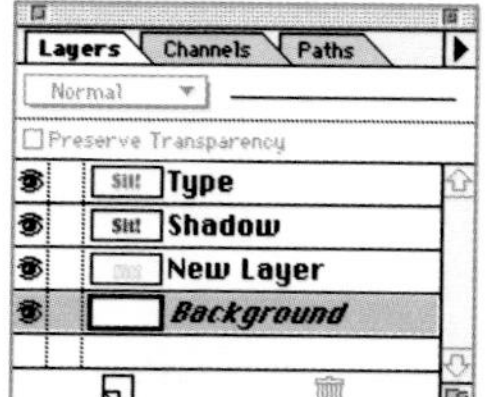

Sit!

KPT Gradient Designer This multicolored drop shadow was created using KPT Gradient Designer to fill in the shadow in Step 4 of the Basic Drop Shadow technique above.

Roll Over!

Alien Skin Drop Shadow 2.0 Filter A much easier way to create a drop shadow is to use the Drop Shadow filter from Alien Skin's Black Box (included on the CD). There's no need to create a new layer. Just enter the text in the composite channel. Choose the foreground color you wish to use for the drop shadow. With the text still selected, choose Filter ➡ Alien Skin ➡ Drop Shadow 2.0.

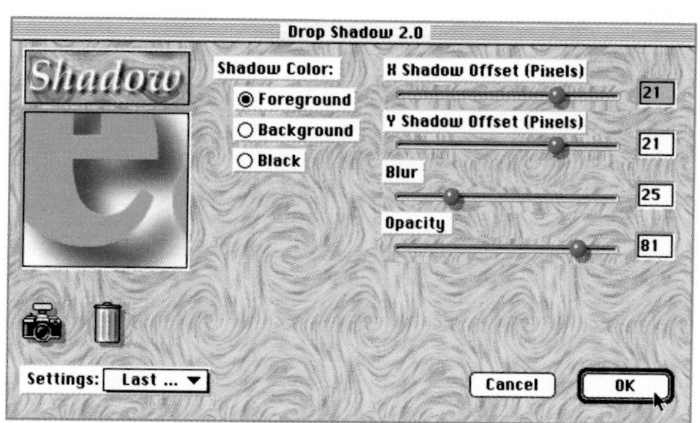

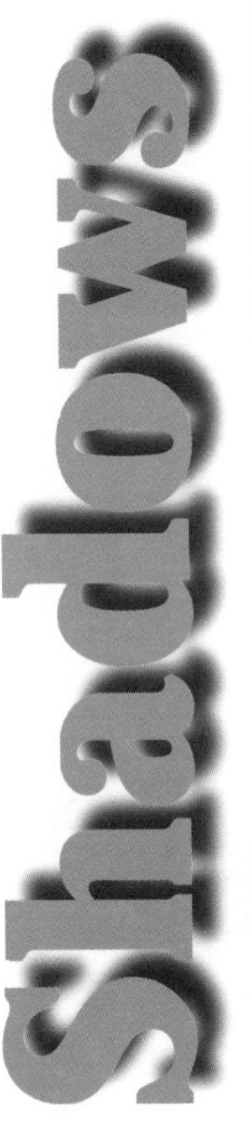

Perspective Shadows

Creating a perspective shadow is virtually the same as creating a drop shadow. You only need to distort the shadow so that it looks like it's falling back on a surface. Complete Steps 1 through 3 of the Basic Drop Shadow section (except don't hide the Type layer), then continue with these steps:

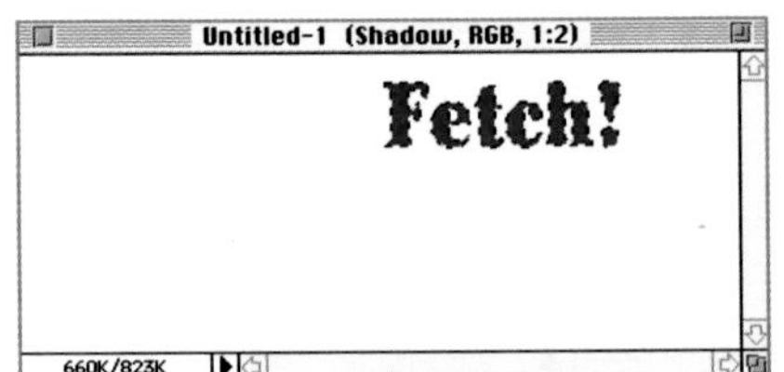

④ Fill the selection with white. (You won't see any change when you fill the selection because the Type layer is on top of the Shadow layer.)

⑤ Since our shadow is coming forward we first had to flip it, and then align it. Choose Image ➡ Flip ➡ Vertical, then drag the flipped text down until the bottoms touch.

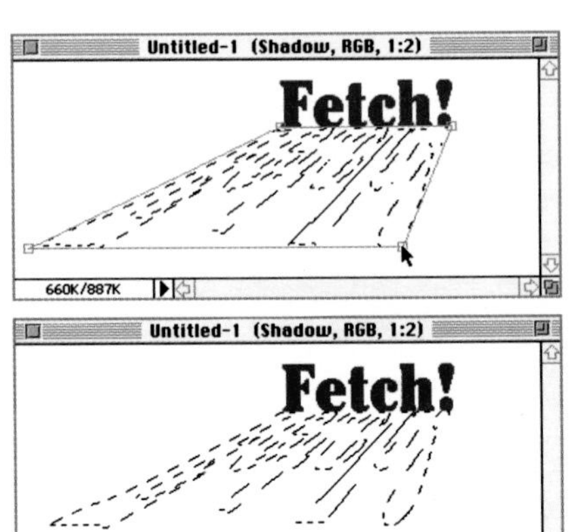

⑥ Photoshop has several distortion tools useful to creating the right form for the shadow, but the most versatile is the Distort tool. Choose Image ➡ Effects ➡ Distort. You can now drag the four corners of the selection in any direction you wish. We dragged the bottom two corners down and to the left. Click the gavel over the type when you're satisfied.

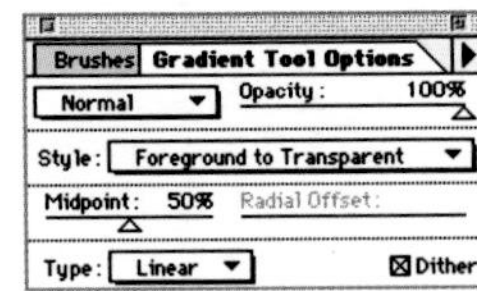

⑦ Now we have the shape for the shadow, but before filling it we're going to fade the near edges of the text. Press Q to enter Quick Mask mode. Double-click on the Gradient tool to select it and open the Gradient Tool floating palette. Make the settings as you see them in this figure.

(8) Click at the bottom of the shadow with the Gradient tool and drag straight up about one-third of the way through the shadow. You should see something like this in Quick Mask mode.

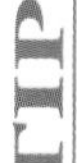

Holding the shift key while dragging the Gradient tool keeps the gradient straight.

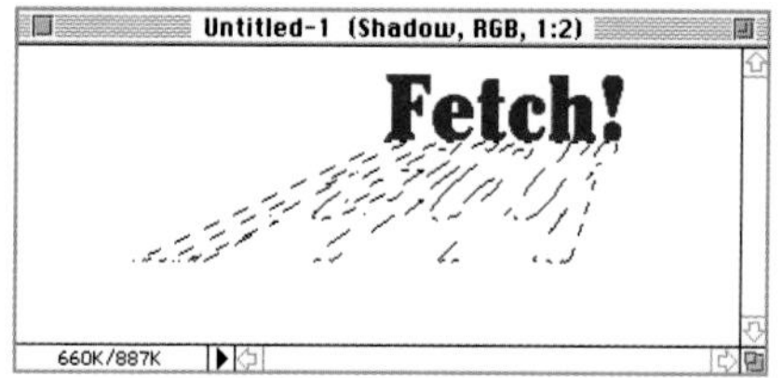

(9) Press Q to exit Quick Mask mode. Save the selection. Press Command-A to select the entire layer, then press delete to clear up the residue that often hangs around on layers after distorting selections. Load the selection just saved.

(10) Choose Select ➡ Feather (2 pixels) to soften the selection. Set the foreground color to a color for the shadow. Press Option-Delete to fill the shadow.

To create this floating type, the original text was distorted with the Image ➡ Effects ➡ Distort tool (as described in the Perspective Shadow steps above), then we followed the Basic Drop Shadow steps on page 168. ■

This is your one-step guide to shattered type. For this effect, we've done all the work for you.

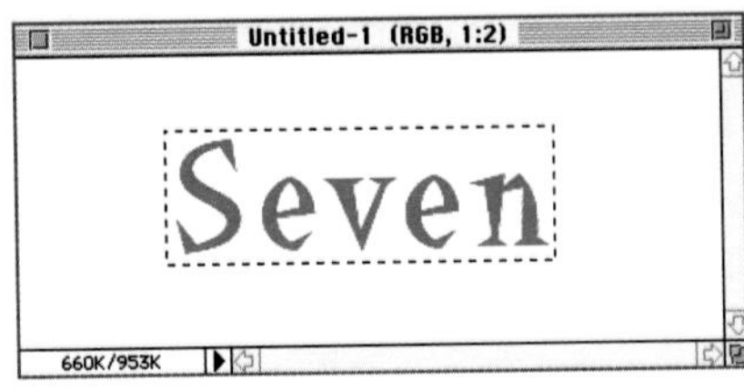

① Create a new file, and use the Type tool to enter the text. We used La Bamba at 80 points. You may want to increase the letter spacing in the Type dialog box to give the letters some room for splintering. The spacing for this example is set at 5. Deselect the text (Command-D).

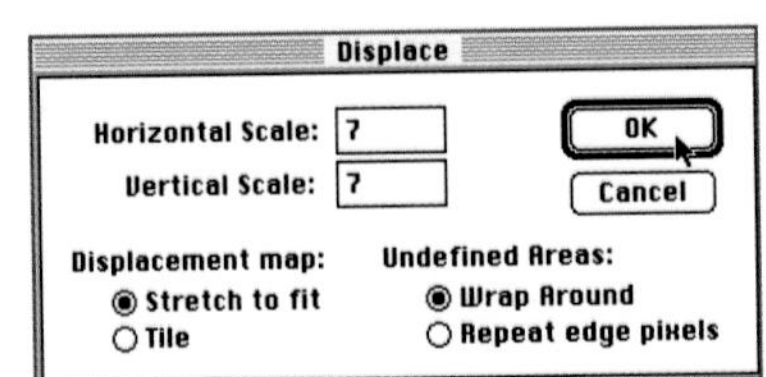

② Use the rectangular Selection tool to select an area surrounding the type. Grab some of the surrounding area, but not too much.

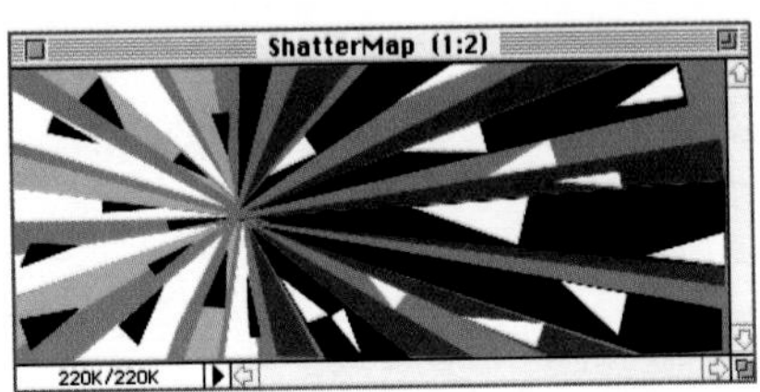

③ Choose Filter ➥ Distort ➥ Displace. Use these settings: Horizontal Scale 7, Vertical Scale 7, Stretch to fit, Wrap Around. Click OK.

ShatterMap (1:2)

220K/220K

④ A dialog box will appear asking you to choose a displacement map. Find the ShatterMap preset file from the CD. This file is a grayscale displacement map that we created. It shifts parts of the image (or text) according to the lightness or darkness in areas of the displacement map. Although you won't see this figure, we wanted to show you what the displacement map looks like.

TOOLBOX

ShatterMap preset file

⑤ Click OK, and that's it. If the displacement map distorts your text too much or too little, then either adjust the size of the area you select around the text in Step 2 or adjust the values in Step 3.

VARIATIONS

For this variation, we applied the Displace filter a second time with the same displacement map and the same settings.

Before deselecting the text in Step 1, we opened a stock photo from D'Pix, copied it, returned to our text file and chose Edit ➥ Paste into.

First, we rendered the type using the Marquee effect on page 102, then followed Steps 2 through 4 above to create this type. ■

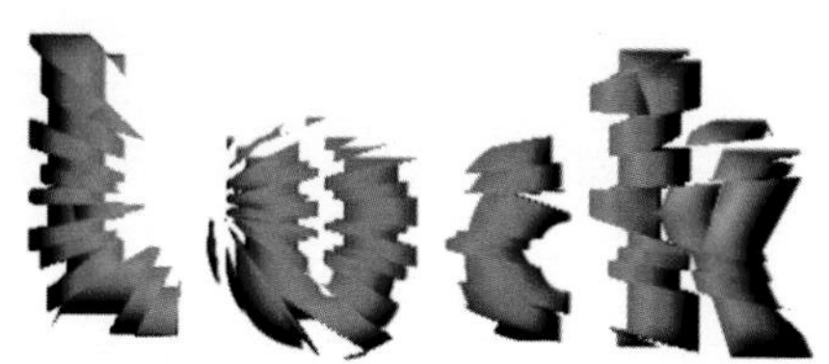

Smoke

©Digital Stock 1995

Depending on how you use this effect, it can also look like fog.

① Create a new file or open a file containing the image you want to place the foggy or smoky text over. We used a stock photo from Digital Stock.

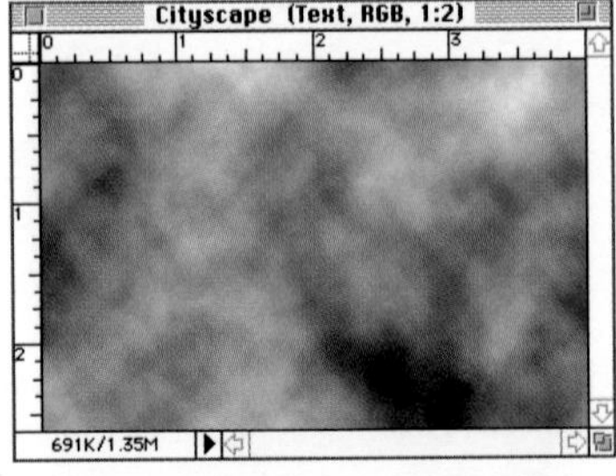

② Create a new layer, and name it "Text". In the new Text layer, choose Filter ➡ Render ➡ Clouds.

③ Add a layer mask for this layer. Hold the Option key and click on the layer mask, so only the mask is visible. Set the foreground and background colors to their defaults (Press D), and fill the mask with black. Press X to switch the foreground and background colors to white and black, respectively. Enter the text. We used BL Frutiger Black font at 50 points, with bold applied. Deselect the text (Command-D).

④ Choose Image ➡ Rotate ➡ 90° CW, then Filter ➡ Stylize ➡ Wind (Wind, Right). Reapply the filter (Command-F).

VARIATIONS

These variations give you some minor adjustments you can use to make your type look a little better.

Use the Smudge tool to improve the look of the smoke or fog. If you click on the layer mask for the Text layer to make it active, you can use the Smudge tool on the text while viewing the results to the entire image without affecting the other layers. Set the Smudge tool Pressure to 50%.

If you want to strengthen the text, then make the Clouds layer mask active and choose Image ➥ Adjust ➥ Brightness/Contrast and raise the Contrast. You can also do this to the Text layer window. If raising the Contrast is too harsh, then try adjusting the Levels (Command-L).

You probably noticed that after Step 7 and before Step 8, clouds were floating in front of the entire image. If you like that effect, but want the text to stand out more, then stop after step 7 and choose Image ➥ Adjust ➥ Brightness/Contrast. Raise the Contrast all the way to 100, and slide the Brightness slider either all the way up or all the way down.

Add some color to the text by selecting a foreground color after creating the new layer in Step 2, or filling the Clouds layer with a solid color instead of white. ■

Stitched

This effect uses Photoshop 3.0's new Lighting Effects filter. Included on the CD are several preset LightingStyles files to be used with this filter. To find out what you need to do to load these files, turn to page 206 in Appendix A, *What's on the CD-ROM*. Also, to use the Lighting Effects filter the file must be in RGB mode.

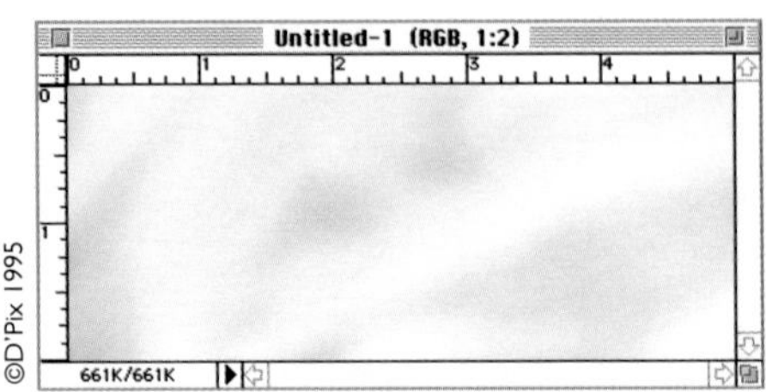

©D'Pix 1995

① Create a new file (RGB), or open a file containing the background that you want to stitch. We used a stock photo of silk from D'Pix. (which we manipulated to soften it). Whatever you use, it must be an RGB file in order for the Lighting Effects filter to work.

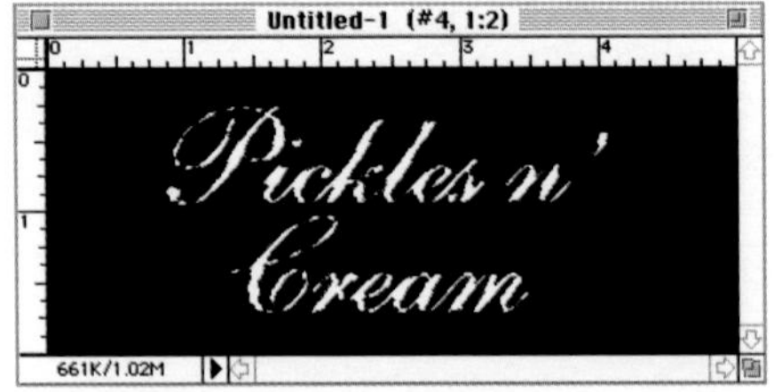

② Create a new channel (Channel #4). Use the Type tool to enter the text in the new channel. This effect was created with a script font, such as Shelley Andante (which we used here at 70 points), in mind. Save the active type selection in another new channel (Channel #5).

③ Don't lose the selection after entering the text. Press Command-J to defloat the text. Choose Filter ➡ Blur ➡ Gaussian Blur (3 pixels) to blur the inside of the text selection only.

④ Choose Select ➡ Inverse, then Filter ➡ Blur ➡ Gaussian Blur (5.5 pixels), to blur only the outside of the text selection. Now, you can get rid of that annoying active selection (press Command-D).

TOOLBOX

EmbossLightingStyles preset file
Adobe Illustrator 5.5

⑤ Choose Filter ➥ Stylize ➥ Find Edges.

⑥ We are building a grayscale texture channel to be used with the Lighting Effects filter. Right now, things are a bit too harsh for a stitched-on-silk look. Choose Image ➥ Adjust ➥ Brightness/Contrast and use settings near these: Brightness 22, Contrast -46.

⑦ For a final softening choose Filter ➥ Blur ➥ Gaussian Blur (1 pixel).

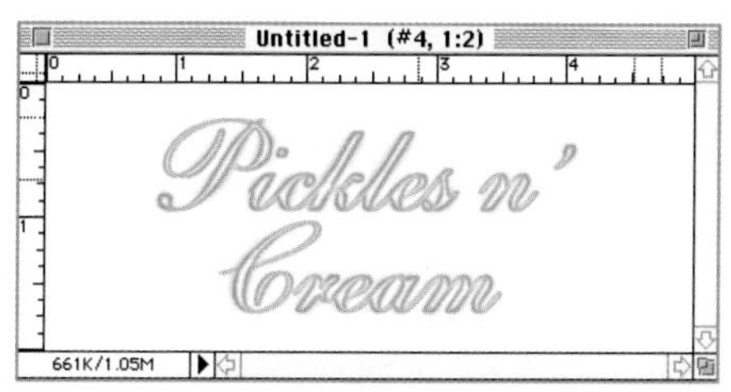

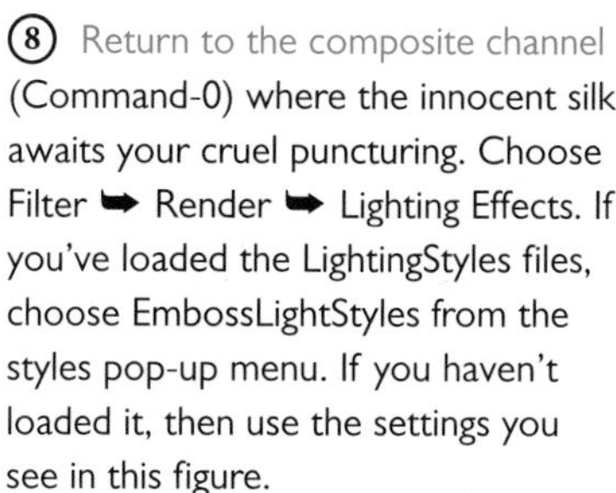

⑧ Return to the composite channel (Command-0) where the innocent silk awaits your cruel puncturing. Choose Filter ➥ Render ➥ Lighting Effects. If you've loaded the LightingStyles files, choose EmbossLightStyles from the styles pop-up menu. If you haven't loaded it, then use the settings you see in this figure.

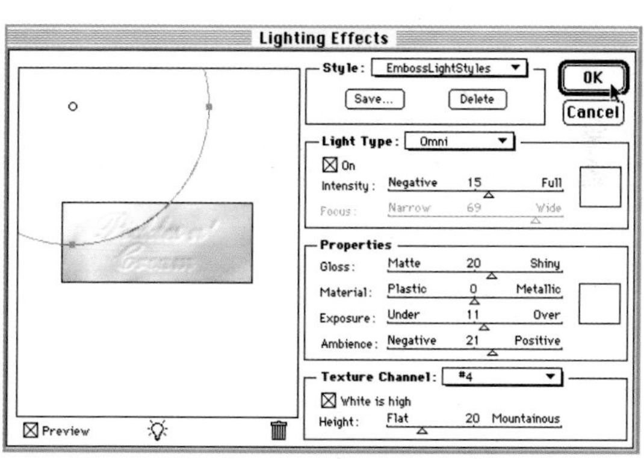

You should see something like this.

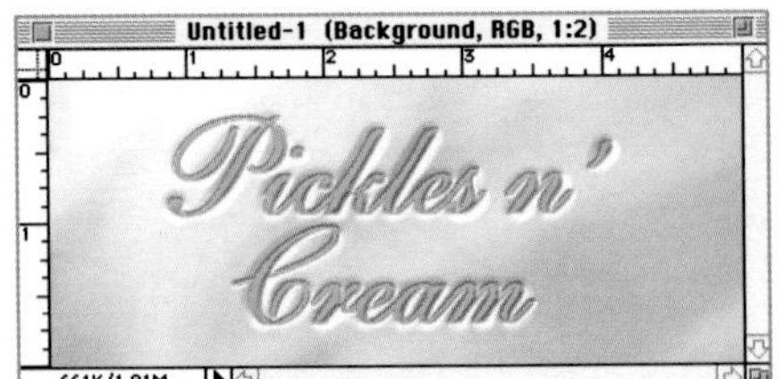

⑨ To change the color of the type, load channel #5 (the original type selection), and choose Image ➥ Adjust ➥ Hue/Saturation. You may or may not want to check the Colorize checkbox. If you don't, then the Hue slider is only going to effect the darker areas of the type. Use the sliders to find the color you want. Here are the settings we used for this example: Hue: 95, Saturation: 74, Lightness: -42.

VARIATIONS

Adding Stitches

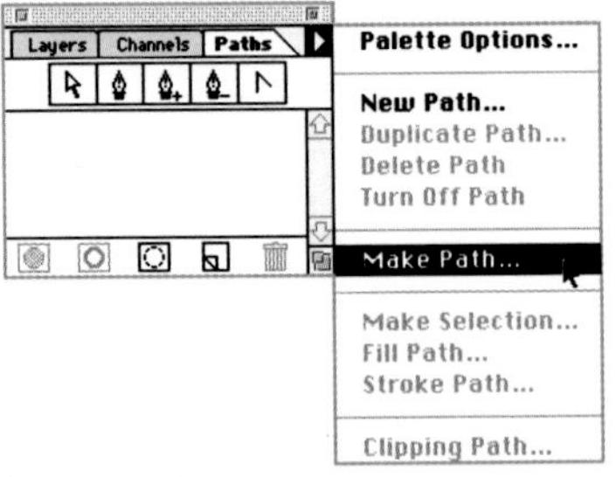

① We used Adobe Illustrator to create the stitches. Open Adobe Illustrator, and open a new file. Return to Photoshop while Illustrator runs in the background. Load the selection for Channel #5, open the Paths palette and choose **Make Path** (1 pixel) from the arrow menu.

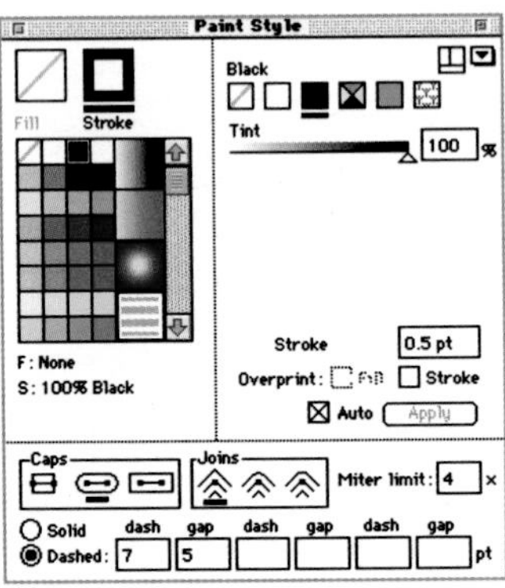

② Copy the path to the clipboard (Command-C). Now, switch to Adobe Illustrator. On the empty page, paste in the path from the clipboard. The path will appear in Illustrator. Do not lose the selection. In the Paint Styles palette, choose black for the stroke color. Make the stroke weight .5 points. Switch the line style to Dashed with a 7 pt. dash and a 5 pt. gap. Make the ends round. Your settings should match what you see in this figure.

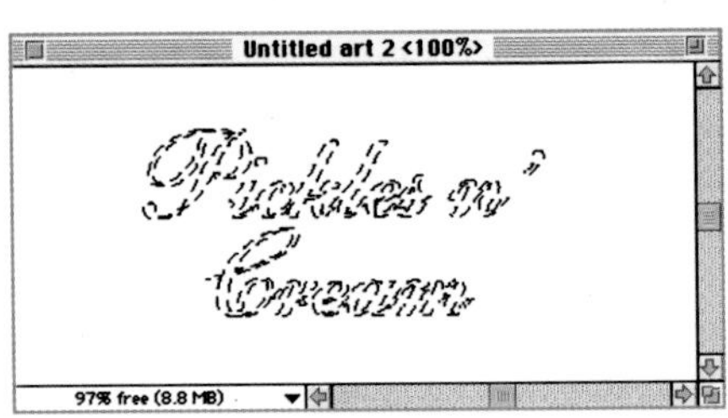

And the text path should look like this (press Command-Shift-H to hide the blue guides).

③ Copy the path to the Clipboard (Command-C). Return to Photoshop. **Choose Turn off Path** from the Paths palette arrow menu. Load the selection for Channel #5, and paste in the clipboard (Command-V). A dialog box will appear; choose Paste as Pixels (anti-aliased) and click OK. Choose Select ➥ Save Selection to make Channel #6.

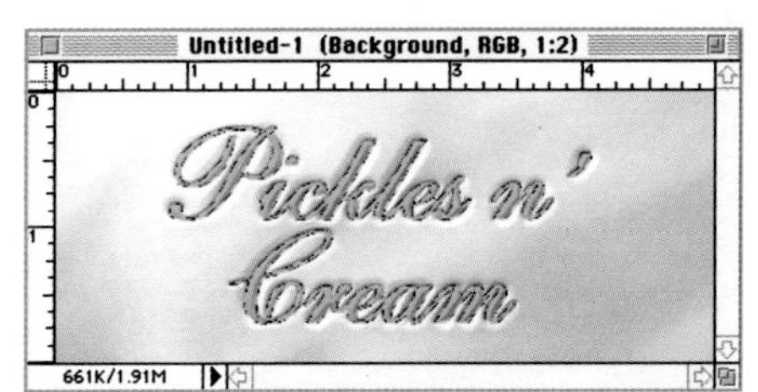

④ Press Command-H to Hide the Edges. You can see the stitches are black now. If you want to change their color or soften them, then Choose Image ➥ Adjust ➥ Hue/Saturation. For this example we checked the Colorize box and used these settings: Hue: 180, Saturation: 100, Lightness: +16.

More Stitches If you want to make the stitches look more raised, after Step 7 complete Steps 1 through 3 of Adding Stitches with one exception: choose white as the stroke color in Step 2. Deselect the stitches (Command-D) and finish Steps 8 and 9. The image should now include a row of indentations that gives the impression of stitches.

To add color to More Stitches, load the stitches selection (Channel #6). Hold down the command and option keys and press the up arrow and left arrow once each. Then choose Select ➥ Feather (1 pixel). Choose Image ➥ Adjust ➥ Hue/Saturation. We used these settings: Hue: -25, Saturation: 100, Lightness: 0. ■

This effect is gonna take some patience—and a lot of trial and error. Save often and get friendly with the Undo command!

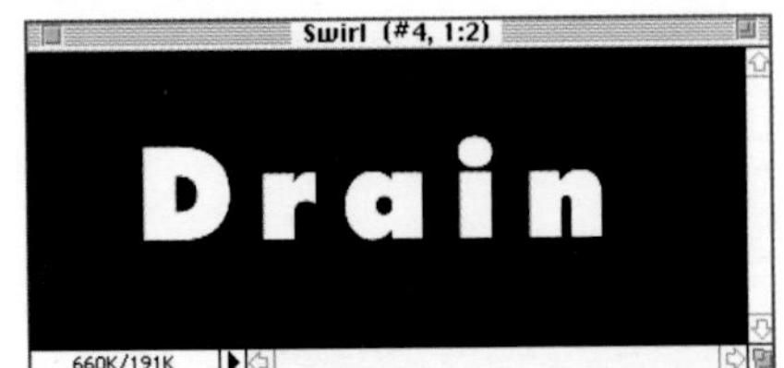

① Open a new file, and create a new channel. Press D to change the foreground color to black and the background color to white. Use the Type tool to enter your text into the new channel. For this example, we used Futura Extra Bold at 60 points, with the spacing set at 12 to provide some extra room between the letters.

② Change the Selection tool shape to Elliptical and the Style to a Constrained Aspect Ratio with Width: 1 and Height: 1. This will give you a perfect circle.

③ Select a part of one of the letters, keeping the body of the letter less than halfway through the circle. If part of the letter goes over halfway through the circle, the result will be the background bleeding into the letter rather than a spike coming out of the letter (just try it…you'll see what we mean). If you need to move the marquee, but don't want to change the size, hold down the Option and Command keys while click-dragging the selection. Only the marquee will move—not what's in it!

④ Bring up Filter ➥ Distort ➥ Twirl. Move the slider back and forth until you like what you see in the preview window. If you can't get what you want, cancel and move the selection a bit or try using a different size selection. Both of these changes can have profound effects on the filter.

TOOLBOX

Alien Skin's Swirl 2.0 filter
KPT Gradient on Paths

Now you've got the first one.

⑤ Move the selection or make a new one and continue swirling until you have a finished product.

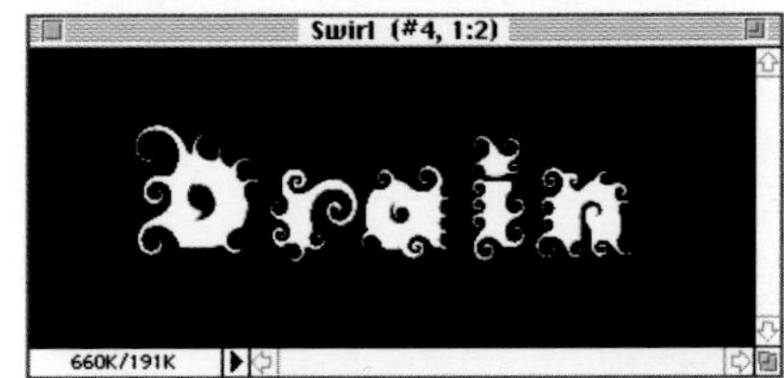

⑥ Return the composite RGB Channel and fill the area with any color or texture you want to appear in your type. Here we used a texture from Kai's Power Tools and applied Filter ➥ Alien Skin ➥ Swirl 2.0 (Spacing: 22, Length:7, Twist: 90, and Detail: 100). (Warp and Smooth were both checked, too.)

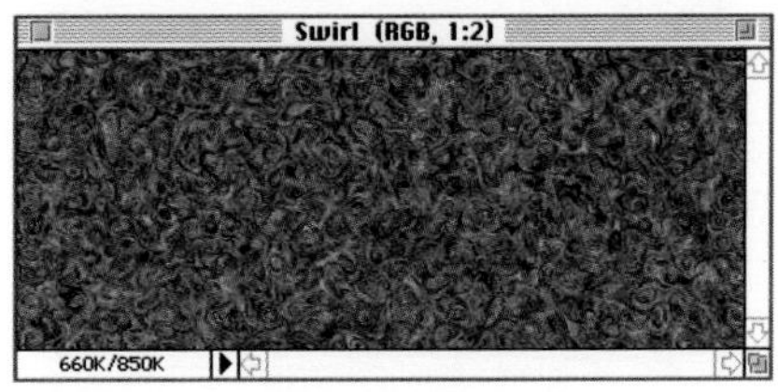

⑦ Select ➥ Load Selection (Channel #4) and Select ➥ Inverse (or you could have clicked the Invert box in the Load Selection dialog box.) Press Delete to fill the selection with white. You're left with the letters filled with a pattern!

VARIATIONS

You can treat your swirled type just as you could anything typed with the Type tool, meaning you can apply a barrage of other effects from this book. For instance, try some Neon (page 112)—we feathered the selection 3 pixels, then used KPT Gradient on Paths with a custom gradient.

Or try Flaming (page 68). A few extra swirls really add to that "hot" effect, don't they? ■

TOOLBOX

Adobe Dimensions 2.0
KPT Texture Explorer 2.1

Although it is possible to create type that looks three dimensional within Photoshop, there are several other applications which make this task a lot easier. On the CD are demo versions of a few of these three-dimensional rendering applications, including: Adobe Dimensions, Infini-D, and StrataType 3d. There is also a demo version of Andromeda Software's 3-D Photoshop filter. We're going to use Dimensions to model some 3-D type, then take it into Photoshop and dress it up.

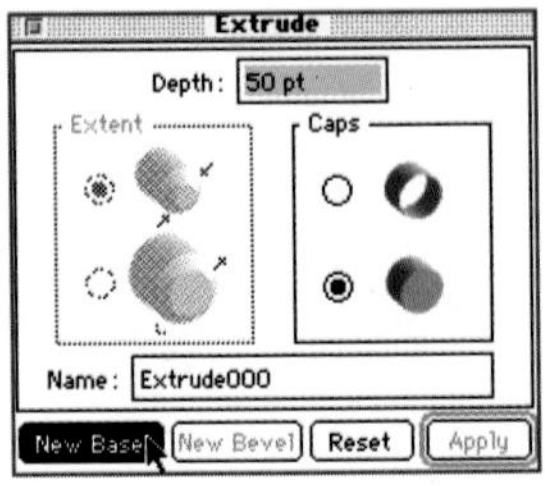

① Open Adobe Dimensions 2.0. A new document window will automatically open. Press Command-E to make sure that you are working in Edit Mode, where everything runs faster. Then choose Operations ➥ Extrude (Command-Shift-E). The Extrude floating palette will pop up on the screen. Click on the New Base button on the palette.

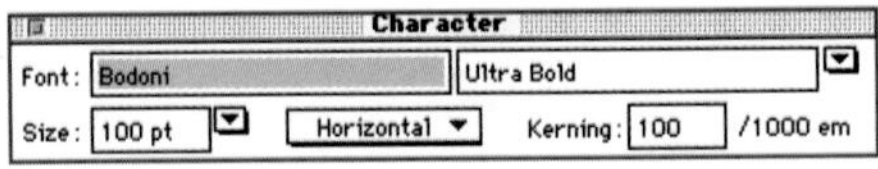

② A new untitled window will open up on screen, and the icons in the toolbar will change. Double-click on the Type tool to select it and open the Character floating palette. Make your selections in the Character palette. We use 100-point Bodoni UltraBold for this example.

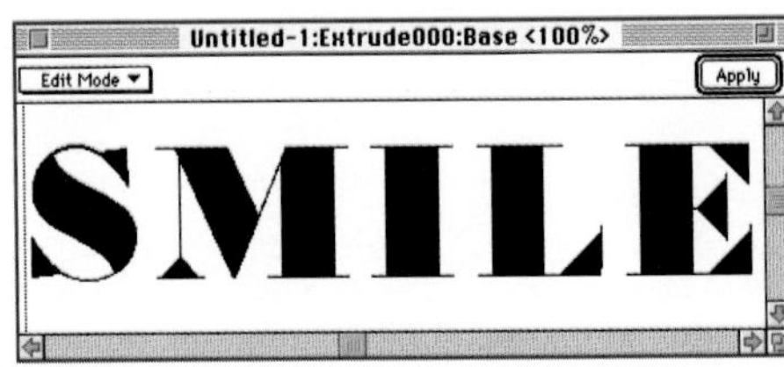

③ With the Type tool, click in the extrude window that opened in Step 2. A cursor will appear. Type in the text.

If you want beveled type, then see Steps 3, 4, and 5 in the Beveled type section on page 28, then skip to Step 5 of this section.

④ Find the Extrude floating palette. Enter, in points, the depth you want the text to extrude. We used a value of 25 points. We also choose the end caps option. Click the Apply button on the Extrude floating palette.

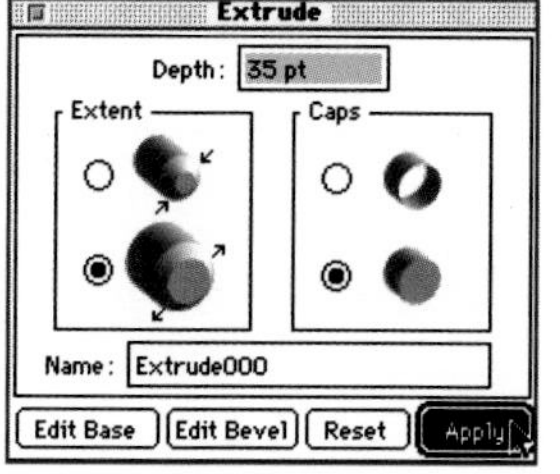

⑤ To go back to the original image window choose Window ➡ Untitled-1. Now you can see that the text has been extruded. What you see is actually a wireframe model of the type. Before rendering the final image, we're going to set its color.

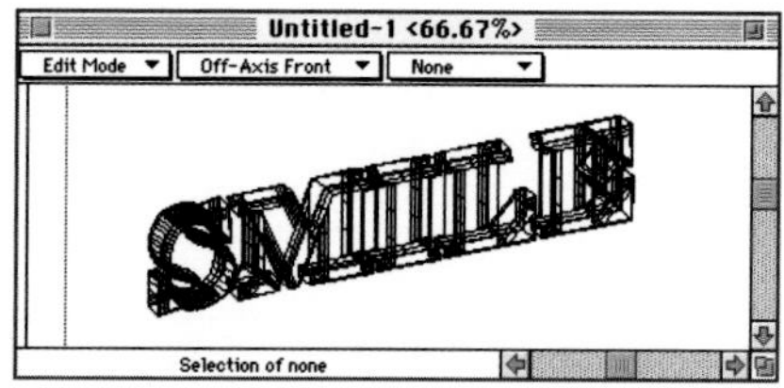

⑥ Choose Appearance ➡ Surface Properties. A floating palette will appear. The figure here explains its features. For the Fill (text) color, we used these CMYK values: 0/95/80/0. For the Shade (shadow) color, we used black. We left the Stroke (edge) color at none. Click on the Reflectance icon, then the Plastic icon, and use the values shown in the figure. Click the Apply button when you're finished.

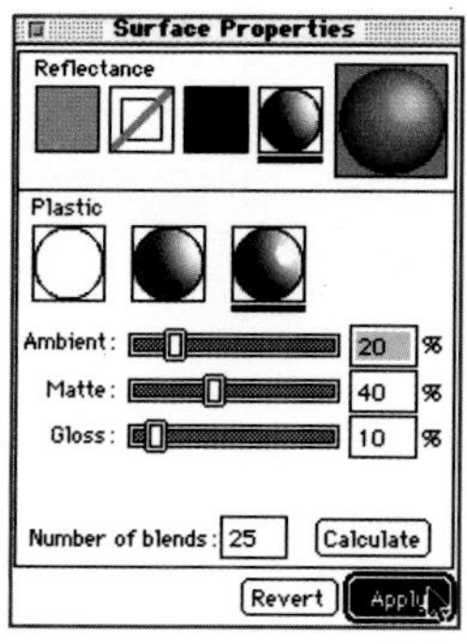

⑦ To show off more of the perspective of the type, we selected View ➡ Custom Perspective and set the angle to 115°. Then we moved the type straight down so the perspective would affect the type even more.

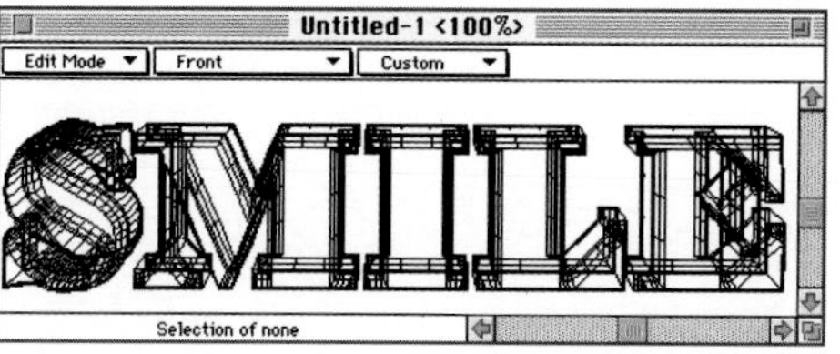

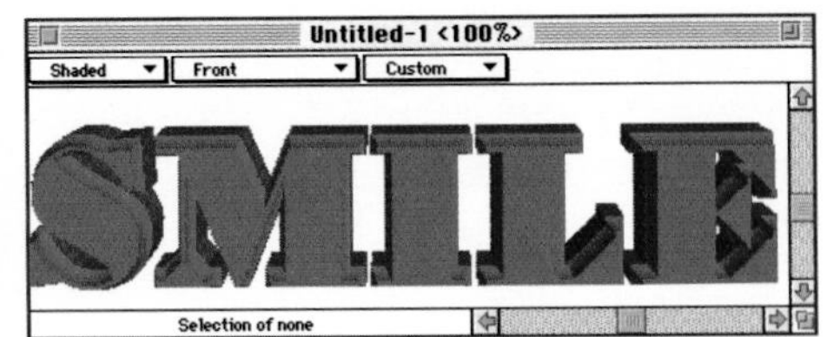

⑧ You won't see any changes in the text because you're not in a render mode yet. Choose View ➥ Shaded Render. (Complex type may take some time to render—ours took about 15 minutes.) If you don't like what you see, you can simply use the Surface Properties palette to make appearance changes or go back to the Extrude palette and use the Edit buttons to alter the text. Remember, it's always quicker to work in Edit mode (View ➥ Edit Mode).

Art for Chapters
Photoshop T...
3d.1
3D.2
3D.3
3D.4
3D.5
Eject
Desktop
New
Cancel
Export to:
SMILE
Export
Preview: Color Macintosh™
Compatability: Adobe Illustrator 5

⑨ When you are satisfied with the type, deselect the type (Command-Shift-A), and choose File ➥ Export. Choose Color Macintosh and Adobe Illustrator 5 from the pop-up menus. Quit Dimensions (Command-Q). No need to save changes—we already exported what we wanted.

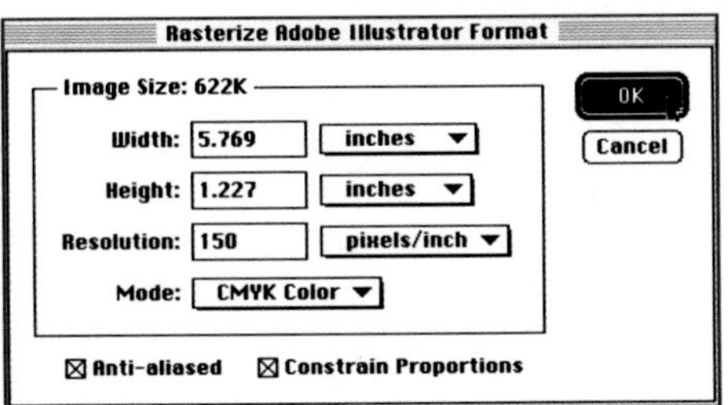

⑩ Open Photoshop, and open the file you just exported from Adobe Dimensions. Here are the settings we used in the Rasterizer box.

⑪ The text will open into Layer 1 and there will be no background layer. It is complete and ready for you to embellish with Photoshop.

⑫ The rest of the steps demonstrate how to map a pattern onto the 3-D type. First duplicate Layer 1 to make Layer 1 copy. Then, choose Luminosity from the Layers palette composite controls menu.

⑬ Make Layer 1 active, and press Command-Option-T to select the outline of the type. While the selection is active, fill the selection with white.

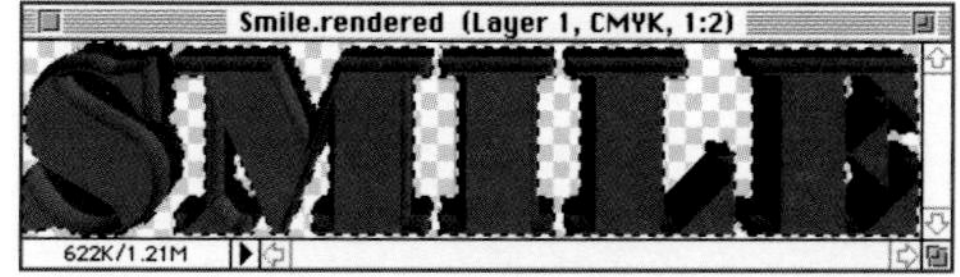

⑭ Now choose Filter ➥ KPT 2.1 ➥ KPT Texture Explorer. Once you find something you like, click OK, then flatten the image.

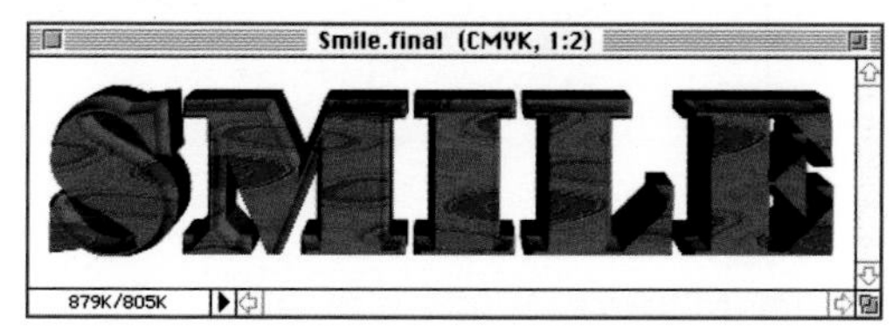

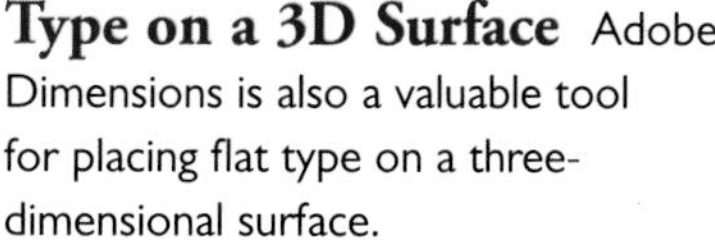

TIP

To map a stock photo texture onto to the type, open the photo, select the area you want to use, copy it to the clipboard (Command-C), and close the file. In Step 13, instead of filling the text with white, choose Edit ➥ Paste Into.

Type on a 3D Surface Adobe Dimensions is also a valuable tool for placing flat type on a three-dimensional surface.

① Again, open Adobe Dimensions 2.0. A new window will automatically appear. The toolbar includes tools to create boxes, spheres, cones, and cylinders. We decided to put our type on a sphere. Click on the sphere tool on the tool palette to select it, then use the crosshairs to draw a box in the Untitled-1 window area. To make a perfectly round sphere, hold the Shift key to keep all the dimensions the same.

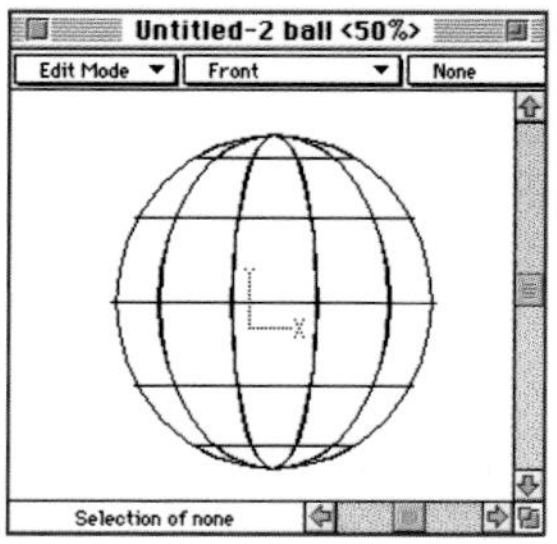

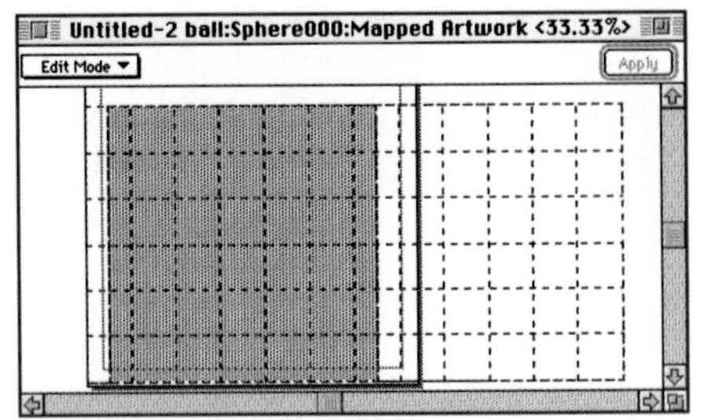

② Choose Appearance ➡ Map Artwork (Command-Option-M). A new window will open and the tools in the toolbar will change. The grid in the new window is a "map" of the sphere. The gray areas are the areas of the sphere which are currently hidden from view in the Untitled-1 window.

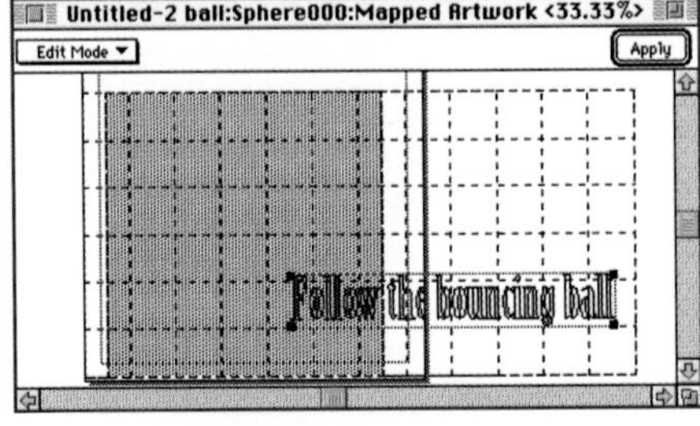

③ Double-click on the Type tool to select it and open the Character floating dialog box. Type in the text, press Return, then move the text where you want it on the map.

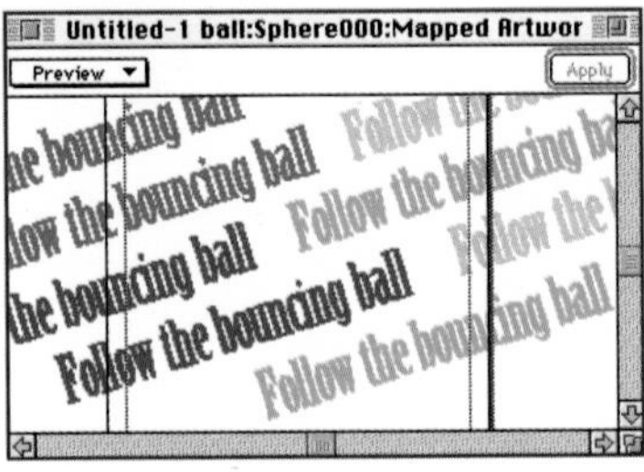

④ Press Command-Y to see a preview of the text only. To change the fill or stroke color of the text press Command-I to open the Surface Properties floating dialog box.

TIP

If you want to edit the type while still in the Map Artwork window, go back to the Edit mode (Command-E) and use the Type tool to select the text and the floating Character dialog box to make any changes.

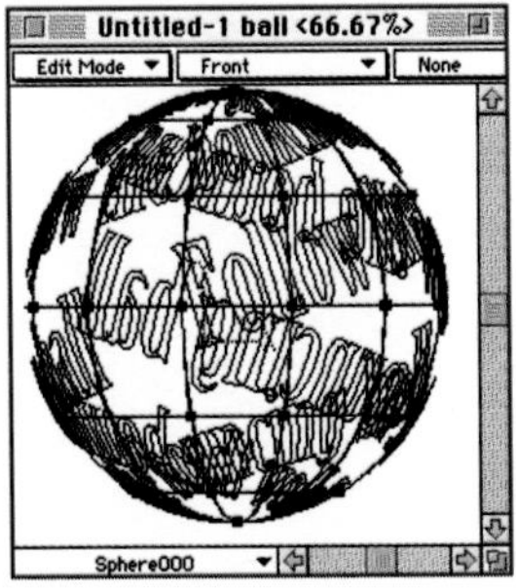

⑤ Click on the Apply button in the upper right corner of the Map Artwork window, then choose Window ➡ Untitled-1 to see the type mapped onto the sphere.

⑥ Now, since we don't want to see the sphere, but only the type, we have to make sure the Surface Properties of the sphere are set to none. Press Command-I to open the Surface Properties dialog box and set the Fill and Stroke colors to None. Be sure to click the Apply button to activate your changes.

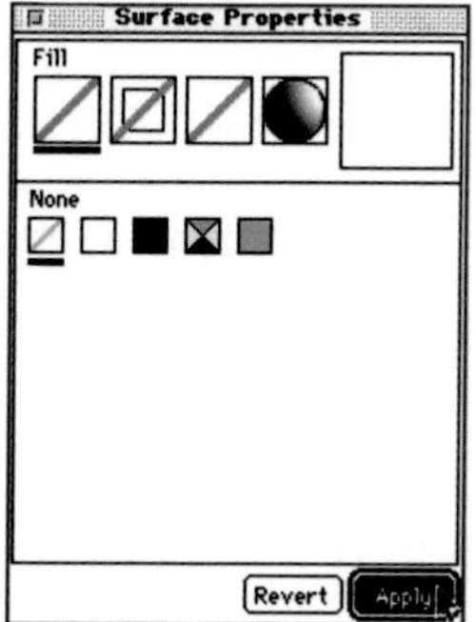

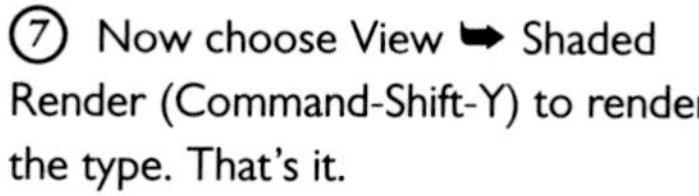

⑦ Now choose View ➥ Shaded Render (Command-Shift-Y) to render the type. That's it.

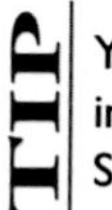

TIP

You can import this type for use in a Photoshop file by following Steps 9 and 10 above. ■

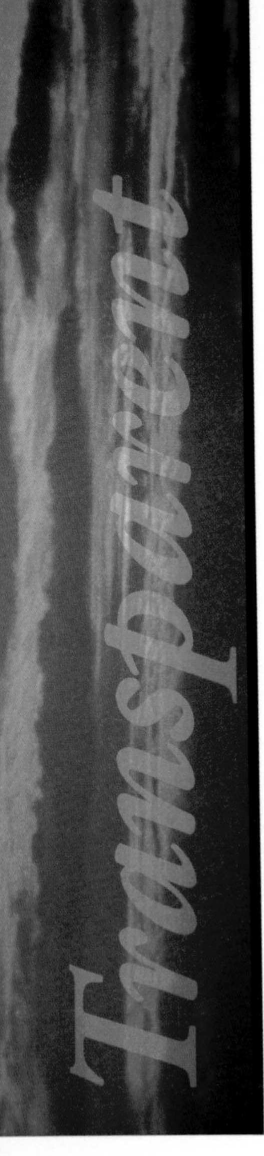

Photoshop's new layer features make this one a breeze.

©Digital Stock 1995

① Open the file containing the background you want to lay the type over. We used a stock photo from Digital Stock here.

② Create a new layer. Change the foreground color to white. Use the Type tool to enter the text.

③ To make this type transparent, all you have to do is lower the opacity of this new layer. Grab the Opacity slider in the Layers palette and slide it to the left.

VARIATIONS

This technique is so simple it gives you lots of time to experiment.

To make the text a little brighter in this image, we chose **Overlay** from the Layers palette composite pop-up menu.

You don't have to keep the text white. For this variation, we made the text 100% Cyan and chose Screen from the pop-up menu.

Another quick way to work with this effect is to type the text into a channel. Then return to the composite channel and load the selection. You can now manipulate the selection anyway you like. In this variation, we chose Image ➥ Adjust ➥ Brightness/Contrast, and bumped the brightness all the way up to 100. Use the Levels sliders (Image ➥ Adjust ➥ Levels) for more control.

©Digital Stock 1995

You can also knock words out of a transparent overlay. First, in a new layer above the background photo (this one's from Digital Stock), we filled a box with white and lowered its opacity. Then after creating each word with the Type tool, we defloated the text (Command-J) and pressed Delete.

If you want a foggy or smoky transparency, flip to page 176 and take a look at the Smoke technique. ■

① Create a new file, and create a new channel (Channel #4).

② Choose the font you wish to use. In this example, we used Copperplate 33 BC at 70 points. Use the Type tool to enter the text in the new channel. Choose Select ➡ None.

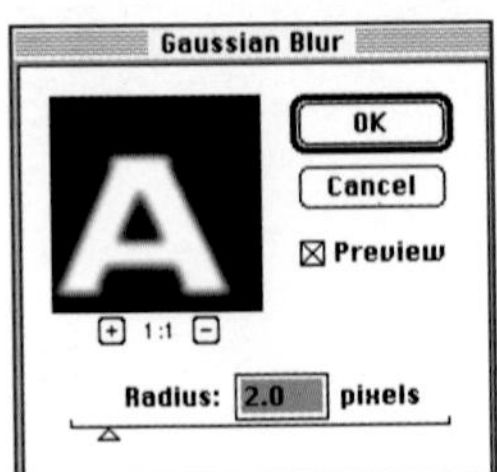

③ Use Filter ➡ Blur ➡ Gaussian Blur (2 pixels) to soften the edges of the text.

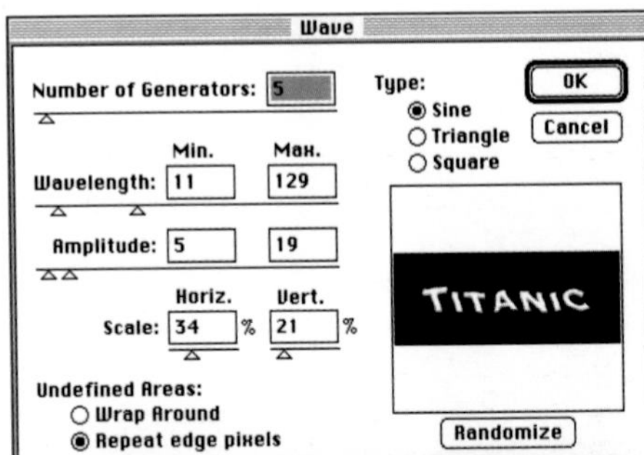

④ Apply Filter ➡ Distort ➡ Wave (Type: Sine; Generators: 5; Wavelength: 11, 129; Amplitude: 5,19; Horiz.: 34%; Vert.: 21%).

Click the Randomize button a few times until the thumbnail has a watery look to it (this randomizes settings based on the values you entered). Your text should look something like this.

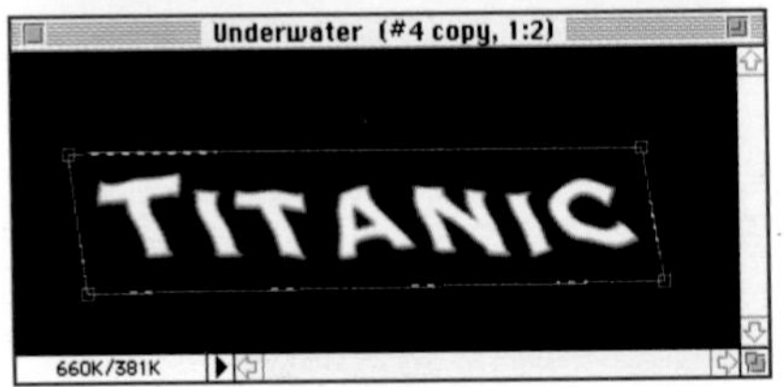

⑤ To make the shadow, duplicate channel (#4). In the duplicate channel (Channel #4 copy) select the text with the rectangular Selection Tool. Use Image ➡ Effects ➡ Distort to offset and warp the text a little more (remember, this will be a shadow so you may want to move the layer around a little using the Move tool).

⑥ Use Filter ➡ Blur ➡ Gaussian Blur (6 pixels) to blur the shadow channel.

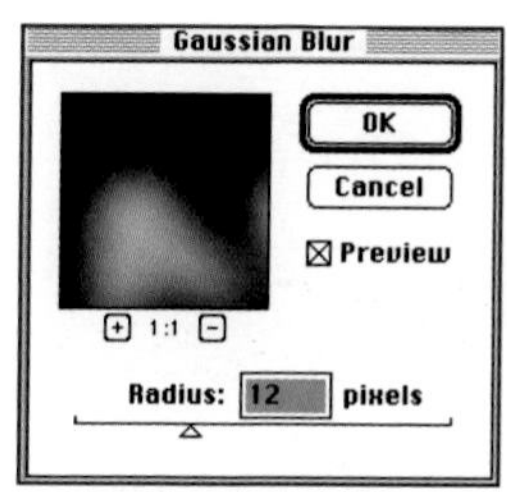

⑦ For the water, create a new channel (Channel #6). Apply Filter ➡ Pixelate ➡ Mezzotint using the Medium strokes option. Repeat this two more times (press Command-F twice).

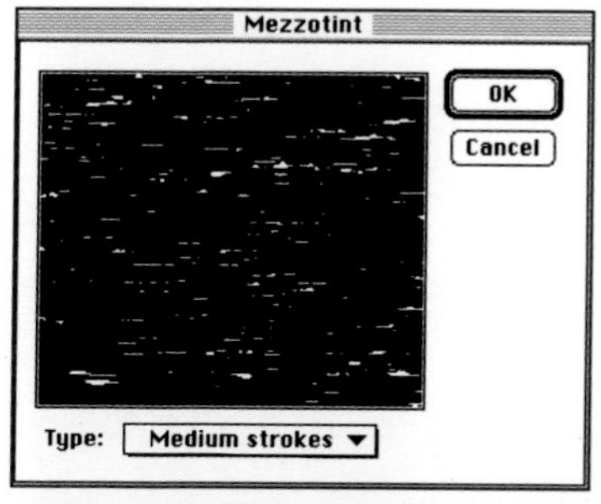

Channel #5 should now look something like this.

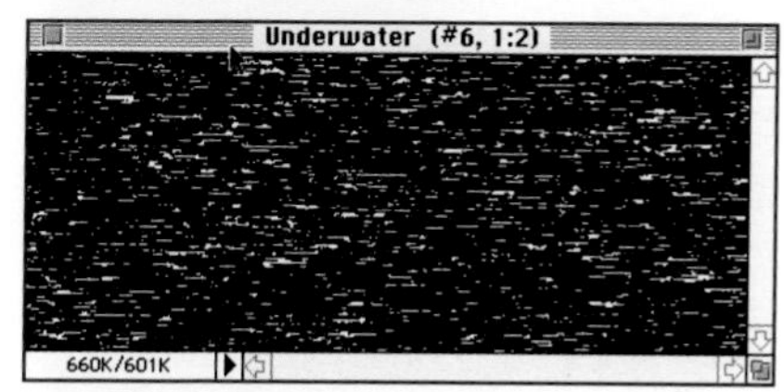

⑧ Apply Filter ➡ Blur ➡ Gaussian Blur (4 pixels).

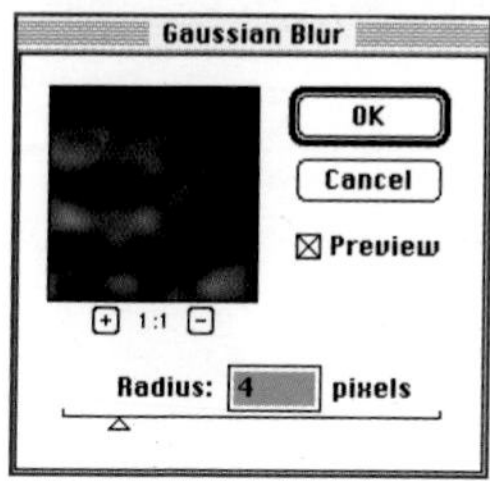

⑨ Apply Filter ➡ Other ➡ Minimum (3 pixels.) This will create the spider-web look for sunlight shimmering on the water.

You should get something like this.

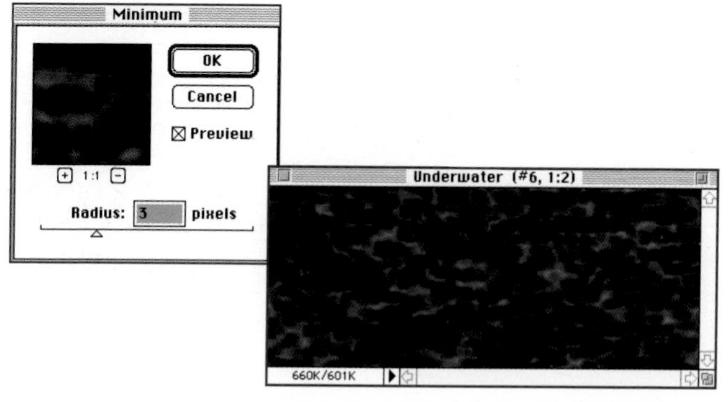

UNDERWATER

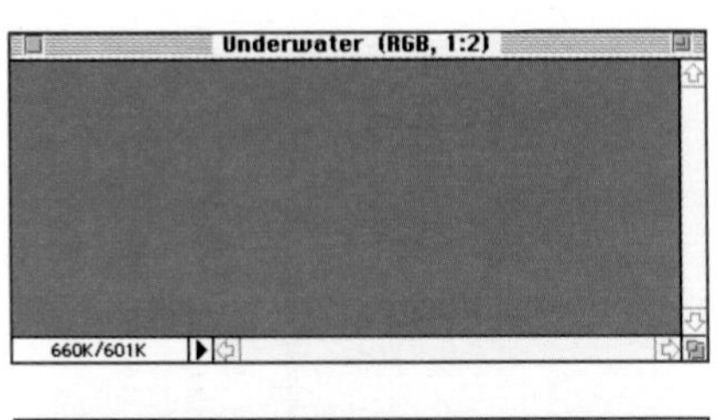

⑩ Now it's time to create the visible image. Return to the composite RGB Channel. Choose a color for the water. We used a medium cyan color here. Press Option-Delete to fill the entire image with the chosen color.

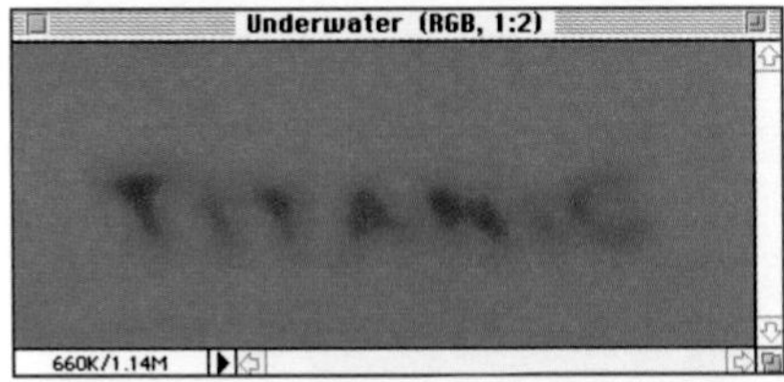

⑪ Select ➡ Load Selection and load Channel #4 copy (the shadow channel). Set the foreground color to a medium sandy brown color for the shadow. Press Option-Delete to fill the selection.

⑫ Use Select ➡ Load Selection to load Channel #4 (the text channel). Set the foreground color to the color you'd like the text to be. Here we used a forest green. Press Option-Delete to fill the selection.

⑬ Finally, Select ➡ Load Selection and load Channel #6 (the highlight channel). Set the background color to white and press Delete to fill the selection. Don't lose the selection yet!

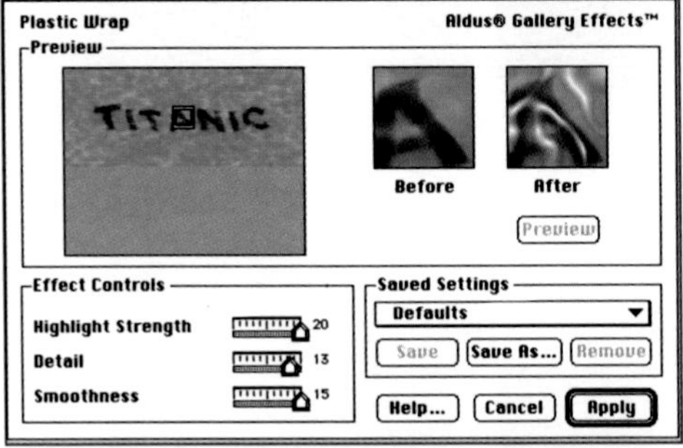

⑭ To add a few more highlights, apply Filter ➡ Gallery Effects: Classic Art 3 ➡ GE Plastic Wrap with the settings Highlight Strength: 20, Detail: 13, Smoothness: 15. Don't worry what the preview looks like—it doesn't take into account the various levels of your selection.

Presto! Don't forget to breathe!

VARIATIONS

To create the watery text without the background, follow Steps 1 to 9. Then,

(10) Select ➥ Load Selection (Channel #4 copy) to load the shadow channel. Set the foreground color to a color for the shadow. Here we used cyan. Press Option-Delete to fill the selection. If the shadow isn't dark enough, press Option-Delete again as we did here.

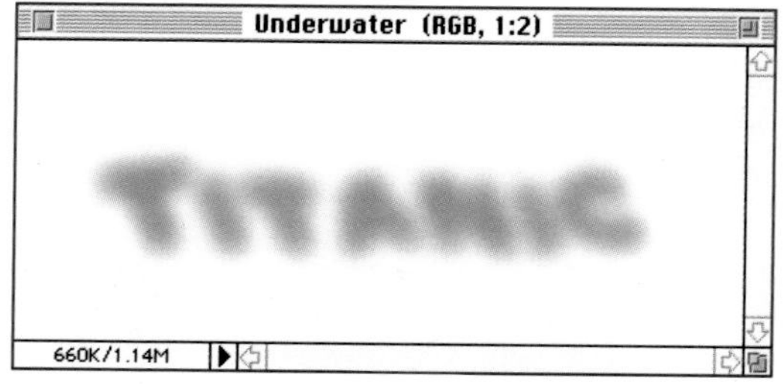

(11) Select ➥ Load Selection (Channel #4) to load the text channel. Change the foreground color the color you'd like the text to be. We used a dark blue color. Press Option-Delete to fill the selection.

(12) Select ➥ Load Selection (Channel #6) to load the highlight channel. Set the background color to white. Press Delete to fill the selection. If you want the highlights brighter, press Delete again. (Using the GE Plastic Wrap filter will cause some dark streaks in the large white areas of the image which are much more noticeable on white than on a colored background.) ■

This effect works best if you intend to use it for onscreen display. In other words, if you are going to use it as an RGB image. You just can't get that glowing green color in a CMYK image.

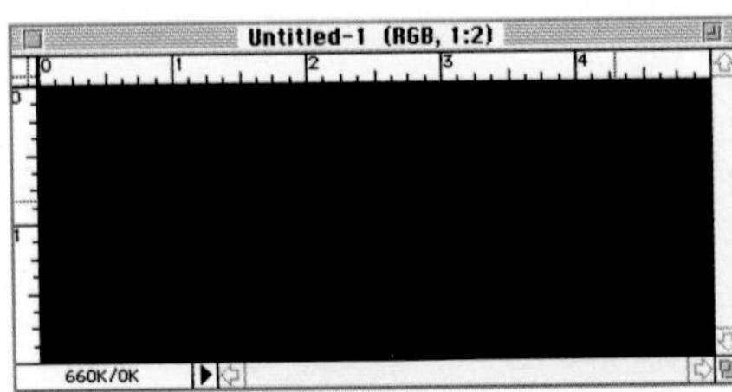

① Create a new file. Change the foreground color to black (press D), and press Option-Delete to fill the image with black.

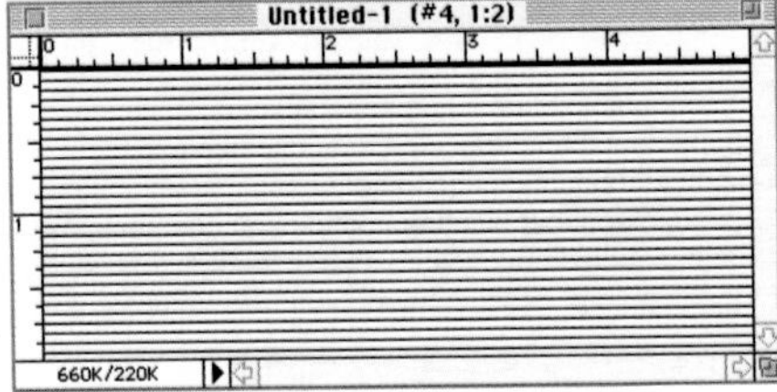

② Create a new channel (#4), choose Filter ➥ Render ➥ Texture Fill, and load the StripesForVDT file. Or, create the stripes yourself: First, use the rectangular Selection tool to select the left half of the new channel, and fill the selection with white. Then choose Filter ➥ Distort ➥ Wave (Type: square; Generators: 1; Wavelength: 1, 50; Amplitude: 999,999; Horiz.: 100; Vert.: 0). Be sure to choose the Repeat Edge Pixels option. Choose Filter ➥ Other ➥ Maximum (amount: 1) to fatten the white stripes and thin down the black stripes.

TIP

Use the upper limit value of the Wavelength in the Wave filter to control the thickness of the lines if you are using a different size type. If you increase this value, then slightly increase the value used when applying the Maximum filter to this channel.

TOOLBOX

Xaos Tools Paint Alchemy 2.0
StripesForVDT file

③ Create another new channel (#5), change the foreground color to black (press D), and use the type tool to enter the text you want to use. The Chicago typeface has the right feel for this effect. We used 50-point type.

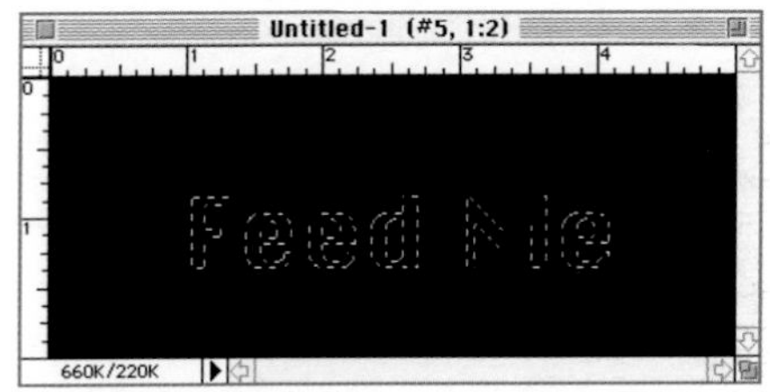

④ To find the intersection of the stripes with your text, hold the command, option, and shift keys and click on the channel created in Step 1 (#4 if you are working in an RGB file).

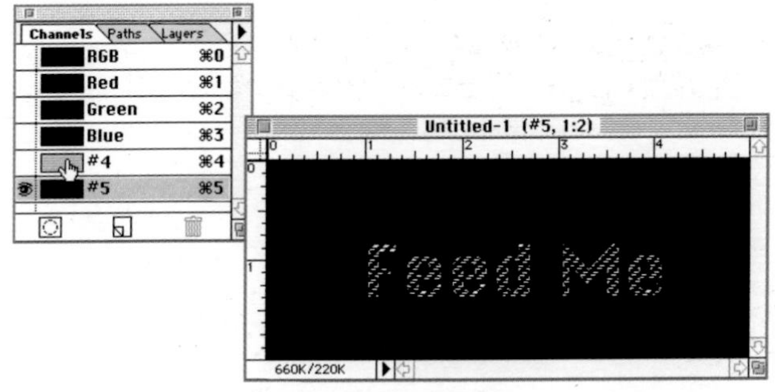

⑤ Choose Filter ➥ Modify ➥ Smooth (1 pixel). Change the foreground color to white (press D, then X), then press Option-Delete to fill the selection with white.

⑥ Choose Filter ➥ Blur ➥ Gaussian Blur (5 pixels). Deselect the type (Command-D).

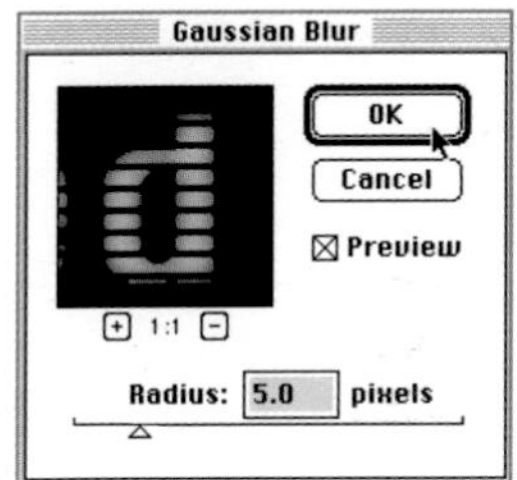

⑦ Choose Image ➥ Adjust ➥ Brightness/Contrast (Command-B) and raise the contrast to 25.

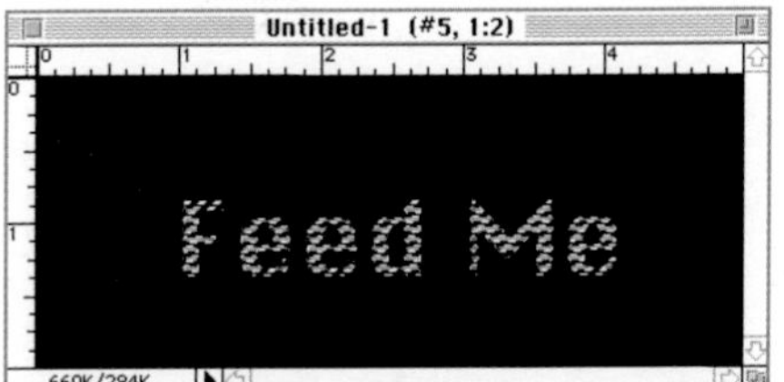

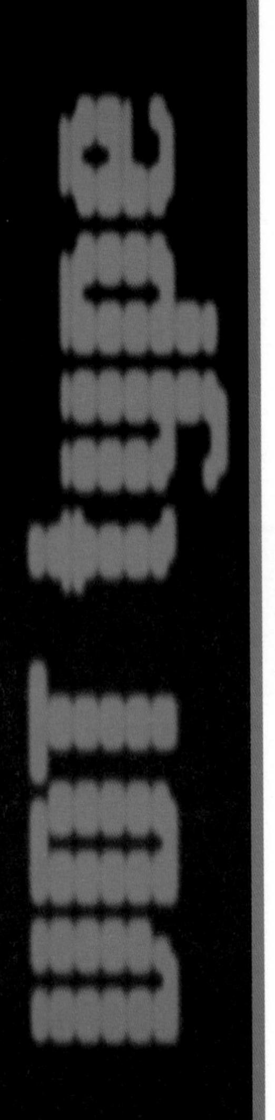

⑧ Choose Filter ➥ Blur ➥ Motion Blur (Angle: 0; Distance: 10). Choose Filter ➥ Blur ➥ Gaussian Blur (1 pixel).

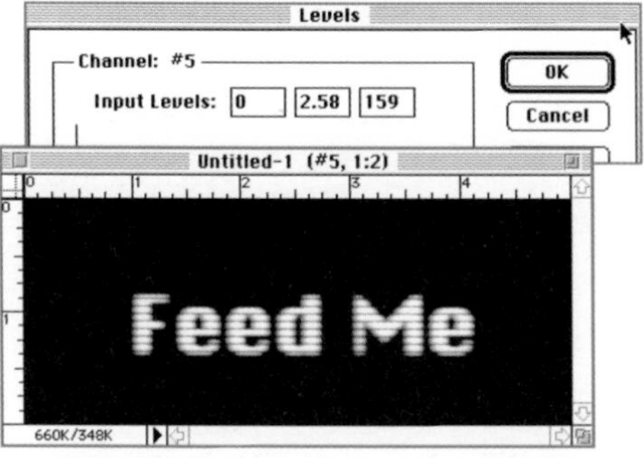

⑨ Choose Image ➥ Adjust ➥ Levels (settings: 0, 2.58, 159).

⑩ Switch to the composite channel (Command-0), and select a foreground color. Here, we used R: 0, G: 255, B: 0. Load the blurred text selection (Select ➥ Load Selection, and choose Channel #5). Press Option-Delete two or three times to fill the selection to the desired brightness.

TIP If you plan on using this text as a CMYK file, it would be best to convert to CMYK mode (Mode ➥ CMYK Mode) before selecting the foreground color. That way you won't be shocked when you convert to CMYK mode and find all the brightness stripped from your otherwise-glorious VDT text.

⑪ Press Command-D to deselect the text. A final blurring will finish it off. Choose Filter ➥ Blur ➥ Gaussian Blur (4 pixels).

VARIATIONS

Apply Filter ➡ Xaos Tools ➡ Paint Alchemy (Video Styles ➡ Blue Video). Gilded CD font was used for these examples.

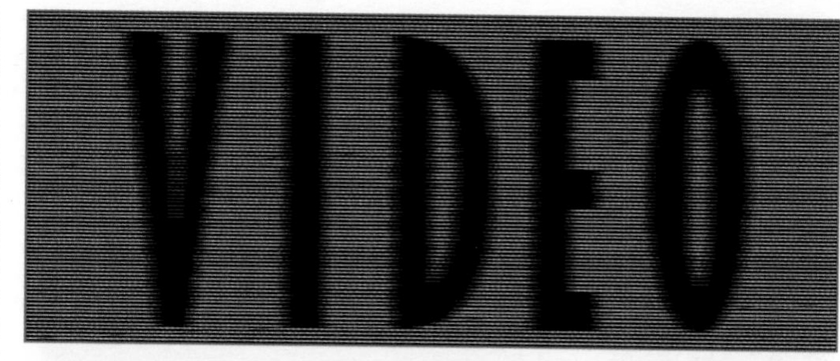

If green is your favorite color, color the type black and apply Filter ➡ Xaos Tools ➡ Paint Alchemy (Video Styles ➡ Green Video). That's all there is to it.

WET CEMENT

©D'Pix 1995

① Open a file containing a cement background. The file must be in RGB format since this effect uses the Lighting Effects filter. We manipulated a stock photo of stucco from D'Pix.

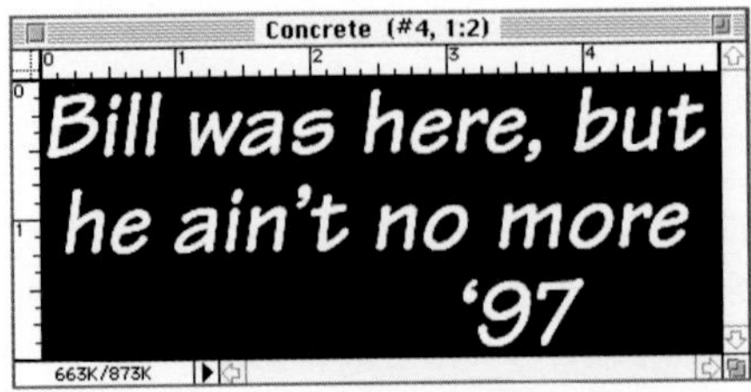

② Create a new channel (#4). Use the Type tool to enter the text. Use a font that looks like it has been handwritten or distort the text to make it look handwritten. Deselect the text (Command-D).

③ Duplicate Channel #4. In the new channel, choose Filter ➥ Stylize ➥ Diffuse (Lighten Only). Press Command-F four or five times to re-apply the filter.

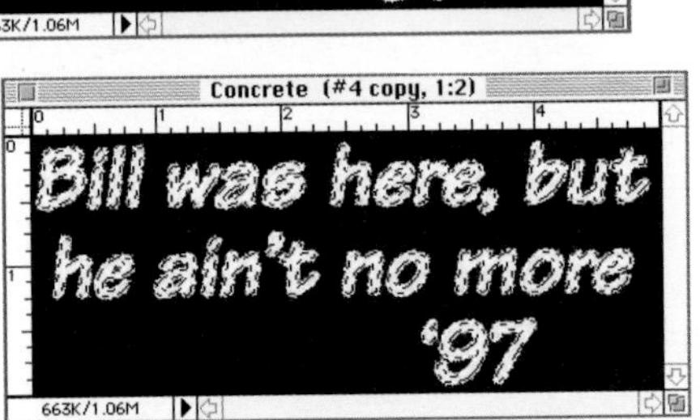

④ Load the original text channel selection created in Step 1 (Channel #4). Choose Filter ➥ Blur ➥ Gaussian Blur (4 pixels).

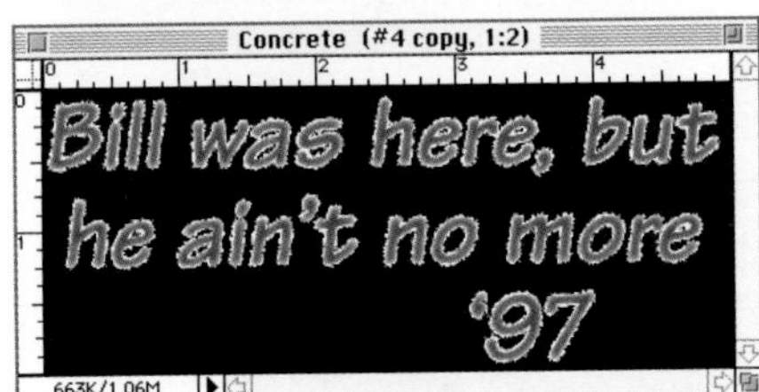

⑤ Press Command-I to invert the area within the selection. Choose Brightness/Contrast and raise the Brightness to about 55 and the Contrast to 20. Deselect the text (Command-D).

⑥ Return to the composite channel. Choose Filter ➥ Render ➥ Lighting Effects. Choose the PlasticLightStyles from the pop-up menu. Choose **#4 copy** for the texture channel, change the Height to about 45. To move the light so it doesn't wash out the type, click on it in the preview and drag it to its new location.

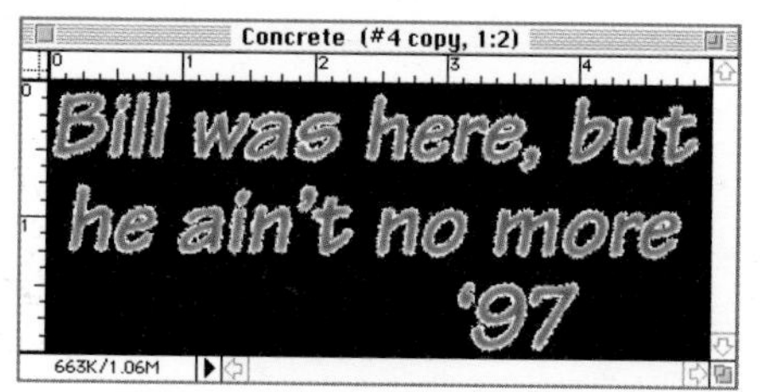

TIP

If the PlasticLightStyles does not appear in the menu, then you need to load it into your Adobe Photoshop folder. See Appendix A, *What's on the CD-ROM*, on page 206 for more info.

VARIATIONS

To make the text look more handwritten, use the Paintbrush tool to draw the letters. Choose a hard edged brush and follow the rest of the steps.

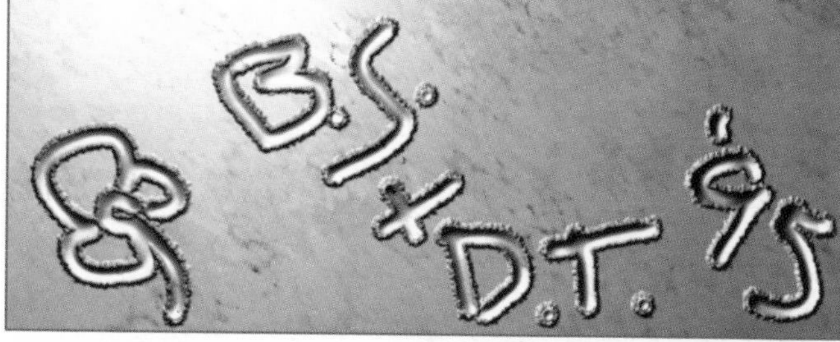

Try using a rougher font like BrushStrokeFast. Before deselecting the text in Step 5, choose Filter ➥ Stylize ➥ Diffuse (Lighten Only). Reapply the filter (Command-F), deselect the text (Command-D), do Step 6, and you're done.

If you want to make a mess, before deselecting the text in Step 5, choose Filter ➥ Stylize ➥ Find Edges. Follow Step 6. Return to Channel #4 copy, Set the Magic Wand tool tolerance to 10, and use it to click in the white area surrounding the text (also, hold the shift key and click in white areas in the middle of letters like O and Q). Return to the composite channel. Set the foreground color to white and press Option-Delete to fill the selection with white. ■

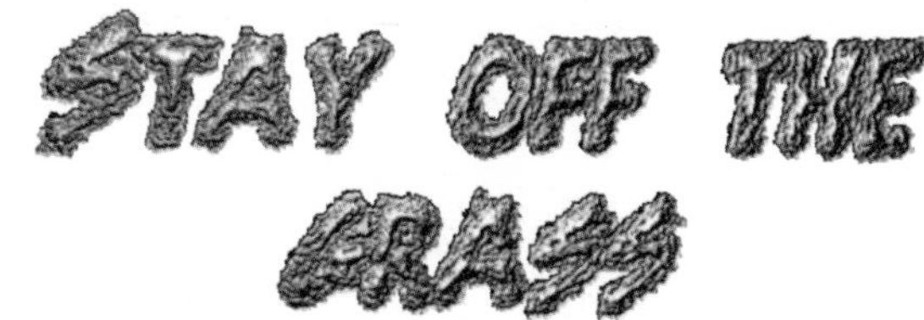

What's on the CD-ROM

The CD-ROM that comes with this book is readable on both Macintosh and Windows CD-ROM drives. Because you've almost certainly checked out parts of the CD-ROM already, you probably have some familiarity with its contents.

Contents

The CD-ROM is divided into seven folders (Windows folders are shown in parentheses):

• Type Effect Preset Files (TEPF)

This is a collection of ready-to-use files referred to in book discussions. You'll need to refer to these files when following certain tutorials.

• Effects (EFFECTS)

This is a collection of effects for manipulating images in Photoshop. Featured is a sampler of edge effects from Auto F/X.

• Filters

This folder contains lots of different filters you can use to manipulate your images. You can do a variety of things with filters, one of the most powerful features of Photoshop. Some of these filters are freeware, some are shareware, and some are commercial demos.

• Fonts

Here you will find a large selection of fonts on which you can try the various type effects. Some are freeware and some are shareware.

• Images (IMAGES)

You'll need some high-quality images to use as backdrops for some of the type effects described in the book. This collection of images from various commercial stock photo companies will give you plenty of room to play.

• Software (SOFTWARE)

Contained in this folder are demos and working copies of commercial software. Included are demo versions of Adobe Photoshop™, Adobe Illustrator™, Macromedia Fontographer®, Specular LogoMotion™, and Equilibrium DeBabelizer—plus much, much more.

• Special Offers (SPECIALS)

If you are interested in purchasing software and/or collections of images, you'll find some very cool promotions from companies which have contributed to the CD-ROM. Discounts on commercial software and other such offers are located here. You'll need a copy of Adobe Acrobat Reader (included on the CD-ROM) to view these files.

Installation

For detailed instructions on how to install and use the resources we've included on the CD-ROM, please consult the READ ME or ABOUT files in the individual software, filter, effects, and imagery folders. General installation information is as follows:

• Filters

Filters should be copied into the Plug-ins folder, located in the same place as your Adobe Photoshop application. Then, restart your computer, relaunch Photoshop, and find the filters in the Filter menu. You can now access and apply these third-party filters the same way you use Photoshop's filters.

• Preset Files

Before installing the type effect preset files, we recommend you first create a new folder in Photoshop called "PTM" or something similiar. This is the place where you should keep all the presets *except the lighting styles files.* It is *extremely* important that you remember to put BevelLightingStyles, EmbossLightingStyles, GlassLightingStyles, LiquidLightingStyles, and PlasticLightingStyles in the Lighting Styles folder with the other Photoshop lighting styles, otherwise they will not work. Follow this path to open the Lighting Styles folder within Photoshop: Plug-Ins ➥ Filters ➥ Lighting Effects ➥ Lighting Styles.

The other preset files can be opened via the Select a Document dialog box. To bring up this box, you can either choose File ➥ Open or wait till Photoshop automatically opens it for you, as in the Liquid chapter when you choose Load Settings in the Curve dialog box to load LiquidCurve. In either situation, you'll open the Photoshop folder on your hard disk, find the preset folder you created at the start, and access your preset files in this fashion.

• Fonts

Fonts should go into the Fonts folder, which is located in your System Folder. If you would like to try out a specific font, drag it to your closed System Folder. You should see a message stating that the fonts will be moved to the Fonts folder. In the case of Type I fonts, you might need to drag multiple files to your closed System Folder.

• Stock imagery and textures

The stock photos and textures located in the Images folder do not need to be copied to your hard drive. Because many of them are very large, you'll want to open them from the CD-ROM which won't eat up your computer's memory. For most files, you can double-click on them, and they will open in Photoshop. If they don't, try opening Photoshop first, and then go to the File menu and select **Open**. Then, open the image or texture you want to use. If you particularly like a certain image, and would like to access it quickly, by all means copy it to your hard drive.

Some of the software can be run straight off the CD-ROM while other packages must be installed onto your hard drive. Refer to the READ ME files accompanying each of these products for more information.

A note about shareware

If you use any shareware items beyond an initial trial period, you are obligated to follow the guidelines set forth by the author; this is usually in the form of a reasonable shareware payment forwarded to the author. Your purchase of this book and accompanying CD-ROM does not release you from this obligation. Refer to the READ ME and other information files which accompany each of the programs for additional information.

Appendix B: Contributors Listing

For more information on the software, filters, stock photography, and textures we used to make these type effects, contact the following companies.

Software & Filters

Adobe Systems, Inc.
1585 Charleston Rd.
Mountain View, CA 94039
voice: 415/961-4400
800/833-6687
fax: 415/961-3769
http://www.adobe.com

Photoshop
Illustrator
Dimensions
Aldus Gallery Effects
Texture Maker

Alien Skin Software
2522 Clark Ave.
Raleigh, NC 27607
voice: 919/832-4124
fax: 919/832-4065
alien skin@aol.com

Black Box filters
TextureShop

Andromeda Software
699 Hampshire Rd. - Suite 109
Westlake Village
City of Thousand Oaks, CA 91361
voice: 805/379-4109
800/547-0055
fax: 805/379-5253
andromed@aol.com

Velocity filter
Reflection filter

Naoto Arakawa
GCA00443@niftyserve.or.jp

SuckingFish filters

HSC Software Corp.
6306 Carpinteria Ave.
Carpinteria, CA 93013
voice: 805/566-6200
800/472-9025
fax: 805/566-6385
KPTSupport@aol.com

Kai's Power Tools
KPT Gradient Designer
KPT Fractal Explorer
KPT Texture Explorer

MicroFrontier
P.O. Box 71190
Des Moines, IA 50322
voice: 515/270-8109
800/388-8109
fax: 515/278-6828
MFrontier@aol.com

Pattern Workshop

Specular International
479 West St.
Amherst, MA 01002
voice: 413/253-3100
800/433-7732
fax: 413/253-0540
specular@applelink.apple.com
http://www.specular.com

TextureScape

Xaos Tools Inc.
600 Townsend St. - Suite 270 East
San Francisco, CA 94103
voice: 415/487-7000
800/289-9267
fax: 415/558-9886
macinfo@xaostools.com

Paint Alchemy
Terrazzo

Stock Imagery & Textures

Digital Stock
400 S. Sierra Ave. - Suite 100
Solana Beach, CA 92075
voice: 619/794-4040
800/545-4514
fax: 619/794-4041

D'Pix
Division of Amber Productions, Inc.
414 W. Fourth Ave.
Columbus, OH 43201
voice: 614/299-7192
fax: 614/294-0002

FotoSets
4104 24th St. - #425
San Francisco, CA 94114
voice: 415/621-2061
fax: 415/621-2917

Image Club Graphics
729 Twenty-Fourth Ave. SE
Calgary, AB CANADA
T2G 5K8
voice: 403/262-8008
800/661-9410
fax: 403/261-7013
http://www.adobe.com/imageclub

Photo24 Texture Resource
7948 Faust Ave.
West Hills, CA 91304
voice: 818/999-4184
800/582-9492 (outside CA)
fax: 818/999-5704

PhotoDisc/CMCD
2013 Fourth Ave. - 4th Floor
Seattle, WA 98121
voice: 206/441-9355
800/528-3472
http://www.photodisc.com

Information for inquiring about or ordering the software, filters, stock imagery and textures, and fonts included on the CD-ROM can be located in each company's and/or product's individual folder.